SCIENCE, CULTURE
AND SOCIETY

SCIENCE, CULTURE AND SOCIETY

UNDERSTANDING SCIENCE IN THE TWENTY-FIRST CENTURY

MARK ERICKSON

polity

First published in 2005 by Polity Press

Polity Press
65 Bridge Street
Cambridge CB2 1UR, UK.

Polity Press
350 Main Street
Malden, MA 02148, USA

ISBN: 0-7456-2974-1
ISBN: 0-7456-2975-X (pb)

A catalogue record for this book is available from the British Library.

Typeset in 10.5 on 12 pt Sabon
by SNP Best-set Typesetter Ltd., Hong Kong
Printed and bound in Great Britain by TJ International Ltd, Padstow, Cornwall.

Every effort has been made to trace all copyright holders. However, if any have been inadvertently overlooked, the publishers will be pleased to make the necessary arrangements at the first opportunity.

For further information on Polity, visit our website: www.polity.co.uk

Contents

Boxes

Illustrations

Figures

Acknowledgements

Irving Velody provided many seeds of the ideas that grew into this book. I miss him and regret not having had more opportunity to discuss with him those ideas in more detail. Richard K. Brown provided much inspiration, alongside many books and references, over the years, and my thanks go to him for being a wonderful teacher. This book is dedicated to both of them, and to my father, John Erickson.

This book started as a course I taught at the Department of Cultural Studies and Sociology at the University of Birmingham, and I am grateful to all the students who participated for their comments and suggestions. My colleagues at Birmingham provided a stimulating work environment, and I particularly thank Jan Campbell, Ann Gray, Michael Green, Stuart Hanson, Jorge Larrain, David Parker and Frank Webster for their inspiration and friendship. In a crass act of academic vandalism the University of Birmingham closed the department in 2002, with devastating effect on staff and students alike. However, without the demise of the department I would not have got to work with many other good colleagues, first at Aston University and more recently at the University of Brighton: thanks are due to them for throwing me a lifeline at just the right time.

Much of this book is based on my reflections on doing social research in a number of science laboratories. I thank all those who took part in the various research projects I undertook, for giving their time and knowledge so freely. In particular, Dr Georgina Lloyd of the Department of Biosciences, University of Birmingham, taught me a huge amount about scientific method and biochemistry and allowed me to use her experiments as examples of scientific practice in this book. Her colleagues Dr Ann Barnard and Professor Steve Busby were also extremely generous in giving their time, advice and resources.

The Institute of Physics gave permission to use the photograph on page 137, and Discovery Foods gave permission to use their advert on page 124. *The New Scientist*, HarperCollins, Orbit Books, Penguin and MIT Press also gave permission to use text extracts. Bec Chalkley took the photographs of Paolozzi sculptures and Birmingham shopping centres.

It is. a privilege to be part of a supportive academic community, and Sara Bragg, Steve Fuller, Michael Green, Jackie Hodgson, Tom Shakespeare and Charlie Turner deserve special thanks for reading drafts and offering advice. At Polity Emma Longstaff kept me on my mettle.

Ljubica Erickson supported me throughout and helped with my grammar (although all remaining mistakes are, of course, mine). Finally, my thanks to Sara Bragg who lived through this experience with me, and made it all worthwhile.

Introduction

This is a book about science: what it means in contemporary society and how it is represented in contemporary culture. It explores the resources for making sense of science that are available to people both inside and outside scientific institutions, resources such as histories of science, popular science books, social science accounts of science, and science fiction novels and films. It aims to examine these resources and their interconnections to help us understand what science is, how we can define science, and why science is so significant in contemporary society. It also aims to provide an overview of how scientific knowledge is produced, how scientific communities are structured, and the relationship between the two.

Science and Technology Studies (STS) has emerged as a diverse discipline that sees scientific knowledge and technological artefacts as being constructions. By this is meant that the knowledge that emerges from scientific situations – laboratories, observatories and so on – and the technologies that emerge from scientific knowledge are constructed and contingent on when and where they were made. On this view, scientific knowledge is not discovered, uncovered or found, but is actively made through the actions and interactions of scientists and engineers using the resources that surround them. It therefore opposes a long-standing view of scientific knowledge as 'out there' waiting to be 'discovered' or 'uncovered' by talented individuals. From the STS perspective, science and technology are social activities that reflect the social conditions of their production and the social conditions of those involved in their production. This book is, in part, an examination of the roots and current status of these ways of understanding science and technology.

However, there are a number of issues that arise from the STS position. The first is that many, or even most, people who are involved in producing scientific knowledge and new technologies do not subscribe to the story that STS tells. For them, science is a progressive, neutral activity that produces true knowledge and facts about the natural world through application of a standard method. Most scientists do not think that the knowledge they produce is contingent on social factors or conditions, only that it is constrained by the limits of scientific possibility, material and technical resources, or funding. The understanding of what science is from inside scientific institutions is often very different from what STS scholars suggest it is.

Secondly, understanding that science and technology are socially constructed tells us little about how and why science has a particular status in our society. In fact, it probably does the opposite. The commonly held view in Western industrial societies is that science is a form of knowledge that produces results that are more concrete, 'better' and more factual than other ways of making sense of the world. Our societies are filled with representations of science as a more precise way of understanding, of science as a solution to problems in the world, of science as a prop to shore up political ideologies, of science as creating a better future for us. These images of science rest on an understanding that science produces hard facts, truths, and fixed, uncontestable, immutable knowledge. There is an obvious discrepancy between this widely held view of science and a picture that sees scientific knowledge as a contingent and transient construction that does not embody absolute truths.

A further point needs to be faced at the outset. Whilst many public images of, and attitudes towards, science are very positive, an increasing number are negative. Contemporary scientific activities that are in the public eye often meet with popular resistance. Science's role in genetic modification of food, human cloning, production of improved weaponry, or failure to warn of the dangers of food and other health scares, for instance, are obvious examples. Often the public representations of science confront the idea that science is always the right way forward. This contested status of scientific knowledge challenges the widely held public view of science as a 'good' thing, although it would be unfair to characterize such views as being 'anti-scientific'.

These short descriptions of perspectives on science in society show that science is not a single thing, but a complex social phenomenon that appears in many places in a number of different forms. By taking this as a starting point, this book differs from many Science and Technology Studies approaches. Whilst it may be the case, as STS holds, that scientific knowledge is socially constructed by those involved in its production, this book will argue that science as a whole, the science of our societies, is itself a social construct, which the whole of society is involved in creating. The process of social construction of science does not result in a unitary and essential object, but in a complex, contested and contestable family-resemblance concept that holds a range of different meanings according to where it is being deployed, and by whom.

Our societies are so permeated by science, scientific knowledge and the products of scientific endeavour such as technology that all of us, at some level or other, consume representations of science and incorporate them into our everyday understandings. This happens in many different ways, through education, the media and culture, but also through scientific and medical interventions into our bodies, through working in scientific environments or being subject to scientific work regimes, through being included or excluded by formal scientific institutions, through the consumption of technologies. We constantly and continuously construct what science is in our actions and interactions, through deploying meanings and through having other meanings imposed upon us. Given the prevalence of a dominant story of science in our society, we often don't have much choice in this.

This continuous social construction of science is based upon a range of resources that are available at any given time. This book aims to begin to investigate what these resources are and to look at the interrelations between them. A key resource is what in this book is called 'formal science', the science that is carried out in laboratories and other scientific institutions. At the heart of formal science is the production of scientific knowledge through the work of scientists; examining just how such formal knowledge emerges is instructive not least in revealing the complexity and difficulty of much formal scientific work. Formal science is an important topic for this analysis, as it is the substrate that a number of other resources consume to construct their own versions of science. Yet the reverse is also the case: professional scientists working in scientific locations are constructing scientific knowledge, but are doing so with reference to the same external resources that the non-scientific public are using. These external resources are legion, and this book has space only to scratch the surface by looking at a small range: that of popular science and science fiction narratives. These external accounts of science represent different understandings of what science 'is', and such representations serve to both reinforce a dominant story of science and to obscure aspects of the operation of formal science. Here I investigate the tensions between internal and external accounts, between esoteric and exoteric.

This book is divided into four parts. The first presents an example of the relationship between science, culture and society, and introduces the main contexts and theoretical frameworks that will be used to make sense of science.

Part II examines in detail how science is carried out in a formal scientific location. Making sense of this is an important component of understanding what science means, and this book contends that, as investigators of science from a social perspective, we need to have some understanding of what formal science is doing, how it is structured, and what the main theories and ideas underpinning it are. Chapters 3 and 4 introduce the key academic theories that have emerged from investigating the history, philosophy and social organization of science. Understanding the history, philosophy and social organization of science, and how accounts of these have changed over time, provides a picture of social analysis of science, and gives an overview of the main aspects of social studies of science today.

Part III explores some of the more widely distributed resources for the social construction of science. The two chapters each present an example of how science is socially constructed in different discourses.

Popular science books are one way in which images and ideas about formal science enter the popular imagination, although, as will be shown, this is often a process that serves to reinforce the boundaries between science and non-science, as the discourse of popular science can serve to reinforce the idea of science as somehow separate and superior to other forms of knowledge. Popular science also serves to maintain an illusion of science as a unified and united whole, whereas science is fragmented and contested. Popular science texts are often written by people who have been involved in formal scientific work, and some have been hugely successful. One need only think about the continuing popularity of a book like Stephen Hawking's *A Brief History of Time* (Hawking 1988), which captured positions on the bestseller lists in most industrial societies, and provided agendas for discussion in a range of media.

By contrast, science fictions are often written from a perspective that challenges the role and status of science in society, with plot lines that use, for example, dystopian images of planetary crises brought about by mad scientists, or anti-democratic conspiracies where scientists work for shadowy state or industrial organizations. The range of different science fiction texts is vast, and the material presented here is necessarily schematic. However, it tentatively concludes that social science has ignored the construction of science in fictional texts, and has also failed to notice the role that fictional texts play in promoting an image of an essential, unified science. Overall, science fiction provides a different set of resources and constructions of what science is and how we make sense of it.

The fourth part of the book draws together the main themes and offers some strategies and ideas for future research that takes a culturally oriented, anti-essentialist approach. The specific example used in this section is nanotechnology, an emerging area of scientific research, and one that is already surrounded by a degree of public controversy, hope and fear. This part also presents some concluding remarks concerning the relationship between science, culture and society. Focusing on the social construction of science, it proposes that we stop regarding science as a separate part of society, and instead see the boundaries of science and the boundaries of society as inseparable and coterminous.

Many social accounts of science have argued that, to understand science, we need to understand society and its workings. Whilst this book supports that position, it also argues the reverse: that to understand society, we also need an understanding of science. To achieve this, we need to understand what formal science in scientific institutions is, and how scholars have made sense of it over the years. But we also have to recognize that society actively attaches meanings to science, making sense of science through using the resources at hand. We need to see the cultural resources that are used in this process, and understand the relationship between science, culture and society if we are to get to grips with what science is, why it is so important, and why our societies are inextricably linked to it.

Part I

Language, Art and Science

Someone says to me: 'Show the children a game.' I teach them gaming with dice, and the other says 'I didn't mean that sort of game.' Must the exclusion of the game with dice have come before his mind when he gave me the order?

Ludwig Wittgenstein, Philosophical Investigations, *p. 33*

Sir Eduardo Paolozzi, RA, *Faraday* (2000). Photo by Bec Chalkley.

I

Paolozzi and Faraday: Science and Art

What is science?

Much of this book is taken up with trying to define and describe science. Having this as a goal might seem strange – most people know what science is and use the word quite frequently in their everyday lives; scientists work away in their laboratories and produce scientific knowledge; social scientists use the word to describe a range of things that they see; and our culture is full of representations of science. Yet many scientists find it hard to explain even what their own work is and what it means to other people, let alone what the whole project of science is and what that means. By contrast, social scientists and philosophers of science can often offer descriptions of what science as a whole means to us, and know what science as a project is, but find it difficult to explain the connection between this and the individual actions that take place in laboratories, or the role that science has in society. Our media and culture also 'know' what science is, and present us with images and understandings of science, but on closer inspection these representations often turn out to be crude stereotypes that reflect the prejudices and traditions of analysis that are bound up in the media community, rather than reflecting what science and scientists actually are. As for the 'lay public' – non-scientists – when we begin to look at everyday uses of the word 'science', we can see that it comprises a range of meanings, few of which match up to dictionary or academic definitions of science.

As we start to define science, we realize that our definitions are often of a negative form: we define science by saying what it is not, not what it actually is, yet we can see that science is very important to us. Science appears all around us, is part of our lives; but when we try to explain it to ourselves or to others, we run into major problems, and often fall back on clichés. Science is a complex and complicated thing. We have problems looking at it due to its complexity, but these are compounded by a widespread belief that science is unitary and easily definable.

Science today – science in technoscientific worlds

What are we talking about when we speak of science? The word 'science' becomes attached to a great many different things in contemporary society and culture, from laboratory practices to hair shampoos and political programmes. This profusion of attachments implies that there are problems of definition associated with the word 'science', and it may be that these are impossible to resolve. Not only that, we may be wrong in trying to make sense of science in isolation, of trying to look at it on its own. This is clear from the difficulty in contemporary society to distinguish science from technology: when we look at technological objects in our lives, we often think of science – and likewise, when we think of science, we often think of the technology that science facilitates. This conflation and fusion of science and technology has been called 'technoscience' by some commentators (Latour 1987; Aronowitz and DiFazio 1994; Haraway 1997), and it is a term that will be often used in this book. However, identifying the conflation of science and technology is only the starting point for a range of different perspectives on what technoscience actually is.

Bruno Latour, and Stanley Aronowitz and William DiFazio, whilst approaching this topic from very different perspectives, agree that the defining feature of technoscience is the indivisibility of science and technology, where we simply cannot distinguish science from technology, and vice versa, any more. As well as describing the inseparability of the objects of technology from the practice and knowledge of science, technoscience can also designate a state of affairs (a time and place – in this case Western industrial societies in the early twenty-first century) in which intellectual problems of the day become increasingly dominated by technical and mechanical considerations and, often, solutions. This is what a number of writers, including Haraway, do:

This discourse takes shape from the material, social, and literary technologies that bind us together as entities within the region of historical hyperspace called technoscience. *Hyper* means 'over' or 'beyond', in the sense of 'overshooting' or 'extravagance'. Thus, technoscience indicates a time–space modality that is extravagant, that overshoots passages through naked or unmarked history. Technoscience extravagantly exceeds the distinction between science and technology as well as those between nature and society, subjects and objects, and the natural and artificial that structured the imaginary time called modernity. (Haraway 1997: 3)

Technoscience, as Haraway explains it, is thus both an object of inquiry and a context that our inquiry can be located within, and technoscience 'exceeds' science and technology – it is bigger than the sum of its parts. Technoscience is also a language and a grammar that we are using to describe the world around us and our selves within the world. If we follow Haraway's sophisticated understanding of technoscience, we will find it impossible to break it down into its constituent components: we will not find it possible to look at an object and see what is 'scientific' about it and what is 'technological' (Haraway would want to go much further and say that we cannot identify 'objects' in contradistinction to 'subjects', that such distinctions have been rendered meaningless by our changing relationships to artefacts and non-human actors). This isn't simply due to the fusing together of science and technology, it is also due to the changing shape of our language and grammar of meaning. Our lives are now described by technoscientific language, our meanings are constructed around technoscientific viewpoints on the world. We cannot easily escape this frame of reference, this form of life.

As such, it will be difficult to identify a starting point for technoscience: rather, we will find that when we talk about technoscience, we are identifying trends and traces rather than facts and figures. One such trace we can identify is, ironically, in the world of artistic production. This is ironic in the sense that the world of art is often considered to be removed – remote – from the concreteness of scientific knowledge and the tangible impact of technology.

Representing technoscience – Paolozzi and Faraday

The work of Eduardo Paolozzi has been inspired by technoscience – the fusing together of science and technology – since the 1950s (for examples see Kirkpatrick 1970). The themes of his art and sculpture are often 'scientific' in the sense that they express the significance of scientific knowledge and scientists in our society, and he often executes works using the technology of our everyday lives – domestic appliances, engines, radios, robotic toys – and placing it in new, sometimes surreal, contexts and conjunctions. Paolozzi's commitment to modernism and to the progressive character of modernity is clear, and his art expresses a strong faith in the power of science to transform and change the world, although the results are sometimes unexpected or even surreal. Paolozzi's works show that science has creative power (in the senses both of being a product of creative processes like human imagination and creating things), transformative power (changing nature and society and the self) and visual power (science looks good). His work also suggests that science is inescapable: it is an integral part of the modern world that we live in, and Paolozzi's art celebrates this, whilst at the same time showing the dangers of science and the power that science and technology have over us.

Michael Faraday, one of Britain's greatest scientists, made huge theoretical and practical contributions to the study and understanding of electrical phenomena in the early nineteenth century. Faraday's understanding of science was based upon the idea that the world was a structured whole, formed by continuously interacting natural agents or powers; the task of the scientist was then to discover the regular patterns in nature and to describe the laws that govern the behaviour of natural phenomena (Agassi 1971; Harré 1981: 177). In many ways, as we shall see, Faraday's understanding of science was little different from that of many people – scientists and non-scientists alike – in contemporary society: we are often told that science is a form of knowledge and a set of techniques that provides a truthful account of the natural world by breaking it down into its component parts and identifying the rules and laws that govern the behaviour of those parts. Among Faraday's achievements were a series of experiments that showed that different varieties of electricity – that is, electrical phenomena produced by different means such as chemical or mechanical processes – were all manifestations of the same phenomenon. Through this Faraday unified the understanding of electricity in a way similar to Newton's unification of the laws of motion in the seventeenth century. Faraday was both an experimenter and a theorist, a point emphasized in Agassi's definitive biography (Agassi 1971), and his experimental work produced two of the most important inventions of modernity: the electrical generator and the electrical transformer. His practical and theoretical works are of huge importance: the electrification of the world and the entry of electricity and electrical modes of being are a direct consequence of Faraday's work. It is unsurprising that Paolozzi chose Faraday as a theme and subject for a recent sculpture (see photograph on the reverse of the Part I title-page).

Paolozzi completed *Faraday* in 2000 – it is a millennial piece of art, a celebration of modernity. The sculpture shows a seated figure, monumental (over 5 metres high), powerful, superhuman, raised above the viewer on a large pedestal. The humanoid form that is represented here is a figure that is fragmented and invaded by geometrical machine-made forms. The figure holds rods – symbols of power and law – that extrude cables that encircle the piece. These lines of power evoke those that encircle our world and encircle the self. The self is transformed through this power, changing from the organic version of a human being to a transformed 'modern' human, fractured and reconstructed by science and, by association, modernity. This is most visible in the 'cubist' way that Paolozzi represents the head of this sculpture (see illustration 1.1): Paolozzi saw the cubist heads that he began to produce in the 1990s as inspired by computer graphics that had been pared down to a series of geometrical facets. He described these cubist heads as 'Mondrian Heads' 'because they reminded him of Mondrian's late "boogie-woogie" paintings' (Pearson 1999: 74). The shift from an organic human form to an inorganic, machine-made, humanoid form suggests that our human selves have been transformed by technology and by science, that we have become cyborgs (see chapter 7 for more about cyborgs).

What does this sculpture say about our relationship to science? Science is an agent here, changing our lives and changing our bodies, changing society and changing nature. Science is powerful, exuding energy that can change the self and can transform the whole world. But science is also dangerous, transforming the human into the

Illustration 1.1.   Detail of *Faraday*, head. Photo by Bec Chalkley.

inhuman. The understanding of science that is being represented here is not the same as that expressed by Faraday himself; nor is it the same as the dominant story of science that we are told in contemporary society.

The science of the *Faraday* sculpture, the science of today, is not the unified and essentialist science of the past – that is, a form of science where there are clear foundations and rules that unify all scientific endeavours. Science in the past has been characterized by the *unity* of the enterprise – science was seen as a combined, unified project that all scientific knowledge was a part of, and all scientists subscribed to the core values and goals of this project. Here, when we look at *Faraday*, we see a *void* at the core of the form, the scientist, and, by implication – for scientists are as much a part of society as the rest of us – a void at the heart of all of us. There is no core to science: instead there is a rather glaring absence, one that is surrounded by strength and power, but an absence none the less. Our science today is fragmented and is being constantly reconstructed by its interaction with society and culture. Our science is not a pure form of knowledge and practice but a confused and confusing set of enterprises, activities and representations that make up our techno-scientific reality. There is no centre to 'science', because science has expanded far past its original boundaries and has entered and colonized realms that also have no centres.

It takes the power and insight of an artist like Paolozzi to see this and to produce an image of this that begins to express what that absence means. We tell ourselves a story of science as unified, as powerful, as transformative and, above all, as having a continuous history and a continuous future. We experience science as an essential force, as something that has an essence, a core that is true and permanent. However, as Paolozzi's *Faraday* suggests, we need not look at science this way. Thinking of Paolozzi's sculpture, and particularly his cubist heads, gives us another way of configuring and understanding what science is.

Paolozzi's cubist heads are made up of geometric fragments that have been recombined and reconstructed, and we can think of science as having a similar form. Science can be imagined as being a semi-opaque, three-dimensional object with many faces – a dodecahedron, for example – an object that we imagine turning around in our heads such that, as we turn it, a new face comes into view.

As we turn our dodecahedron around in our mind, each face we see expresses a different aspect of science. We may start with the face that shows us the production of scientific knowledge in the lab, and we can examine this face to further understand what this process of knowledge production entails. As we look at this face of science, we see that adjoining it are other faces that are impinging on the production of scientific knowledge – the history of science, the materiality of lab work, the scientists' understanding of their own project – and we will find it easier to understand the process of knowledge production by making reference to the adjoining faces. Later, we can turn the dodecahedron around and look at another face – perhaps the representation of science in popular culture. Again, we can examine this face to better make sense of how such representations are produced and how they are connected to, for example, the science of popular science books or the practices of laboratory workers. The more we look at the dodecahedron, the more we see the connections, tensions and interconnections between the different faces of science. We also begin to see that the dodecahedron is, actually, much more multi-faceted: there are far more than twelve sides to this imaginary object. And because the imaginary object is semi-opaque, we also see inside it that, like Paolozzi's *Faraday*, it has no core, no centre, no essence. Each facet of the object of science, like each facet of the head of *Faraday*, has a reality and an existence of its own, and is related to other facets; yet no one facet expresses all of the object, or has a necessary superiority to other facets.

When we look at an art object, say a sculpture or a painting, we often find ourselves looking at one particular feature – the eyes of a portrait, or the foreground of a landscape. That we focus on, say, the eyes of Paolozzi's *Faraday* is a feature of our culture, not a feature of the sculpture; similarly, it is a feature of our culture, and not an expression of some integral quality or essence of science, that we look at science and describe its form of knowledge as being superior to other forms of knowledge. This need not be the case, although our investigations will show that there are features of scientific knowledge that make it different from other forms of knowledge.

We can describe science as a multi-faceted object that we can pick up, turn this way and that, peer inside and scrutinize; but science also has its own agency. With Haraway we must admit that it is no longer possible to maintain a strong separation between subject and object: things that appear to be passive and subject to external influence often turn out to be active and capable of effecting change themselves (Haraway 1997). We objectify science, but do this through our subjectivity, which is itself constituted by our technoscientific lives. This means that we need to look at ourselves, our relationship to science, and how we embody science, to start to understand it. But also we need to scrutinize science appropriately and recognize that we cannot grasp it all at once as a whole.

Two key thinkers

We can see science as a fragmented and multi-faceted object. This is a perspective that is supported by two key thinkers – Ludwig Wittgenstein and Ludwik Fleck – who offer, respectively, some tools for making sense of the grammar and language of science, and of the social relationships inside and surrounding science.

Ludwig Wittgenstein

The later philosophy of Ludwig Wittgenstein provides us with a way of understanding how a concept such as 'science', which appears to have such a tight and formal definition, can come to have so many different meanings, and how such a complex concept can occupy such a central position in social thought. Ironically, it is Wittgenstein's early philosophy (see box 1.1) that provides the opposite conception of science, the position held by logical positivists such as Rudolf Carnap and A. J. Ayer (see chapter 3), where science is seen as being a unified project with a unitary method: the most important, and best, form of knowledge existing in modern society (Ayer 1971). As Ayer notes: 'There is no field of experience which cannot, in principle, be brought under some form of scientific law, and no type of specula-tive knowledge about the world which it is, in principle, beyond the power of science to give' (Ayer 1971: 64).

Wittgenstein's later philosophy radically departs from his earlier work. Whereas he had seen the world as being a totality of logical propositions which could be described with the regularity of scien-tific endeavour, in his later work Wittgenstein presents an under-standing of the meanings of words as being constructed through their use – the meanings of words are contingent upon their use in every-day speech. This means that there are no fixed meanings for words, and that meanings can shift and change according to how, where and by whom they are being used. Wittgenstein thought that some con-cepts in our language were 'family-resemblance concepts', in that they do not fall into simple 'true–false' bipolar distinctions (like a colour being described as red or not-red, one or the other) and are really amalgamations of a constellation of meanings. He uses the example of 'games' to illustrate this point:

> Consider for example the proceedings that we call 'games'. I mean board-games, card-games, ball-games, Olympic games, and so on.

Box 1.1   Ludwig Wittgenstein

Wittgenstein (1889–1951) was born into a wealthy Viennese family. He initially studied engineering before moving on to study philosophy at Cambridge in the years before the First World War. His first book, *Tractatus Logico-Philosophicus* (published in 1921) was hailed as a work of genius. Wittgenstein thought that it had solved all of the current philosophical problems and abandoned philosophy after it was published. The book presents in a rigidly logical way a series of propositions that describe the relationship of language to the world, and at the heart of the book is Wittgenstein's picture theory of meaning, which states that language consists of propositions which picture the world. Wittgenstein realized in the late 1920s that the doctrine of the *Tractatus* was wrong and returned to philosophy, taking up a chair at Cambridge. His second book, *Philosophical Investigations* (published posthumously in 1953), is also about the relationship of language to the world. However, in this book Wittgenstein abandons the idea that propositions have fixed meanings that can be broken down into their logical elements. He moves away from the formal analytical frame of reference and looks at how meanings become attached to words. The meanings of words are constructed through their use, and thus cannot be understood when taken out of their linguistic context. Breaking sentences down into atomic elements to find meanings will never work, as the meanings are attached as language is deployed. Wittgenstein called the whole situation where meanings become attached to words 'language-games'.

What is common to them all? – Don't say: 'There *must* be something common, or they would not be called "games" ' – but *look and see* whether there is anything common to all. – For if you look at them you will not see something that is common to *all*, but similarities, relationships, and a whole series of them at that. . . . Look for example at board-games, with their multifarious relationships. Now pass to card-games; here you find many correspondences with the first group, but many common features drop out, and others appear. When we pass next to ball-games, much that is common is retained, but much is lost. – Are they all 'amusing'? Compare chess with noughts and crosses. Or is there always winning and losing, or competition between players? Think of patience. . . . Think now of a game like ring-a-ring-a-roses; here is the element of amusement, but how many other characteristic features have disappeared!

> And the result of this examination is: we see a complicated network
> of similarities overlapping and criss-crossing: sometimes overall simi-
> larities, sometimes similarities of detail. (Wittgenstein 1958: §66)

I would propose that we consider 'science' to be such a family-
resemblance concept (Wittgenstein 1958: §67; Phillips 1977), where
it is not possible to consider phenomena as either 'science' or 'not
science'. Rather, we will see that much of what we formally categorize as science in contemporary society is not as 'scientific' as we
thought, and much of what we think of as being unscientific actually
contains elements of science. However, it isn't simply that our use of
the word 'science' (or 'scientist', 'scientific', etc.) is ambiguous and
open to a range of meanings. We need to recognize that, in the same
way that when we deploy the word 'game' in everyday language, we
cannot help starting to look for game-like features, so when we
deploy the word 'science', we start looking for 'scientific' features.
Given the open-textured definition of the words that we use, it
is likely that we will find such features when we start looking.
Wittgenstein uses the example of 'natural law' and the use of the term
by scientists to show that simply using particular words means that
we will end up carrying out certain forms of investigation, or will
start to look at the world in a certain way. When we use the term
'natural law' we immediately start looking for certain things, and
start thinking in a certain way:

> First of all, the idea of compulsion already lies in the word 'law'. The
> word 'law' suggests more than an observed regularity which we take
> it will go on.
>   The usage of the word natural law connects, one might say, to a
> certain kind of fatalism. What will happen is laid down somewhere ...
> if we got hold of the book in which natural laws were really laid down.
> The rules were laid down by a Deity – written in a book. Rules in physics
> are a guess: 'I suppose that is the law'. (Wittgenstein 1993: 430)

For Wittgenstein, the use by science of terms like 'natural law' means
that science will *always* see the world as if there is a set of already
written laws that it simply needs to uncover. It is not that our language 'compels' us inescapably to see things in certain ways (this
would be too deterministic and mechanistic for Wittgenstein), but
that there is an element of compulsion there, and that it is only by
great effort that we can escape from the view of the world that our
language imposes upon us. We can use Wittgenstein's philosophy as
a therapeutic intervention into the world of ideas and words to help
us see where it is that language is leading us, and to identify alternative understandings of the world around us.

By applying Wittgenstein's philosophy to the case of science, we can begin to see the concept of science as a complex constellation of meanings that bring together a wide range of different practices and knowledges. Unlike Wittgenstein's example of 'game', this family-resemblance concept is much more difficult to unpack because one of the central modes of understanding the contemporary world is based upon a version of scientific knowledge, scientific method and scientific practice. There is no formal theory of games that makes us look at games in our society as if there was a hierarchy of practices – with, say, chess at the top and football at the bottom. However, there is a strong perception in our society that scientific knowledge is better than other sorts of knowledge, and that scientific practice is a more reliable mode of investigation than other forms of inquiry. For example, a recent book on cyborg theory states:

> I'd encountered the idea that we were all cyborgs once or twice before, but usually in writings on gender or in postmodernist . . . studies of text. What struck me in July 1997 was that this kind of story was the *literal and scientific truth*. (Clark 2003: 4, my emphasis)

Similarly, a recent editorial in *Scientific American* (December 2002) stated: 'No endeavor rivals science in its incremental progress towards a more complete understanding of the observable world.' Because of this we will find it difficult to see the other uses of science, or the other locations of science, as having similar status to what we can call formal science (broadly akin to the natural science that is taught at university).

The dominant story of science comes from a number of different sources: education would seem to be the most likely starting point for its internalization, but we are currently surrounded by it in our technoscientifically oriented media. This story reinforces science's image of being a method for achieving truth, a discourse that is neutral in its origin and consequences. We can identify a number of different locations where this story is presented to us, and where we interact with it. We can call these different locations where stories of the world we inhabit are told and retold thought communities.

Ludwik Fleck

The idea of thought communities comes from the work of the Polish microbiologist and sociologist of science Ludwik Fleck (1896–1961) (see box 1.2). A thought community is a group of individuals who share ideas, concepts and theories: they share a particular 'thought style'. Fleck suggests that such thought communities are multiple, vary in size, and vary in composition. For Fleck, it was important to see scientists as being members of a thought community: new scientific ideas could only 'progress' once they were accepted by the thought community that would be using them.

Box 1.2   Ludwik Fleck

Fleck (1896–1961) was a Polish microbiologist who took a keen interest in the philosophy and sociology of science. His groundbreaking book *Genesis and Development of a Scientific Fact* was published in 1935. In it, Fleck describes how scientific communities come together, and how the esoteric (internal) knowledge of a scientific community will be related to the exoteric (external) knowledge of other thought communities. In addition, Fleck offers an account of the history of science which is discontinuous, unlike the seamless progressive standard accounts.

Fleck's life is quite astonishing in other ways. By 1935 he was head of the bacteriological laboratory in the city of Lvov, but was sacked that year as part of the anti-Jewish measures taken by the Polish state. *Genesis and Development of a Scientific Fact* was published that year, but in Switzerland – as Fleck was Jewish, he could not get it published in Poland or Germany due to anti-Semitic prejudice and laws. Up to 1939 Fleck survived as a private researcher, but then the Russian occupation of that part of Poland saw him being made director of Lvov city microbiology laboratory and appointed to the state medical school. The Nazi invasion of Russia in 1941 saw Fleck sacked (again) and confined to the ghetto – he became director of the bacteriological laboratory at the Jewish hospital, a post he held until December 1942.

During this period there was an outbreak of typhoid, and Fleck – without proper equipment, lab supplies or funds – managed to invent and develop a diagnostic test for typhus, allowing infected patients to be confined at a much earlier stage (thus preventing the infection spreading), and started working on a vaccine which he extracted from the urine of infected patients. He used his family to test this out, but before he could check the results in a fully scientific way, by vaccinating a large group, the Nazis liquidated the ghetto. Fleck was sent to Auschwitz, where he was forced to produce his vaccine for use by the Wehrmacht on the Eastern Front.

Fleck agreed to do this, and was supplied with a team and a small lab in one of the isolation huts, where all the inmates were already dying of typhoid. Fleck produced a large quantity of vaccine from the urine of German soldiers (the Nazis would not allow him to use Jewish urine to produce vaccine for their troops, of course). This 'vaccine' was inert – effectively sterile – and did not protect against typhoid. Fleck's team also produced a small quantity of real vaccine that did work – thus allowing them to convince the Nazis that what they were injecting into their soldiers was a real vaccine. This real vaccine they kept for themselves and for the inmates of Auschwitz, as many of whom as possible were secretly inoculated. Fleck was upset that he could not keep proper scientific records of how effective these inoculations were, as the Nazis would kill or relocate his research subjects frequently.

Fleck survived Auschwitz, and no doubt countless others also survived because of the vaccine he produced there. After the war Fleck was made professor of microbiology at Lublin University, and a fellow of the Polish Academy of Sciences in 1954. He emigrated to Israel in 1957 and died in 1961.

In his major work *Genesis and Development of a Scientific Fact* ([1935] 1979) Fleck looks at how one thought community of scientists – microbiologists who were investigating syphilis – came to accept and understand a specific scientific test. Crucially, Fleck notes that the thought community of scientists would be affected and altered by the individual scientists' membership of other thought communities. For example, a scientist will be a member of her own thought community – say microbiologists – but will also be a member of a number of other thought communities: her family, maybe a political party, a workers' association, a local community, etc. Each of these thought communities has its own thought style, its own way of making sense of and understanding the world. The scientist cannot abandon all of these other – possibly competing – thought styles at the door to the laboratory, however much she may want to. The result is a thought community of scientists – what we may choose to call a scientific community – whose scientific knowledge, although seen as a neutral and pure product, is actually made up of knowledges that incorporate, at least to some extent, the thought styles of the communities external to that scientific community. Hence, for Fleck, societies end up with scientific knowledge that reflects the social conditions of that society as well as of our understanding of the natural world.

This is a powerful challenge to our dominant story of the neutrality and truthfulness of scientific knowledge. Whereas our dominant story tells us that scientific knowledge is the result of a precise endeavour that produces facts about the natural world – facts that are either true or false – Fleck's understanding (and Wittgenstein's too) is quite different. Fleck categorically rejects the idea that currently recognized 'facts' are more true than facts were in the past, and proposes that we understand 'facts' as contingent on place and use in a particular location – on their genesis inside a thought community.

It isn't only those inside an esoteric scientific community who are responsible for constructing science. Those of us in exoteric thought communities, ones external to where science is produced, are also involved in making up science through representing, discussing and reproducing the ideas of science.

Scientism

What we 'lay people' (as we are significantly called) mostly notice about the sciences is simply their power. Technology impresses us so deeply that we are not much surprised by the claim that scientific methods ought to be extended to cover the rest of our thought. (Midgley 2001: 59)

Fleck's theory of thought communities provides us with a complex understanding of the contingency of scientific knowledge, but also begins to explain the expansion and colonization of science into our everyday lives. The thought communities we are a part of become infused (infected?) with the ideas and ethos of science to the extent that we begin to see science as a dominant or superior mode of understanding our world. We can call this infection 'scientism' – the belief or general feeling that science is the best mode of explanation for things in the world. Scientism delivers to us a dominant story of science in our contemporary society: a contested story that attracts dissenting voices and, at times, alienates many people from its core narrative, but a powerful and prevalent story none the less. Scientism, as Mary Midgley demonstrates in her book *Science and Poetry* (2001) is part of our current situation, where we ask for more science to be provided (this may be in the form of explanation of things, culture, technology) and for science to be more prevalent in our lives. This is often inappropriate:

Irrelevant notions about how to make thought 'hard' and scientific by imitating physical science still constantly distort the social sciences and many other areas of our thought, notably psychiatry. Though the entire enterprise of making all our thought on human affairs conform to physical patterns has never been at all successful, the idea that we must somehow do this impossible thing still haunts us. Many people find the prospect of abandoning that attempt unbearable. (Midgley 2001: 150)

Midgley is undoubtedly correct in her description of the relationship between the social and the natural sciences, and in her general depiction of the prevalence of scientism in society as a whole. Yet we can also see a number of challenges to the hegemony of science and scientistic thinking in our technoscientific postmodernity. Ironically, given the dire predictions made by thinkers such as Max Weber and Herbert Marcuse early in the twentieth century, we are not seeing the increasing rationalization of *all* aspects of our lives (although that is certainly happening to large parts of our lives). We are seeing a decrease in rationalization in, for example, the expansion of New Age thought, the increase in opposition to 'scientific' interventions in our health and food, and the increasing rejection of scientific education by young people. Our thought communities, it would appear, are becoming more profuse, more diverse and more distinctive from one another, and the grip of the ideas of science inside them would appear to be loosening.

Science is everywhere

Our technoscientific world is suffused with science: scientific knowledge is imperative for the maintenance of our modern life-styles; our understanding of the world often relies on modes of thinking that, at the very least, owe a debt to the tradition of scientific investigation; our culture – popular, high, underground – relies on science and technology for the material means of production and reproduction, and science and technology are frequent themes for the content of science – from science fiction to the subject matter for the sculptures of Paolozzi. Science is a central tool in the search for power, allowing us to control our environment, and legitimating the forms of domination that exist in our industrialized societies; science is a central component of the operation of capitalist enterprises, providing the knowledge that enables the development of new goods and services, and providing wealth for those who control it.

Our understanding of science will inevitably be affected by the stories we have already been told about it, the most dominant one being scientism. Scientism presents us with a picture of science as a neutral, objective set of tools that are the best way of describing the world around us. Whilst it is appropriate to argue that the best mode of understanding basic biochemical processes, for example, should be based on the methods, tools and understandings of science, many would challenge the imposition of scientific thought elsewhere. We can also note that scientism, for all its prevalence, actually doesn't describe much of our world – our personal experiences are often at odds with the claims made by scientism. This may be due to our membership of thought communities that are becoming less easily penetrable by scientism, and our membership of various thought communities will also affect our understanding of science in society. Those who are part of a community that has suffered badly from the imposition and failure of technologies in their lives (such as the residents of the communities adjoining the Chernobyl nuclear power stations), or from the domination by a scientific elite (victims of unethical experiments carried out by pharmaceutical companies), will have perspectives concerning the role of science in society that are at odds with those who are members of communities and societies that are 'winning' because of the role of science in their lives.

This means that we need to understand science in a range of contexts: our scientistic, technoscientific frame of reference may not always be appropriate. Further, we must also recognize that our frame of reference prioritizes and fetishizes science in certain locations: we 'know' where real science is – in the laboratory, the textbook, the documentary – and we 'know' where the non-science is – on the TV screen and in the science fiction book and the art gallery. We need to challenge this way of looking at science to really understand what science means to us and where it is located.

When we start to do this, we begin to see that science is located almost everywhere in our society: obviously in some places – the laboratory, the school – but also in culture, in our everyday descriptions of the world, in the operation of our economic systems. Each of these sites tells us something different about science, sometimes reinforcing and sometimes contradicting our dominant story of science. Examining science as a complex object that has multiple, interdependent locations leads us to a number of key conclusions:

- Science is multi-faceted.
- Science is a complex and contestable concept.

- There is no essential core to what we call 'science' in contemporary society. Each facet of science leads us to an understanding of a different reality of science, and each has some validity.
- Placing a hierarchical order on top of these multiple realities is a social construct, not a necessary feature of science itself.

As we begin to explore science, each facet that we see brings new and different meanings with it. Our understanding of science, technology and technoscience – to name but three important things – changes according to which face of science is confronting us. In doing this, we should reflect also that we ourselves are responsible for bringing some of each of these meanings and themes with us – all of us are actively involved in constructing the meaning of science and the contexts within which it is located.

We will start our exploration of the different facets and locations of science by considering what many of us would identify as being 'real' science: the laboratory work from which a lot of scientific knowledge emerges. Although the laboratory has become a metaphor for control and simplification in our society, what we find when we enter the actual laboratory worlds of scientists is incredible complexity.

Part II

Doing Science

Photographs *of Einstein show him standing next to a blackboard covered with mathematical signs of obvious complexity; but* cartoons *of Einstein show him chalk still in hand, and having just written on an empty blackboard, as if without preparation, the magic formula of the world.*

Roland Barthes, The Brain of Einstein

2

In the Laboratory

In this chapter the word 'laboratory' is used as shorthand for any location where scientists are involved in the production of scientific knowledge. Such locations include observatories, field studies and also virtual computer-generated experimental areas. Although science permeates all of society and is visible in multiple locations, the laboratory remains the prime location for the enactment and execution of formal science. The formal scientific knowledge that emerges from scientific work-places provides a significant resource for wider societal understandings of science and, by extension, technology. In this chapter a laboratory experiment will be examined in detail, to introduce the themes of formal scientific method and scientific experimentation (see box 2.1). Before that, a quick overview will be given of some key themes that will be encountered when looking inside formal scientific locations.

Looking at how science is done starts with making sense of laboratory work, and this will provide some familiarity with the language and meaning construction that is occurring inside formal scientific work-places. The following example may present a challenge to readers who are not familiar with formal scientific knowledge, but it is worth persevering with this illustration of what is, at root, the basic substance of the 'science' that is so prevalent in society and culture. The experiment discussed here is not necessarily typical or representative of formal scientific experiments in general – finding a typical experiment is not possible given the range and variety of experimental techniques and scientific disciplines – but it does illustrate how

Box 2.1   Experiments

Why do scientists do experiments? The answer seems as obvious as the question seems banal: to find out about nature (Harré 1981: 5) Experiments are the basis of tightly disciplined means for the acquisition of certified practical knowledge (Harré 1981: 2)

Experiments are a key component of the formal scientific method. In formal science, this method begins with the collection of observed facts, and the construction of a model, a hypothesis, to explain the observed facts. The hypothesis may or may not be correct, and needs to be tested. Experiments are designed where the parameters contained in the hypothesis can be controlled and manipulated such that measurable results can be collected. The results will, ideally, confirm or deny the hypothesis. Assuming the hypothesis is confirmed by experiment, it can begin to change its status. Rather than just being an educated guess that has some evidence to back it up, the hypothesis will be tested rigorously in a number of ways. It will begin to take on the status of a scientific theory.

Although this outline of scientific method is widely held by those involved in formal scientific experimental work (although, as Steve Fuller, notes many scientists consider it to be a 'caricature' (Fuller 1997: 12)), it has come to be strongly challenged by many sociologists and philosophers of science, as we shall see later in this chapter.

formal scientific method (see box 2.2) is put into practice by scientific researchers.

The experiment described below shows a number of things. It illustrates the complexity of formal scientific activity, and the degree of detail that experimenters routinely work with. It also shows that the connections between the 'big problems' of science and the actual practical activity of many scientists are loose and stretched. The experiment also reveals the site of the production of formal scientific knowledge, and the site of the expression and application of formal scientific method.

Box 2.2   Scientific knowledge and scientific method

The standard account of formal science, and the account that is still largely held by most scientists and by most lay observers of formal science, is based around the idea of scientific method being a special way of discovering facts, where facts are individual packets of truth that describe the natural world, or nature. Science, on this account, has a privileged relationship to nature: it can provide us with truthful accounts of what nature really is. Not only that, science can act as an exemplar for other forms of human inquiry, such as investigation into the form and structure of the social world or of individual mental states.

Schematically, the standard account of formal science looks like this:

- Scientific theories generate hypotheses which can be translated into specific testable questions.
- Experiments are designed which will provide answers, in the form of facts, to those questions.
- Facts are compiled to confirm or deny the validity of the theory.
- Science thus proceeds by the operation of theory in close relationship to the facts generated by scientific endeavours using scientific method.

This position, broadly speaking, is congruent with what we call *positivism* (Chalmers 1999).

This idea would appear to distinguish scientific from other kinds of knowledge in a quite marked way. Whilst we, in our everyday lives, may know many things, there are few things that we can, or need to, prove. Science, on the standard account, proceeds through proving things beyond reasonable doubt, and by compiling facts and making fact-like statements, and through extending theories of the natural world.

Formal scientific knowledge can look as though it is written in a different language. It isn't, but it may be helpful to consider formal scientific papers to be written in a 'dialect'. To understand what is happening in these papers, a process of translation is necessary, moving from the tightly controlled formal scientific dialect to looser, everyday language. Ironically, this process is in many ways the oppo-site of the process that leads to the construction of the scientific paper, where the pragmatic methods of a team of experimenters, with asso-ciated uncertainty, informal understandings and 'making do' are turned into the formal scientific knowledge and discourse of a science journal article (see box 2.3).

Throughout the description of this example a process of transla-tion takes place. The experiments carried out in this laboratory are described by the researchers doing the work, and by the formal record of the work (i.e. scientific papers) in a 'dialect' that relies upon a large number of tightly defined, but esoteric, terms, such as 'enzyme', 'polymerase', 'molecule'. To fully understand what is happening in laboratory situations, we need to translate these terms into a language that is more familiar to us, the 'lay' public. In this process there is an inevitable change in meaning – we are moving from one thought com-munity, one language situation, to another. The context of the words and terms being used is dramatically different: in the laboratory sit-uation, or in the scientific paper, the words being used must have very precise and tightly defined meanings to ensure clarity of expression and comprehensibility across the scientific community to which the discourse is being addressed. Readers of the scientific paper who are inside the community of researchers will attach meanings to terms such as 'subunit' and 'polymerase' according to their past experience, their training, their practical activities of using the things with those names. They understand the esoteric terminology and language. For outsiders, these terms will retain their esoteric character, and it may be difficult to attach meanings to these words in ways similar to insid-ers. This process of translation from scientific dialect to everyday lan-guage can never be perfect, and no attempt is made here to try and perfect this process. What may happen is that readers will become more familiar with some of the discursive constructions taking place inside this scientific work-place, and will see how a thought com-munity structures its activities around a shared set of practices, atti-tudes and linguistic descriptions of the[ir] world.

In the biochemistry laboratory – investigating the structure and function of a protein

Before we look in detail at how this experiment is done, we need to think about why it is done, and therefore we need a little background and context. The basic principles that inform this experiment are the

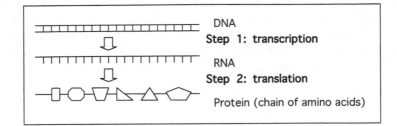

Fig. 2.1.   Schematic stages in protein production.

same as those that inform a great many current topics in biology, such as the Human Genome Project, cloning and genetic modification of organisms.

All living cells operate according to similar principles. Each cell contains DNA *(deoxyribose nucleic acid)*, which is the chemical that contains the genetic code for the production of proteins. All life processes in all living cells are carried out by proteins, which are complex molecules, and understanding how proteins are made inside cells is central to understanding any biochemical system.

In schematic form, the production of proteins in cells is a simple two-step process (see fig. 2.1). The first step is called transcription: a single stranded transcript of the double stranded DNA molecule is made by an enzyme (enzymes are also proteins) called RNA polymerase (RNAP). It does this by 'unzipping' the double-stranded DNA molecule, 'reading' the code that DNA contains, and transcribing this on to a new, single-stranded molecule called RNA (ribonucleic acid). This single-stranded molecule contains the code for a sequence of amino acids (simple nitrogen–carbon compounds) which will make a protein molecule, and the RNA is subsequently translated, in step 2, into a protein.

The experiment is concerned with the first stage in this process: transcription. Specifically, the experiment will investigate the structure and function of the enzyme RNAP and some of the factors that affect transcription of RNA. RNAP is a large, complex molecule which is made up of a number of components: rather than look at RNAP as a whole, this experiment investigates the role and structure of one particular part of RNAP, the subunit known as α (alpha). The experiment was carried out by Dr Georgina Lloyd of the School of Biosciences, University of Birmingham, as part of a long sequence of experiments investigating the alpha subunit of RNAP. The experiment discussed here, when combined with other complementary experiments, provides results that allow us to draw inferences about the architecture and operation of RNAP. Full details of this range of experiments can be found in Lloyd et al. 2002, entitled 'Requirement for two copies of RNA polymerase alpha subunit C-terminal domain for synergistic transcription activation at complex bacterial promoters'.

Box 2.3 Formal scientific language

The Lloyd et al. 2002 paper collects together a number of experiments and presents a range of results. The following quotation illustrates the format that discussion of complex experimental results will often take:

> Our finding that a single αCTD suffices to manifest the full synergistic effect of CRP and an adjacent single UP-element subsite (Fig. 5, lanes 2, 5) has a further implication; namely, a single αCTD can interact productively with both CRP and DNA. This supports the proposal that αCTD has distinct, nonoverlapping functional determinants for interaction with CRP and DNA, and that αCTD interacts simultaneously with CRP and DNA in CRP-dependent transcription complexes (Blatter et al. 1994; Busby and Ebright 1994, 1999; Tang et al. 1994; Zhou et al. 1994b; Savery et al. 1998, 2002) and is less easy to reconcile with the alternative proposal that the same surface of αCTD interacts with both CRP and DNA (Murakami et al. 1996; Ishihama 1997; Ozoline et al. 2000). We suggest that αCTD interacts simultaneously with activator and DNA in many, possibly all, activator-dependent, αCTD-dependent transcription complexes. (Lloyd et al. 2002: 2562)

Summarizing complex experimental results is a difficult task, but Lloyd et al. do this in a few sentences, and place their results in a wider context by making explicit reference to the two opposing sides in a debate about the action of the alpha (α) subunit of CRP: those who agree with Lloyd et al. (represented by the list of references beginning with Blatter et al. 1994) and the opposing camp who think that the α subunit interacts with both CRP and DNA (represented by the list of references beginning Murakami et al. 1996).

Why carry out experiments to investigate the architecture and operation of RNAP? It could be said that science is about finding things out about nature, and that everything in the natural world, including these molecules, is fair and appropriate subject matter for science. But such a response is not sufficient. We really need to start trying to answer the question 'Why investigate this enzyme and not some other?' A starting point to answering this question is to see that RNAP is central to the process of transcription, and that without this enzyme functioning correctly a cell will die. This experiment investigates the architecture of RNAP in bacteria: greater knowledge of the structure of this molecule might allow researchers to design new forms of antibiotics that, for example, inhibit the operation of RNAP in bacterial cells, but not in mammalian cells.

Constructing a hypothesis using previous experimental results

Researchers cannot 'see' RNAP (it is far too small), but they know that it exists from other experiments that have isolated this protein and discovered its chemical composition. However, simply knowing that RNAP is composed of a chain of amino acids that are themselves composed of certain numbers of atoms of nitrogen, carbon and hydrogen is insufficient to explain why RNAP works in the way that it does. Sequencing – that is, working out the precise order of the specific amino acids that constitute RNAP – is a step towards understanding the complex structure of RNAP, and prior experiments doing this have found that RNAP is made up of a number of subunits, which have been designated α_2, β, β', ω, σ (Ebright 2000). This designation means that there are six subunits of RNAP: two alphas (the designation α_2 means that there are two of these), two betas (β and β'), one omega (ω), and one sigma (σ). Each subunit carries out a different function in the transcription of DNA, such as helping RNAP to recognize the right part of the DNA to be transcribed, or interacting with additional factors such as proteins or chemicals which help the transcription reaction to take place. By making different versions of RNAP which have subtle variations in the composition of the subunits, and then measuring how effective each version of RNAP is in transcribing a piece of DNA, researchers can draw inferences about what each subunit is doing in the reaction as a whole, and how each subunit interacts with other subunits and other factors involved in the transcription process. Most crucially here, RNAP will use an additional factor called cyclic AMP receptor protein (CRP) to facilitate transcription of DNA: RNAP and CRP work together to maximize RNA production, but their precise interaction is not fully understood. The experiment discussed here investigates how RNAP and CRP interact with each other, and extends the understanding of how RNAP, CRP and DNA interact with one another.

The experiment uses different versions of RNAP. The alpha subunit of RNAP is composed of two separate units that are connected to each other. In the experiments that led to the Lloyd et al. 2002 publication, these separate parts of the alpha subunit were manipulated and altered. The results allow inferences to be drawn about the role and the architecture of RNAP as a whole.

Doing the experiment

The experiment can be broken down into three main phases: preparation of reactions, collection of data, analysis of data.

1 Preparation of reactions   A comprehensive list of all reactants and reagents to be used in the experiment is drawn up. The experiment relies on precise comparisons between different versions of RNAP producing a RNA transcript. The transcript will be identified by tagging it with a radioactive molecule and measuring the amount of radiation that is emitted by the reaction products: more radioactivity indicates that more reaction product has been made. To ensure that the comparisons are valid, measurement must be very precise at all stages of the experiment: for example, if too much RNAP were to be added to one of the test-tubes containing the reaction, then the amount of reaction product would be increased inadvertently, and this would invalidate the results. Precise administration of the chemicals needed is carried out using a micropipette (see illustration 2.3).

The original code for the reaction products is a piece of DNA that has been artificially manufactured in the laboratory using a PCR machine (also called a 'thermal cycler') (see illustration 2.1) that can synthesize DNA pieces using a chemical process called Polymerase Chain Reaction (PCR). (For a sociological history of PCR, see Rabinow 1996.) The PCR machine makes multiple copies of a straight piece of DNA which is subsequently inserted into a loop of

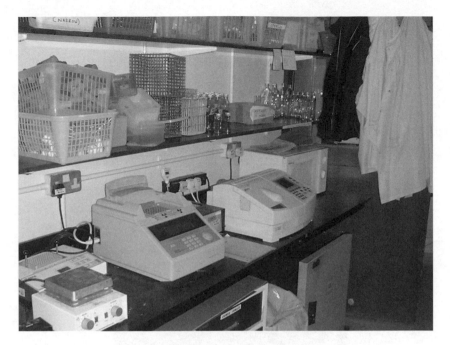

Illustration 2.1.   PCR machine. Photo by author.

DNA called a plasmid. The process of inserting the straight piece of DNA into the plasmid is called *cloning* (see box 2.4).

Box 2.4   Cloning

In biochemistry cloning means the copying of a piece of DNA or RNA such that an exact replica is made. However, cloning has taken on a much wider meaning in contemporary culture and society. The word 'cloning' is now used to refer to the copying of entire organisms, rather than just their DNA.

Working from a protocol that lists all the ingredients needed for the experiment, the appropriate chemicals are added to individual test-tubes. In this experiment twenty-one different reactions will be carried out, so twenty-one separate test-tubes are prepared, each with its own cocktail of chemicals. Each test-tube needs to contain some

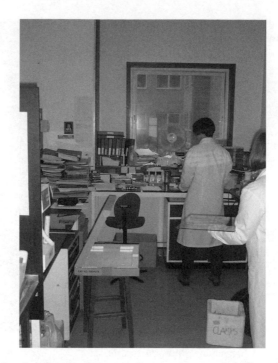

Illustration 2.2.   Lab bench where experiments are prepared. Photo by author.

medium for the reaction to take place in. This is provided by a solution that imitates conditions inside a bacterial cell, and contains the chemicals that are needed to construct the reaction products (RNA and a CRP-dependent RNA). The test-tube will also contain a version of RNAP, and may contain a version of CRP. The initial preparation of these ingredients takes place at the lab bench (illustration 2.2), and the addition of radioactive isotopes to tag the reaction products takes place in the 'hot room' (illustration 2.3) where, for safety reasons, all radioactive reagents are stored. This experiment is taking place *in vitro* (which means in glass). The conditions inside each test-tube are an approximation of what happens in real life (*in vivo*).

The reactions are allowed to proceed for 15 minutes at 30°C. Because so many reactions are taking place at the same time, the experiment is split into two halves, with the first group of reactions being completed, then put on ice, while the second group of reactions are completed. The reactions are stopped by adding a solution which denatures the active RNAP molecules in each test-tube.

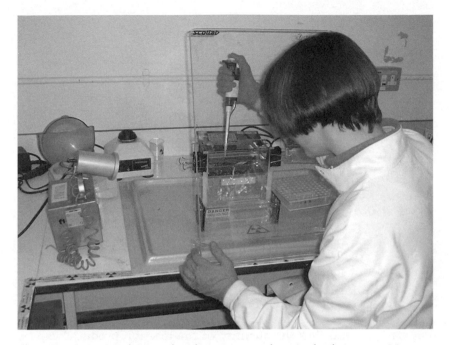

Illustration 2.3. Loading a gel with reaction products in the 'hot' room. Note use of micropipette. At far left is a Geiger counter to measure radioactivity. Photo by author.

2 Collection of data At the end of the experiment each test-tube contains a cocktail of chemicals: some of the original reagents will still be present, some will be transformed into the reaction products that the experiment aims to measure, and there will be additional products. The experimenter needs to filter out just the reaction products that the experiment is designed to measure, and a process called gel electrophoresis is used. This process uses the different electrical properties of different molecules to separate them from each other. A chemical gel is made at the lab bench (the process is fairly similar to making jelly/jello at home), and a fixed, precise amount of the contents of each test-tube is placed in a well at the top of the gel. Because the reaction products are radioactive, the gel is loaded in the hot room.

A gentle electric current is applied to the gel, and this 'pulls' the reaction products from the top of the gel to the bottom. In this experiment current is applied to the gel for approximately 90 minutes, and the gel is then dried. The gel is then placed inside a phosphorimager which displays the intensity of radiation at different parts of the gel.

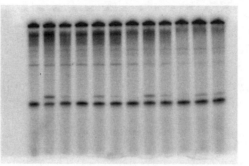

Illustration 2.4. Visual results from the phosphorimager. Photo by Dr G. Lloyd. Published with Dr Lloyd's permission, © author.

3 Analysis of data The results from the phosphorimager are produced in the form of a photograph which shows the radioactive reaction products as black bands on a lighter background (see illustration 2.4). Using a piece of software called ImageQuant the intensity of the black bands, and thus the quantity of the reaction products, can be measured.

The results of the experiment are collated and added to the collection of results from other experiments. The experimental results will vary in quality, in that they may be close to the predicted results or far away from what is expected. The experiment will be repeated a number of times using exactly the same method until at least three sets of results are obtained that have broadly similar data.

Results

The results show that RNAP operates at different levels of efficiency according to how its structure has been altered. Each experiment that is carried out compares the modified versions of RNAP to the original 'wild type' (i.e. unaltered) form of RNAP. By compiling a large number of different observations of RNAP's performance under different conditions and with different structures, inferences about RNAP's structure can be drawn. Lloyd et al. drew a range of conclusions concerning RNAP, most crucially that it requires both parts of the alpha subunit to be present when carrying out a CRP-dependent reaction. This means that the alpha subunit must be carrying out two functions: binding RNAP to the DNA *and* binding RNAP to CRP. A further inference can be drawn: the alpha subunit of RNAP must have two active binding sites – one for DNA and one for CRP – rather than having only one active binding site (which would mean it having to simultaneously bind to CRP and DNA at the same physical location).

However, the above description is a 'translation' of two more formal scientific discourses. The first is that presented verbally in this laboratory, where researchers will discuss with each other what the results of experiments show. These discussions take place over a long period of time – a series of experiments may be carried out over a number of years, and the researchers may only fully understand their results after a long process of thought, reflection, further reading and discussion. Discussions will take place in formal settings, such as presenting research findings at seminars and conferences, or informally through team meetings in the lab or during rest breaks. The second is the formal scientific discourse that is in the Lloyd et al. 2002 publication in the journal *Genes & Development*. Looking at the formal scientific discourse in Lloyd et al. 2002, the dialect of this branch of biochemistry becomes fairly clear. Not only do outsiders need to recognize key terms such as CRP and DNA; they also need to make sense of the deployment of such terms in active constructions, where meaning is being argued over. In addition, they need to have an understanding of the construction and representation of debates that take place in a specific scientific community, where the social components of these – such as informal discussion, emails, chatting – will be 'hidden' by a highly formal description of a state of affairs.

Some observations on this experiment

Space This is a complex experiment that requires a great deal of precision. However, the experiment can be completed with fairly basic equipment, and does not require a great deal of space. As can be seen in illustration 2.2, the laboratory being used is quite cluttered, and this fairly small space is shared by two experimenters. The hot room is shared by about twelve researchers. Much of the equipment being used – refrigerators (illustration 2.5), microwave ovens, sinks, water purifiers – would not be out of place in an ordinary kitchen. The laboratory is a busy place, with a lot of activity and discussion of aspects of experiments (as well as other conversa-

Illustration 2.5. Corridor and refrigerators outside main laboratory work-space. Photo by author.

tions) taking place almost constantly. Close co-ordination of work and the ability to co-operate and work as a part of a team are important here.

Time and space The experiment described above takes two days to complete. The first day is taken up with preparation of reagents, completing the reactions, and separating the reaction components on the gel. The second is devoted to collecting results from the phospho-imager, analysis of these results, and collation of results with other experiments. However, although the experiment takes relatively little time, the experiment must be repeated at least three times, and the development stage, where the original experimental technique is designed, tried and tested can take a number of years. This experiment relies on experiments being carried out in the same lab, and at other facilities around the world, most notable of which is a laboratory at the Howard Hughes Medical Institute, Rutgers University, USA. Amongst other things, chemicals, ideas and results are shared between these two laboratories.

Outcomes

What happens to the results from these experiments? We can point to a number of different specific outcomes. The first is the obvious product of specific publications, in this case a paper in the peer-reviewed journal *Genes & Development* (see box 2.5).

The paper will inform other researchers working on similar experiments, and adds to a general body of knowledge surrounding RNAP and CRP. Other researchers may choose to replicate some aspects of this work to confirm the results, although it is unlikely that exactly the same experiments would be carried out at other laboratories. It is more likely that the results presented in the paper will be the starting point for further examinations of aspects of RNAP's architecture.

The published paper doesn't describe everything that takes place in the production of the results of the experiment. It is an edited and truncated description of the experimental procedure which focuses on the successful experiments, not the unsuccessful ones, and which provides only the absolutely necessary information for someone skilled in a similar range of techniques on a similar range of objects to make sense of the results. Significantly, the paper omits general discussion of the principles of polymerase chain reaction, the structure and function of DNA and RNA, and the general scheme of transcription: it is assumed that the audience of the paper will know all this already. Effectively the paper is a translation, and a condensation, of a large amount of formal and informal interaction (e.g. discussion between researchers in the laboratory) that has taken place over a number of years. The point here is that it is the laboratory practice of working for an extended period in a very specific area, designing a large number of experiments (many of which will be failures), refining techniques through discussion with colleagues in a team and in other laboratories, confirming and rejecting hypotheses, and moving from existing theories on a subject to extend knowledge of an area that is the formal scientific method. The scientific paper is a pale reflection of this process, and a reflection that hides key features of the collective and non-linear processes that make up scientific research work.

A second outcome is confirmation of the techniques and procedures being used by a team of researchers as a whole. The results of these successful experiments with RNAP and CRP confirm that the experimental technique of comparing different versions of RNAP and analysing the results using gel electrophoresis and a phosphoimager is a 'good' method. This is important, because the researchers inves-

Box 2.5 Peer review

Securing publication in a reputable scientific journal is a significant goal for most academic scientists: the very act of publishing
verifies the quality and 'correctness' of the research. This ascription of status to formal scientific knowledge is made possible by
the peer review process, whereby other researchers who are familiar with the general field of the research described in a paper are
asked to comment on the merits and demerits of the paper on
behalf of the journal. Peer reviewing in the natural sciences is, in
general, a one-way anonymous process: the reviewer will know
the identity of the author of a paper, but the author will not know
the identity of the reviewer (however, it is likely that they can guess
the identity). Peer review is at the heart of the process of the validation of scientific knowledge, and is also a mainstay of the
process of awarding research grants: it is seen as being a way of
guaranteeing the quality of scientific research.

However, as Steve Fuller points out, there are problems with
the process of peer review. Given the complexity of the work
carried out in many experiments, and the very high degree of spe-
cialization, it is unlikely that the peer reviewer will have extensive
knowledge of the material presented in the paper, and almost
inconceivable that the peer reviewer will have the time or the
resources to replicate the experiments being described. At best, the
reviewer will be able to judge from their experience that the work
described is plausible, competently executed, and produces results
that are consistent with others. Fuller describes the peer review
process in terms of a collective insurance policy that a scientific
community takes out (Fuller 1997: 65). But the peer review
process systematically reproduces structural problems built into
scientific communities:

> [B]ecause each scientific speciality is dominated by a few gatekeep-
> ers who pass judgement on everyone else in the field, failure to
> appease these 'peers' can be disastrous, much like the failure to pay
> money to the local mafia boss. Not surprisingly, scientists tend to
> underplay their own originality and overplay that of their signifi-
> cant colleagues. (Fuller 1997: 65)

tigating RNAP could choose from a range of different methods. For
example, they could adopt a completely different approach and
decide to use X-ray crystallography to produce images of the RNAP
molecule that would 'show' the fine detail of RNAP's structure.

By choosing and confirming the worth of their chosen method, the researchers are increasing their confidence in the method as a whole and its applicability to solving certain types of biochemical puzzles.

A third outcome is confirmation of the models being hypothesized. At the most basic level, the results of this experiment confirm that DNA is transcribed to make RNA by an enzyme called RNA polymerase (RNAP). However, at a much more detailed level, the results confirm that the sequence of events in the hypothesized transcription process have been correctly modelled, and that RNAP and CRP are important factors in this. Further, the experiment confirms that there are different subunits in the RNAP molecule, and that these subunits are discrete.

Formal science

From the outside, formal science can look like a number of very large projects that are working on big 'problems' – the problem of gene therapy, the problem of what matter is really made of, the problem of bacterial resistance to antibiotics, the war on cancer, and so on – but from the inside it becomes clear that there is often a very large gap between an individual experimenter's work and the big 'problem' that their work is trying to address. Science in our present society proceeds by breaking down big problems into ever smaller problems, solving these as best it can, and then amalgamating (if possible) results from a whole series of small-scale experiments to try and shed light on the original big problem. However, even this abstract description makes it appear as if science is a kind of hierarchical conspiracy, in which there are some people who control the research strategy as a whole. This simply is not the case: bringing together the elementary researches of the mass of scientists involved in a broadly similar field does not take place in a systematic way. Rather, it is fairly haphazard (particularly if we take a global view of formal scientific endeavour) with new research projects combining previous work with new experiments in the hope that a synthesis of ideas will produce useful results. The complexity of what formal science as a whole is trying to do can be illustrated by considering an example.

If we take a disciplinary area like biochemistry, and look at a significant problem that biochemistry is trying to tackle, such as the emergence of bacterial resistance to antibiotics, with a view to providing a new generation of more effective antibiotics, we find that a huge number of different projects are involved in this endeavour.

Some projects will appear to be 'closer' to the main topic than others, simply by virtue of their self-descriptions, and these may or may not be the projects that will bring about the next generation of antibiotics. All knowledge, all information relating to how bacteria develop resistance to antibiotics and what sorts of chemicals inhibit bacterial growth, will clearly be of use in tackling and solving the big problem. But it may be that the next generation of antibiotics emerges from work being done in genetic engineering, by investigating how bacteria replicate themselves. New antibiotics may not look anything like old antibiotics (indeed, it is even possible that the next leap forward in anti-bacterial treatments could come from nanotechnology, a branch of physics, as argued by Eric Drexler (1990) – see chapter 8). The complexity of trying to resolve one, on the surface, fairly straightforward problem is revealed only when we really start to break down the problem. The current focus on the biochemical approach to producing new antibiotics is a reflection of the sense in science and society that genetic knowledge is the most appropriate knowledge for changing, and improving, our world. (See Lewontin 1993 and Nelkin and Lindee 1995 for a more in-depth analysis of these themes.)

Looking at one specific research project in particular will reveal very little about the problem as a whole, but will tell us a lot about why a complete understanding of this problem has not yet been found, and why it is that science is so hard to make sense of.

It appears that the natural world is fairly straightforward to understand because we are told that it works according to rules and laws, and we think that the social world is much more difficult to make sense of because we cannot identify those rules and laws. What we fail to notice is just how incredibly complicated the natural world actually is: simply having the rules and laws helps very little when we are dealing with complex and disparate phenomena. Some sociologists of science have described this everyday laboratory work as 'puzzle-solving' (see section on T. S. Kuhn in chapter 3), but what we are really seeing is the application of proven tools to new areas of inquiry to produce descriptions of the workings of, for example, the mammalian cell. There is no puzzle here, in the sense that there is a theoretical prediction that can be tested and, if it doesn't match up to expected results, will be, perhaps eventually, falsified. What most scientists have is a set of laws, rules, techniques and prior examples that can be applied to the vast number of cases that have yet to be investigated. Knowing that the production of one protein is regulated by another enzyme does not tell us about how a different protein is regulated, not to mention how two proteins are regulated separately when they are being produced simultaneously inside a cell, although it may provide us with clues that will help us investigate further cases. Our knowledge of the workings of one protein can help us to formulate a hypothesis to test in a future experiment investigating a different protein.

Different kinds of formal science

Although our common understanding of science, and our experience of formal science at school, tends to focus on experiments, not all scientific endeavour proceeds by the method of testing hypotheses through controlling variables and finding experimental results. *Experimental* sciences do this. However, there are some scientific activities that simply can't proceed by testing things in experiments, yet they are also classified as being science by most observers: we generally call these *discovering* sciences. An example is astronomy, and other 'discovering' sciences are geology, botany and palaeontology. However, all of these will use, at times, experimental technique, and a separation between experimental and discovering sciences is in many ways an artificial one. We should also note that many commentators, indeed many practising natural scientists, would consider the social sciences of sociology, psychology, economics and politics to be 'discovering' sciences. Much of what astronomers do involves observing things, cataloguing these phenomena, and then drawing conclusions that try to provide answers to the 'why' questions that are raised by the phenomena. Astronomers are 'discovering' things about how the universe works through observing it, albeit in very systematic ways. For example, astronomers may observe some new phenomenon in the night sky. They will then attempt to find similar examples, and will then try and find commonalities in terms of the data they have collected which will help to explain why the phenomena have the characteristics that they do. We can note that significant characteristics of this form of method would be the attempt to carry out observation systematically, to measure phenomena as precisely as possible, to record data as accurately as possible, and to apply existing rules to results, or to construct new rules that can explain the main features of the phenomena in question, all aspects of a general scientific method.

The experimental/discovering dichotomy is by no means the only distinction that we can use to categorize scientific enterprises. Most people will be familiar with the distinction of scientific sub-disciplines into the fields of *life* and *physical* sciences. These distinguishing labels are visible not only in media descriptions of the sciences, but also in university structures, where biology may be located in a faculty of life sciences with disciplines such as psychology and pharmacology, as distinct from faculties of physical sciences containing disciplines such as chemistry, physics and astronomy. The split between life and physical sciences is becoming hard to maintain, or even identify, in contemporary formal science. Biology is increasingly being dominated by biochemistry – the chemical study of life processes that often proceeds by experiment – and disciplines such as chemistry and physics are increasingly concerned with the construction and operation of biological systems.

A further twist to these distinctions is provided by scientific endeavours that neither carry out experiments nor observe the natural world. Formal science that proceeds by creating computer-generated scenarios and analysing the outcomes of changing variables in these are not particularly new, but are much more common now. It is quite possible for scientists to present research findings on new chemical compounds that have been 'created' entirely inside the memories of computers.

What are experiments for?

The experiment we looked at shows that laboratory practices generate specific data about specific phenomena. The data collected in the experiments are used to infer knowledge about the objects in question. In this case, the results of the biochemistry experiments are used to make inferences about the structure of RNAP. We can therefore see clearly that one of the stated goals of the project of science – the expansion of certified knowledge of the natural world – would appear to have been achieved by this experiment. However, some philosophers of science would question the validity of the knowledge being produced, in that they would challenge the reality of the objects being studied. This is not something that most scientists would do, and in the case of the experiment looked at here the experimenters consider that the object of inquiry – RNAP – actually exists and can be considered to be 'real' because 'real' data are produced about it. For the moment we will suspend judgement on this point. The connection between the data collected in experiments and the knowledge that is produced in scientific publications and other forms of scientific discourses will be discussed in chapter 3.

Although it can be said that a goal of the project of science has been achieved by producing and extending certified knowledge of the natural world, this may not be sufficient reason for carrying out the experiments. These experiments result in publications that will inform a small part of the scientific community, but the knowledge that appears in the publications will, in all likelihood, not be used by anyone immediately, and may not be used by anyone ever, or at least not for a considerable period of time. This does raise the question of why bother to carry out the experiments in the first place, and considering this question in the light of understanding what the experiments entail shows something important about contemporary science.

The biochemistry experiment is at the cutting edge of the discipline: it provides new knowledge of the world that has not been seen by people before. The researchers carrying out these experiments are part of quite small networks of researchers around the world who are carrying out similar researches using similar experimental techniques. These scientific communities are engaged in complex experiments into very specific things that do not, at least immediately, have connections to other fields of study in their discipline. Unlike the representations of science that are often presented within popular culture, where experimenters are directly working on projects with specific applicability (for examples, a 'cure for cancer'), most science – particularly the science carried out in academic environments – is like the experiment shown here. It may be that there will be specific applications that emerge from these experiments: the biochemistry experiments *may* lead to new forms of antibiotics being produced, but equally they may not.

What experiments are doing is extending the reach of researchers into new areas of study. In addition, they are validating a particular experimental procedure, and a way of imagining the natural world. A further point that must be noted is that laboratories are training grounds for a new generation of academic scientists (see chapter 5), and for highly skilled researchers, computer programmers and managers who will go on to work in industry, or elsewhere.

The discussion above begins to address the issue of why these experiments are happening; but there is a final point that needs to be considered. These experiments are happening because there is a tradition of doing experiments like this in these laboratories, and there has been a large amount of money, time and effort invested in previous experiments that the current experiments build upon.

Analysis of the work carried out in laboratories reveals the relationship between the results created in experiments and the narratives that emerge in scientific papers. In addition to the formal outcomes of scientific papers, the research process in the laboratory incorporates a range of social factors implicated in how experiments take place (e.g. team work, group discussion, informal chatting) and some external structural factors (e.g. funding regimes and the peer review process) that affect what is done in the laboratory. A process of translation occurs in the transition between laboratory practice and description of formal scientific knowledge in a scientific paper. However, there is also a process of translation that occurs in the construction of the accounts of laboratory work presented above: they are informal scientific narratives that attempt to approximate the work taking place in the laboratory. Overall, knowledge is being produced at a number of levels, and with different statuses.

Looking inside the experimental processes taking place within laboratories reveals many things. Purely in terms of the descriptions used by researchers, it is possible to note some distinctions. Initial consideration of topic areas and discussion with colleagues in laboratories are often quite informal, with loose ideas for methods and hypotheses being discussed in informal settings. This is translated into formal scientific method in the form of protocols for experiments. In the course of carrying out experiments, less formal practical features emerge, as researchers adopt pragmatic 'fixes' to get equipment working and ensure that results emerge. Results are formalized by analysis, and experiments are subsequently presented in the highly formal setting, and highly formal language, of the scientific paper. Introducing a social researcher into this flow entails researchers having to translate their internal, esoteric descriptions – the dialect of their thought community – into exoteric general language that outsiders can understand: again, this is a shift between formal and less formal modes of explanation.

The chapter that follows will begin to examine the next aspect of doing science: how formal scientific knowledge is understood by commentators, what the status of formal scientific knowledge is, and what the relationship between formal scientific knowledge and wider understandings of science is. This involves considering the epistemological and historical aspects of formal science, and the construction of general histories and epistemologies of science and scientific knowledge.

Further reading

Sismondo, S. 2004: *An Introduction to Science and Technology Studies.* Malden, Mass.: Blackwell Publishers. This is a good overview of STS, and there is a comprehensive discussion of the emergence of laboratory studies in chapter 9.

Chalmers, A. F. 1999: *What is this Thing called Science?* Buckingham: Open University Press.

Fuller, S. 1997: *Science*. Buckingham: Open University Press.

Harré, R. 1981: *Great Scientific Experiments: Twenty Experiments that Changed our View of the World*. Oxford: Oxford University Press.

For insiders' accounts of scientific work and method a good starting point is to look at general introductory level textbooks for undergraduates. Your local or university library will have a good range of these (look for one-word titles such as *Biochemistry* or *Physics* and try to find up-to-date editions). Almost all of these will contain brief descriptions of what scientific work and method are. It is interesting to compare these descriptions with the versions written by social investigators of science, such as those provided in the next chapter of this book.

3

Scientific Knowledge

Introduction

The previous chapter looked at the production of formal scientific knowledge in scientific work-places. Experiments in laboratories are clear examples of the connection between action and formal knowledge: the actions of experimenters in laboratories result in the production of formal knowledge which appears as scientific papers in journals. Although experiments are not the only method by which formal scientific knowledge is generated, they are the underpinning of formal scientific method and are the core of much formal scientific endeavour. Formal scientific knowledge requires translation between the laboratory and the scientific paper, and subsequently a much greater degree of translation is required as formal scientific knowledge is disseminated in wider society – for example, to social scientists or journalists. Moving away from experiments – that is, shifting the knowledge gained in a laboratory into other places, even just to other formal scientific locations such as specialist journals – means that there is a change in form and meaning. Scientific knowledge will thus take a wide range of different forms, will have a range of content, and will use a variety of different linguistic and discursive constructions.

All philosophical and social science accounts of scientific practice and scientific knowledge serve to create a picture of science in contemporary society: they represent science and scientific knowledge to us. Most philosophy and sociology of science consider scientific knowledge to be an object that is fairly standard, with characteristics that are shared between all the different forms that it takes. In addition, many of the accounts of epistemology of science see scientific knowledge as being separate from, and often superior to, other forms of knowledge. This chapter will examine the relationship between the practical activities of scientists in laboratories and their production of scientific knowledge, the formal scientific knowledge of journals and the different ways in which philosophers and sociologists of science make sense of this knowledge.

A major concern in this chapter is to challenge the standard account of science which sees scientific knowledge as better, bounded and clearly identifiable. The standard account is deeply embedded in our society, promoting scientific knowledge and method as having a status higher than other forms of knowledge and methods of inquiry. The standard account is also deeply embedded in the institutions of science itself, and the dominance of science in education results in a proliferation of this account. It is also clearly visible in many cultural representations of science.

Understanding how scientific knowledge achieves the status that it has in society requires a critical approach to such accounts. Whereas the first picture of science we examined was science taking place in the laboratory with its outcome of formal scientific knowledge, the second will be this: the picture of science created through formal appraisal of scientific knowledge. The formal appraisal of scientific knowledge takes a variety of forms, but in general is described as epistemology of science – the examination of the basis of scientific knowledge.

We have seen in the previous chapter a location and a set of processes that lead to the production of scientific knowledge. We can see a direct relationship between the results created in experiments and the narratives that emerge in scientific papers. We can also identify a range of social factors implicated in how experiments take place (e.g. team work, group discussion), and we can identify some external structural factors (e.g. funding regimes and the peer review process) that affect what is done in the laboratory, and thus what appears in publications. How can we start to make sense of these different elements so as to understand why scientific knowledge emerging from the laboratory has the structure and character that it does? Two main approaches – sociology of science and philosophy of science – are available to us. However, we should also note that the discourses of science are constrained by tradition, a topic that is addressed by the history of science and which will be further investigated in chapter 4. Sociology and philosophy of science have tended to converge around some core interests, principal of which today is the status of scientific knowledge as a construction. In the following chapters a brief overview of key themes in the sociology and philosophy of science will be given.

We will first examine the main general trends in epistemology of science, providing an overview of the terrain. Then we will look specifically at different sociological accounts of what is happening in the production of scientific knowledge. The aim here is to provide some background to answering the question 'How do philosophers and sociologists of science make sense of scientific knowledge today?' A secondary aim is to show how much philosophy and sociology of science, even contemporary post-structural approaches, often serve to construct a picture of science, scientific knowledge and scientists that sees each in essentialist terms.

The standard account

What we will call the standard account is widely held, particularly amongst working scientists, and is a major component of the public image of science in contemporary society. It can be called the standard account of formal scientific knowledge – when applied to single instances of the emergence of scientific knowledge (e.g. in an experiment) – and the standard account of formal science when applied to the analysis of all formal science activities (e.g. when offering a description of the work of a scientific community). At this point we have to note that for the most part STS (Science and Technology Studies) has departed from this account, seeing it as wholly inadequate to describe what is actually happening in the production of scientific knowledge. Yet it remains the case that a huge number of practitioners of scientific method still hold to this account. The standard account of formal science describes a project for science (the discovery of facts about the natural world), and prescribes a method – what we can call formal scientific method – by which this should be carried out. Formal scientific method relies, in experimental sciences (physics, chemistry, biochemistry, etc.), on the construction of experiments where hypotheses derived from theories are tested in conditions that allow for the strict control of all variables. In discovering sciences (e.g. botany, geology, astronomy), the equivalent of experiments can be seen in the construction of strict observational regimes where observational data are collected in precise ways, measurements are made in as accurate a manner as possible, and the theories generated by such a process are based on the collection of as many facts as possible.

The standard account proceeds from this premiss:

Science is a form of knowledge that produces facts and fact-like statements.

This core tenet conflates science and knowledge, seeing them as indivisible. This means that the standard account is *not* defining science by its methods, locations, practitioners or shared value or belief systems. It defines science purely in terms of its goals and its outcomes. By this account, science is the knowledge that emerges from scientific activity, or even from non-scientific activity, if the knowledge conforms to stipulation of facts and fact-like statements. The definition is not about process, location or any other factor that may contain an allegedly 'subjective' element, but just what the statements themselves look like. Finally, the word 'produces' contains some necessary ambiguity. The standard account of science assumes that the natural world is a passive object that objective science can confront in such a way that the underlying rules and laws of its operation can be discovered. Yet the standard account is forced to be vague about *how* these laws and rules emerge from formal scientific endeavour, as they are a product of human activity, not an artefact of nature that has been hidden for us to uncover.

This definition does in one way describe what scientists in laboratories are doing – the end result of their endeavours *is* the production of facts and fact-like statements (although there can be much disagreement about what a 'fact' actually is). But the production of facts and fact-like statements does not necessarily distinguish science from non-science. By this criterion many things we do in everyday life would count as science. As I look at my desk, I can see my iBook (a fact), and I can say 'the iBook is in front of me' which is a fact-like statement. To clarify the distinction between science and non-science, the standard account proceeds to qualify and extend its description of science. The key elements of this extended description are:

- Science is not metaphysics, where metaphysics is a range of sweeping generalizations. Science is a series of factual propositions. These factual propositions are connected to each other by a common subject matter (the natural world) and a project (the extension and completion of knowledge of the natural world).

- Science connects factual propositions through the use of theories. Scientific theories describe what is known about the world and extends science to make predictions about what is not known about the world.
- Science is empirical. It is based upon experience, i.e. actually perceiving things rather than just creating theories about them.
- Scientific knowledge is applied rationality: it is produced using concrete and rigorous methods.
- Scientific knowledge is a direct refutation of religious experience. Religion relies upon faith, science upon facts.
- Scientific knowledge is based upon objectivity and seeks to remove subjectivity from analysis of the world.
- Scientific knowledge has definite outcomes, it makes science 'work'. It does transform our lives through producing technological breakthroughs, cures for illnesses, new ways of understanding our environment, etc.
- Scientific knowledge is cumulative and progressive, through theories coming together and supporting each other. We know more about the natural world than we did in the past, and we build our knowledge on foundations that have been laid down in the past.

These elements of the standard account of science emerged in the centuries following Newton's unification of the laws of physics (we'll discuss the history of science in chapter 4). There is an orthodoxy surrounding these principles. This strong version of science is exemplified and expressed most clearly by adherents of the Vienna Circle, the influential philosophy group that began meeting in the 1920s and included Rudolf Carnap, Viktor Kraft and Moritz Schlick. Their logical positivism relied on an understanding of science that considered scientific knowledge (and mathematics) to be better, more robust and more valid than other forms of knowledge, largely because it constructs theories that describe the world. The Vienna Circle's ideas have a powerful force even today, and many scientists, when asked to describe their understanding of science, will offer explanations that concur with it. The logical positivists of the Vienna Circle thought that theories attain their scientific status through induction (the drawing of inferences from a number of particular cases) and verification. Verification entails that a theory is proposed and the theory makes predictions that can be tested through observation. Scientists will sceptically adopt a theory, and will then test the theory by making many observations. As the observations that confirm the theory accumulate, the theory achieves a scientific status. Therefore a proposition is scientific to the extent that it can be verified by observations, and a scientific theory becomes 'true' when a sufficient number of observations or experiments have been accumulated.

However, an associate of the Vienna Circle, but a dissenting voice to them, Karl Popper, is also influential in the contemporary construction of the standard account. Popper and Carnap appear to be quite opposed regarding some aspects of formal scientific work, but, as Ian Hacking points out, '[t]hey disagreed about much, but only because they agreed on basics' (Hacking 1983: 3). Popper's theory of the logic of scientific theories both refutes and extends the ideas of the Vienna Circle. It refutes them in that the Vienna Circle's theory of verification is disproved by Popper, but extends them in that Popper's defence of science strengthened the logical positivists' arguments that scientific knowledge is superior to non-scientific knowl-·edge. Both Popper and the Vienna Circle agreed that understanding the role of theory is central to this endeavour. 'The empirical sciences are systems of theories. The logic of scientific knowledge can therefore be described as a theory of theories' (Popper 2002: 37).

Popper's understanding of the formation of scientific knowledge rests upon an understanding of theory that was totally new at the time of his writing (*The Logic of Scientific Discovery* was first published in 1935). Popper's refutation of the theory of verification was quite devastating. His theory of falsification (as opposed to verification) suggests a quite different process of theory construction for science. Theories arise in response to pressing problems – they emerge as attempts to solve problems in already existing theory. The new theory will be tested in the same way that the logical positivists suggest – that is, through naming observations and carrying out experiments. But, according to Popper, scientists aren't carrying out observations and experiments to *verify* the theory; rather, they are doing this in an attempt to *falsify* the theory. No scientific theory can ever be proved true, but all scientific theories can be proved false; just because scientists have collected many, many observations that confirm a theory doesn't mean the theory is correct, just that evidence to the contrary has not yet been found.

Popper's account became the dominant story of how formal science proceeded. It describes the actions of scientists in laboratories, seeing them as engaged in efforts to falsify existing theory as a way of advancing scientific knowledge: theories that could not be falsified became 'truthful', although, according to Popper's account, scientists would retain a degree of scepticism about such theories. Similarly, Popper's account describes how the project of science proceeds, through collecting and accumulating different 'truthful' theories that become increasingly reliable. Finally, Popper's account describes why scientific knowledge is 'better' than other sorts of knowledge: because it emerges from theories that are falsifiable. Popper's theory is specifically aimed at validating scientific knowledge, but it is also a clear critique of non-scientific knowledge and theories. Popper famously put it to work against Marxism (Popper 1945), to refute its claims to being a 'science of society'.

This version of scientific knowledge is an insider's account of science. Writing in the 1930s against a political background of competing and murderous ideologies, Popper offered an account of scientific knowledge as a better way of making sense of the world than ideology. His theory proposed that humans could find rational and objective explanations for the world that would not be subject to ideological influence and could be a force for general good. Popper and the Vienna Circle equated science with applied rationality, and science and rationality became, for a time at least, inextricably linked.

An exercise in philosophy of science: are objects really there?

Philosophy of science has, for a long time, offered two separate positions with which to make sense of the objects that appear in scientific experiments: realism and anti-realism. In recent years, a third position of social constructionism, dubbed 'irrealism' by Ian Hacking, has grown in prominence.

These ontological positions address the problem of whether or not the objects that are described by scientific theories and investigated by scientific experiments really exist. This is not as strange a question as may at first be thought. Some of the objects that scientists are concerned with, particularly in the discovering sciences, are obviously 'there' and tangible to the senses: planets, glaciers, human beings. But many objects, particularly in the experimental sciences, are not perceptible to the naked human senses (e.g. atoms, molecules, cosmic rays) and may only be perceptible through inferential (i.e. indirect) procedures. Given that the standard account of science places huge store on an *empirical* method, i.e. a method based upon experience and perception, this can cause some problems. If the experimenter cannot actually see the phenomena in question, are those things described by the theory really there, or is it just a coincidence that the theory is predicting results that are being achieved? This is the core of the disagreement between scientific realists and anti-realists.

Scientific realism is the position that scientific theory construction aims to give us a literally true story of what the world is like, and that acceptance of a scientific theory involves the belief that it is true. Accordingly, anti-realism is a position according to which the aim of science can be well served without giving such a literally true story, and acceptance of a theory may properly involve something less (or other) than belief that it is true. (van Frassen 1980: 9)

Many scientists' form of justification – and also their avoidance of contingency of knowledge – is scientific realism.

Realism

1   We have theories that are correct, theories that we have worked out from extensive experiments and from our current paradigm.
2   Because the theory is correct, the objects that the theory names and manipulates are real. They actually exist: e.g. the theory of vulcanology identifies *volcanoes* as actually existing, and the theory of electricity names *electrons* as actually existing.
3   Until our theory is proved wrong, we can assume that the objects are actually there and treat them as being real rather than as being thought constructs, concepts or possibilities.
4   A major goal of science has always been the construction of correct theories – therefore we do not need to change what we do.

Scientific realism says that entities, states and processes described by correct theories really do exist. Protons, photons, fields of force, and black holes are as real as toe-nails, turbines, eddies in a stream and volcanoes. The weak interactions of those particles are as real as falling in love. Theories about the structure of molecules that carry genetic codes are either true or false, and a genuinely correct theory would be a true one. (Hacking 1983: 21)

Anti-realism

Anti-realism says the opposite to realism. There are no such things as electrons. There is, of course, electricity, but our theories are essentially fictions that we use to help us predict and produce events that interest us. Electrons are fictions on this account. There is no necessary reason to believe that just because there is electricity and we can produce an account that adequately explains electricity, through making up a fictional particle called the electron, we have somehow produced a correct theory. In Hacking's terms: turbines, yes, electrons, no (Hacking 1983: 21). Just because we can make models of the world does not mean that this is actually how the world really is.

Anti-realism is a more difficult doctrine to assume. Our dominant culture 'believes' in realism: the representations of science that surround us affirm this realism. Pictures of DNA molecules that illustrate the achievement of the Human Genome Project, for example, make the molecules look as if they are very concrete objects that are 'really there'. Anti-realists would not try to deny that there are inheritance factors that work in passing on genetic information, but they would say that there may not actually be specific molecules of DNA that *really* look like the ones in the newspaper pictures. For anti-realists the theory of DNA is a model that helps us to organize ideas and data: it is not a literal picture of how things actually are (Hacking 1983: 22). Anti-realists do **not** dispute the results of experiments, or even the status of science, but instead the *form* that theories actually have.

Van Frassen extends this position, and suggests that anti-realists can operationalize their experimental work as *constructive empiricists*: 'Science aims to give us theories that are empirically adequate; and acceptance of a theory involves a belief only that it is empirically adequate' (van Frassen 1980: 12). From this anti-realist position all these constructive empirical accounts must mesh together such that all the phenomena they describe fit into the same model. For van Frassen the achievement of such a model is described by the current situation of scientists being committed to their theories.

Irrealism

Social constructionists see scientists as being actively involved in constructing scientific knowledge, and actively involved in constructing the objects around them. This is clearly not a realist position, but does this make them anti-realists? According to Hacking, we can see social constructionists as being irrealists, i.e. neither realists nor anti-realists (Hacking 1988).

Latour and Woolgar in *Laboratory Life* claim that facts are socially constructed, and that the process of construction involves the use of devices and procedures that serve to hide this process of construction (Latour and Woolgar 1979: 176). This implies a form of anti-realism: theories are just approximations for what actually exists in the world, they are tools for ordering thoughts. But then social constructionists go one step further: once the theory is deployed, and the facts are constructed, those facts become real objects. There is a complex interrelationship between statements about the world and the world itself. The theory, in this irrealist perspective, projects an image of itself into the world which is then 'discovered' by the experimenters and turned into a fact. This perspective suggests a form of linguistic reductionism: it is no surprise that statements made about the world appear to match the entities they name so closely because they are actually the same thing (Latour and Woolgar 1979: 177).

Challenges to the standard account of scientific knowledge

For a long time sociology of science was not concerned with what took place inside laboratories in terms of how experiments were carried out. Practical activities, and the relationship between human actors and non-human objects, were not a concern for sociology of science until the late 1970s. Prior to this point sociology of science – which has a long tradition as a sub-discipline of sociology – had been concerned largely with the institutional structure of science and the scientific community, and with issues of status ascription inside the scientific community. Classic studies in sociology of science, the most influential of which was Merton's delineation of the institutional imperatives of science (Merton 1967), focused on how science as a whole comes together as a set of institutions, why it is superior to non-science, and how science is integrated into wider social structures. Similarly, Hagstrom's analysis of the scientific community looked at the scientific community as a whole, how it circulated ideas internally and disseminated ideas externally (Hagstrom 1965). Merton's and Hagstrom's work on the scientific community will be discussed more fully in chapter 5, but at this point it is worth noting that such studies of scientific communities were common in the 1960s and 1970s, and all took a similar approach: they did not question the nature or status of scientific knowledge (a topic considered to be the preserve of philosophers of science) but focused on institutional aspects of the human organization of scientific activity.

Even Max Weber's critical gaze ignored the status of scientific knowledge, although his essay *Science as a Vocation* (written in 1918) was a highly influential and instructive text (Weber 1989; Erickson 2002). The themes of Weber's paper are still of central importance to sociology of science today. Weber does three things in his essay. First, he describes the external conditions of science as a vocation, primarily concentrating on the institutional organization of science in contemporary Germany and offering some comparisons with the situation in North America. Weber focuses on the rationalization and institutionalization of science, justifying this in a somewhat self-deprecating way as the 'pedantic custom' of political economists such as himself. He also describes the entry route and career path of recruits to the world of academic science, and notes the proletarian-ization of the intellectual through being transformed into a 'special-ist' (Turner 1992: 100). Secondly, he goes on to discuss the inward calling for science that scientists possess, noting that this is what his audience really want him to speak about. Here his focus is on the motivation towards a scientific career that scientists share. Finally, he offers a discussion of what science actually is, and what role it fulfils in society (Erickson 2002: 30).

Standard textbooks such as Barber and Hirsch's *The Sociology of Science* (1962) simply did not question what was happening inside laboratories other than to point out that experimental method had to conform to the norms of the scientific community, and that deviation from such norms would dramatically reduce the status and quality of scientific knowledge, turning it into 'non-scientific' knowl-edge. All of these approaches reinforced an essentialist conception of science, scientific knowledge and scientists. Such sociology of science sees science as being an institution that is in some way separate from, although connected to, the rest of society. It also sees scientific knowl-edge as having an intrinsic superior quality to other forms of knowledge due to its method of production (the scientific method) and its embodiment of rationality and truth. It also sees scientists as being separate and different from other members of society, at least while they are carrying out their experiments in the laboratory. Unlike non-scientists, who are using rough-and-ready forms of practical reasoning to make sense of their world, to produce knowledge and to complete tasks, scientists, from this perspective, are producing knowledge by using a form of purer rationality that allows their results to have a closer connection to truth.

In the late 1970s a new trend in sociology of science emerged, a project that is widely referred to as the sociology of scientific knowl-edge (SSK) which employs a form of social constructionism as its main mode of theorizing the social world. This project has a history that can be traced back to the roots of sociology and sociological analysis, but the term 'social construction' was imported directly from Peter Berger and Thomas Luckmann's *The Social Construction of Reality* (1967), an influential phenomenological approach to making sense of the social world (Sismondo 2004: 52). SSK's first significant manifestation took the form of the Strong Programme, an attempt to understand the content of scientific knowledge in sociological terms. The Strong Programme originated in the sociology of knowledge produced by Barry Barnes and David Bloor, both of whom were working at Edinburgh University (Barnes and Bloor 1982). The Strong Programme appeared in the work of Collins in the late 1970s, and is associated with him and with other social investigators of science who were interested in sociology of scientific knowledge (SSK) and, more recently, the general field called science and technology studies STS (both of which are discussed in more detail below). The relativism of the Strong Programme has been influential on much of science studies since the 1980s. SSK also relied upon earlier work that prepared the ground specifically in the area of science, particularly that of Kuhn and Wittgenstein, and later the 'anarchist' approach of Feyerabend.

The work of Thomas Kuhn (1970) challenged the formal science conception of scientific progress. Rather than science proceeding by an objective process of building fact upon fact such that, eventually, a perfect picture of the natural world would emerge, science actually proceeded by a social process, and scientific progress was, in many ways, illusory. Relativism, previously considered to be inimical to the project of formal science, entered the picture and was seized upon by social scientists investigating science (see box 3.1). In philosophy, the later work of Ludwig Wittgenstein was influential in drawing the attention of philosophers of science to the role of language in the production of scientific knowledge. In the 1970s the work of Paul Feyerabend produced a relativist account in philosophy of science that directly challenged the standard account of scientific knowledge, particularly Popper's theory.

Between them, these relativist approaches, in sociology and philosophy, challenged the standard account of scientific method, scientific knowledge and science as a project. Significantly, they began to converge around a set of ideas that described how scientists were involved in *constructing*, not discovering or finding, scientific knowledge. The relativist challenge to the standard account of science made its mark not by challenging head-on the institutional aspects of science and the scientific community discussed by sociologists of science such as Hagstrom, Barber and Merton, but rather by looking directly into the places where knowledge was produced and chal-

---

Box 3.1   Relativism

'Relativism' is something of a catch-all term that is used in many social sciences. In general, relativism is the theoretical stance which says that things such as knowledge and culture cannot be understood as absolutes but must be understood in relation to one another. Thus a relativist position with respect to knowledge (knowledge relativism) sees that no form of knowledge is 'naturally' superior to any other form, and all claims to knowledge must be qualified by statements showing where they arise from. This gives rise to the current usage of the term 'knowledges' to explain a multiplicity of knowledge claims in the world. Similarly, 'cultural relativism' states that it is not possible to describe one specific culture as superior or inferior to another, as such a statement would rely on the selection of an arbitrary vantage point for analysis.

Note: the relativism of the social sciences is not connected to Einstein's theory of relativity [see box 4.2].

---

lenging the alleged objectivity and formality of scientific practice and experimental method. Overall, a convergence in sociology and philosophy of science takes place, with both disciplines focusing on the status and nature of scientific knowledge, and on how scientific knowledge is validated.

The work of Kuhn and the work of Feyerabend have been enormously influential on contemporary social and philosophical analysis of science. However, they also owe a considerable debt to two earlier thinkers, Ludwik Fleck and Ludwig Wittgenstein. Later we'll look in more detail at Fleck's social analysis of scientific practice. First, a brief examination of the later philosophy of Wittgenstein, and a short examination of Wittgenstein's approach to philosophy and science, will help to highlight some fundamental themes in the contemporary critique of scientific knowledge.

Wittgenstein, language and science

The later philosophy of Ludwig Wittgenstein fundamentally altered the philosophical analysis of language, and the impact of his work can be seen throughout contemporary thought, particularly those forms that describe themselves as being 'anti-foundational', 'post-structural' and/or postmodern. Wittgenstein's work is written in a deceptively simple style, which makes it easy to read and understand, but hard to explain or replicate. Wittgenstein did not often discuss natural science explicitly, so much of what is presented below extrapolates from Wittgenstein's areas of study.

Wittgenstein's philosophy shows that there are no absolute fixed meanings attached to words. He provides us with a dictum – 'the meaning of a word is its use in the language' – to remind us of this (Wittgenstein 1958: §43). Further, Wittgenstein says that understanding a language means understanding a form of life (§19). Thirdly, Wittgenstein notes that there can be no such thing as a 'private language' – all language is shared and relies on this shared aspect for meaning to be intelligible (§243). These basic principles of Wittgensteinian philosophy have major implications for our understanding of science and scientific knowledge.

To start with, the meanings of words are contingent upon their use in language. This means that the meanings of words shift with time and context. Regardless of the fixity of the external world of objects, Wittgenstein is saying that our language will never have fixed points, is never nailed down to the objects it is describing. This creates problems for formal science. Imagine experimenters explaining their work to each other. They appear to be using a number of highly specialized terms to describe things in front of them. Yet these terms rely upon our everyday language for their meaning. Whilst it is possible to see that much of science is concerned with defining objects in tight and rigorous ways, this can never be achieved fully. There will always be some 'looseness' around the meanings that are attached to words, even to very specialized words like 'polymerase chain reaction'. This can be seen quite clearly if we think about how words, even 'tightly defined' scientific terms, change their meaning over time.

If the meanings of words are contingent upon their use, we will have great problems in offering descriptions of reality if we try to adhere to the 'truth' and 'fact' orientation of the project of science. As the meaning of words is internal to the language-game being enacted at any one time, reference to reality or the external world has to gain its meaning from a specific context in a particular human practice (Trigg 1993: 29), not a universal and immutable context and set of practices. Everything thus becomes dependent upon our frame of reference: we can have no external 'God's-eye' view, because if we were to do so, we would need a new, separate and 'private' language.

We cannot do this because our reality is circumscribed by what we can describe using our current language. Constructing new linguistic expressions as an attempt to 'firm things up' cannot work, because those linguistic expressions also rely upon our current language for their meaning. The limits of our world are the limits of the language that we use: changing the language simply changes the limits, not the location from which we are observing the world or describing it.

Thus science, cannot have its own special and separate language; it will always rely upon everyday language to construct meaning. Scientific language may look as though it is 'different' from everyday language, but fundamentally it isn't (Erickson 2004).

Implications for looking at science

This is quite clear when we look at 'translations' taking place between different parts of science as a whole. Inside the lab we can see a group of laboratory workers together talking about what they are doing and seeing. They describe the world in front of them in mundane and everyday terms for the most part, occasionally moving to specialist descriptions to make sure co-workers are identifying the same objects as they are. However, the formal scientific paper that is written on the basis of these activities uses a discourse that is much more rigorous – effectively a translation of the work of the experimenters into the formal scientific discourse of the paper. Subsequently we can see further translations from the formal scientific discourse of a paper into, say, a newspaper or media account, where specialist terms are abandoned in favour of 'easier' ones. All three forms of discourse are intelligible to observers outside of the thought community (see box 3.2) that did the experimental work, and all three discourses are describing the same objects. Different discourses apply in different thought communities, and these discourses will reflect different thought styles and meanings attached to words. Formal scientific discourse may be a 'dialect' in the same way that youth argot may be a dialect, but it is not and cannot be a separate language.

The basic principles of science cannot be given rational justification by Wittgenstein. Ultimately everything comes down to human practices and the construction of systems of belief inside thought communities. There is no correspondence theory of truth – this theory this fact. This is not to say that Wittgenstein is anti-science. However, rationality cannot, on this perspective, have anything transcendentally special about it. It is just another belief and practice like any other, albeit one that has a lot of power attached to it and one that produces real results in terms of organizing our practical investigations of the world. Rationality is a language construct like any other concept.

Science is no longer the privileged location of the truth, just another system of signification. Indeed, we can use Wittgenstein's theory to begin to treat science as being similar to a belief system. Science generates its own rule-governed activities and its own meanings. We may want to say that the language-games of science are more tightly ordered than the narratives that we use in everyday life. But science still relies upon everyday language and narratives to provide meaning and make sense. It is, at the very least, inextricably linked to society.

Ludwik Fleck, thought communities and the social analysis of science

Fleck, working as a microbiologist in the 1930s, produced a remarkable and prescient book that amalgamates historical and social analysis to investigate how scientific communities come to agree on what counts as knowledge (Fleck 1979). Fleck presents a history of syphilis and scientific knowledge about this disease. He looks at its first appearance in Europe in the fifteenth century, how medics at the time made sense of it, and the emergence in the late nineteenth and early twentieth centuries of scientific discourses on syphilis. In particular, Fleck focuses on the Wasserman reaction (a commonly used laboratory procedure), which is used as a proof of the existence of the syphilis bacillus, thus a proof of disease. Interestingly, it was not known why the Wasserman reaction worked, yet it became the standard diagnostic tool in the early 1900s and was in extensive use throughout the first half of the twentieth century.

Fleck starts with the point that sociologists of his day (he cites Comte and Durkheim) were wrong to exempt scientific knowledge from sociological investigation. He argues that we should not accept uncritically accumulated progress in scientific knowledge 'as if our way of thought represented an improvement in the thought styles of previous generations' (Trenn and Merton 1979: 155). He categorically rejects the idea that currently recognized 'facts' are more true, and proposes that we understand 'facts' as being contingent on place and use in a particular location – what he calls a 'thought community' (*Denkgemeinschaft*). A thought community is a group of individuals who share ideas, concepts and theories: they share a particular 'thought style' (see box 3.2). All scientific communities are

---

Box 3.2 Thought communities, thought collectives and thought styles

One of the most useful concepts that the work of Ludwik Fleck has provided is that of *Denkgemeinschaft*. Fleck's use of the term is consistent throughout his work, but the word is variously translated as 'thought collective' or 'thought community' (in Bradley and Trenn's translation (Fleck 1979)) or as 'cognitive community' (in Baldamus's translation (Fleck 1977)). For the sake of simplicity, the term used throughout this book is 'thought community'.

Fleck defines thought community as 'a community of persons mutually exchanging ideas or maintaining intellectual interaction' (Fleck 1979: 39). This definition, whilst clearly applicable to a community of scientists working together on a specific range of problems and experiments, is also applicable to non-scientific communities. Fleck notes that 'there are structural characteristics shared by all communities of thought' (Fleck 1979: 105), and he describes two different sorts of thought communities, esoteric and exoteric:

> The general structure of a thought collective consists of both a small esoteric circle and a larger exoteric circle, each consisting of members belonging to the thought collective and forming around any work of the mind, such as a dogma of faith, a scientific idea, or an artistic musing. A thought collective consists of many such intersecting circles. Any individual may belong to several exoteric circles but probably only to a few, if any esoteric circles. (Fleck 1979: 105)

Individuals can be inducted into the inner, esoteric circle if they are already members of the exoteric circle, assuming they are sufficiently proficient in articulating the thought of the inner circle.

Fleck notes that each thought community is characterized by a particular thought style (*Denkstil*), and that the thought styles operating inside thought communities are never independent, and neither are the members of thought communities. Thought styles inside thought communities are related to other thought styles, first from the interaction between the esoteric and exoteric parts of a thought community, and secondly by benefit of the members of each thought community also being members of a number of other thought communities, each of which also has its own thought style and each of which is just as interdependent as others. Esoteric and exoteric thought communities are useful concepts through which sense can be made of the relationship between the very specific research-oriented experimental communities and wider scientific communities. Further, these concepts allow one to see how scientific thought – on the surface neutral and independent – is actually dependent on social factors external to the workings of scientific practice.

---

thought communities, as are a great many other forms of collective being (families, political parties, groups of friends, etc.), so all of us are members of a number of thought communities. While this concept may not have been new, it enabled Fleck to challenge the idea of the 'lone genius' bringing about a scientific revolution on their own. Scientific revolutions take place, but these are collectively generated. Not only are they collectively generated, but they are also premissed on social and cultural conventions – i.e. factors external to science – that are shared by members of a community. As Fleck says:

> Truth . . . is always, or almost always, completely determined within a thought style. One can never say that the same thought is true for A and false for B. If A and B belong to the same thought collective, the thought will be either true or false for both. But if they belong to different thought collectives, it will just *not* be *the same* thought! It must either be unclear to, or be understood differently by, one of them. (Fleck 1979: 100)

Scientific knowledge is socially and culturally conditioned. Facts vary with time and culture – they are a product of thought styles. Thought styles are specific to thought communities: they are the underlying patterns which structure the production of knowledge in, for example, a scientific community.

Fleck's term *thought style* (*Denkstil*) can be seen to be broadly similar to Kuhn's 'paradigm'. 'Both thinking and facts are changeable, if only because changes in thinking manifest themselves in changed facts. Conversely, fundamentally new facts can be discovered only through new thinking' (Fleck 1979: 50–1). There is no implication of 'progress' here. Fleck notes that the modern understanding of syphilis as being caused by a specific bacterium and being testable by only *one* method means that modern medical science ignores a myriad other important things.

The development of the concept of syphilis as a specific disease is thus incomplete in principle, involved as it is in subsequent discoveries and new features of pathology, microbiology, and epidemiology. In the course of time, the character of the concept has changed from the mystical, through the empirical and generally pathogenetical, to the mainly etiological. This transformation has generated a rich fund of fresh detail, and many details of the original theory were lost in the process. So we are currently learning and teaching very little, if anything at all, about the dependence of syphilis upon climate, season, or the general constitution of the patient. Yet earlier writings contain many such observations. As the concept of syphilis changed, however, new problems arose and new fields of knowledge were established, so that nothing here was really completed. (Fleck 1979: 19)

Fleck's work anticipated that of a number of important writers. He was certainly aware of the Vienna Circle style of thought: he explicitly criticizes it, and his relativistic understanding of scientific knowledge is similar to the later philosophy of Ludwig Wittgenstein. Indeed, both men were living in Vienna in 1927. Although there is no evidence to suggest that they met, if they had, it might begin to explain Fleck's relativistic understanding of issues such as 'truth' and how different groups of people can have different understandings of the same thing. Wittgenstein introduces the concept of 'form of life' to describe the environment in which a particular set of linguistic and grammatical usages will come to have meaning, and suggests that there are a range of forms of life available. Fleck's concept of 'thought communities' is similar to this. Fleck asserted that there will be pre-ideas inside a thought community that will prefigure a later, full-blown idea, and that the adoption of the idea will be through its collectivization in a thought community, and the adoption will look like a revolution.

Three main connections can be identified between Fleck's work and more recent social thought. First, Fleck's analysis of a discontinuous and non-progressive history of medicine is similar to Michel Foucault's (e.g. *Birth of the Clinic*, or *Madness and Civilization* (Foucault 1973 and 1967)). Historical analysis in the Foucauldian style suggests that we simply have different ways of understanding medical problems, different names and different preoccupations. Foucault, of course, wants to point to these different perspectives being socially and culturally determined. Secondly, the connections to Kuhn's work are quite clear (see box 3.3). Kuhn's work appears to be less radical than Fleck's, particularly in terms of its social implications, but because Kuhn used physics, that master-narrative of science, it looks more robust theoret-

---

Box 3.3   Ludwik Fleck and Thomas Kuhn

In *The Structure of Scientific Revolutions* Kuhn mentions an 'almost unknown' German monograph of 1935 that he chanced across at Harvard in 1949 or 1950 (Kuhn 1970: p. vi). It was by Ludwik Fleck, titled *Genesis and Development of a Scientific Fact*, and it remained untranslated until 1979. Fleck's work, although obscure for a long time, is at least as interesting as that of Kuhn. Like Kuhn, although two decades earlier, Fleck combines historical and social analysis of scientific knowledge to produce a radical and relativist account of science. Barry Barnes notes:

> This work anticipates many of Kuhn's ideas, which is possibly why it was passed over on its original appearance. The product of a medical scientist with a real care for the details of actual research, the stature of the book is now clearly evident. Not only is it probably the first ever empirical study in the sociology of scientific knowledge, it is a very good one at that, and one from which much can be learned. (Barnes 1982: 9)

---

ically. Finally, Fleck's work anticipated the current trend in science studies, that of social constructionism. Fleck argues that scientists are involved in 'making up' knowledge. We would possibly identify Fleck as being at the soft end of social constructionism, in that he does think that facts are real, but recognizes that they are culturally validated by a thought community.

The crisis in rationality – Thomas Kuhn's relativist account

Thomas Kuhn produced a relativist approach to the history, philosophy and sociology of science. It has been very influential in these disciplines since its publication in 1962, and a detailed examination of its core ideas will be useful, as many of them underpin contemporary analysis of science. *The Structure of Scientific Revolutions* (Kuhn 1970) not only shattered the core tenets of the standard account of philosophy of science, but also shattered the connection between scientific knowledge and other formal systems of knowledge through challenging the integrity of rationality.

> Philosophers long made a mummy of science. When they finally
> unwrapped the cadaver and saw the remnants of an historical process
> of becoming and discovering, they created for themselves a crisis of
> rationality. That happened around 1960. (Hacking 1983: 1)

Disentangling the history of science from philosophers' accounts
of the epistemology of science is not straightforward, particularly as
the book that challenged the dominance of Popper's version of scientific knowledge is a challenge both to orthodox epistemology and
to history of science.

Kuhn's book was the first widespread account to offer a sociological understanding of scientific knowledge based upon the internal
working of scientific communities and scientific practice. Rather than
looking at how scientists were organized into institutions, or how
social science could emulate scientific theory, Kuhn asked, 'what is it
that makes science distinctive as a practical activity?' The answer for
him was similar in form to that of Popper: the operation and role of
theories. This point became central to Kuhn's understanding of the
relative nature of scientific knowledge, but his understanding of
theories was very different from Popper's.

Kuhn's analysis of science relies on bringing together historical and
social analysis of science. In chapter 4 we will look in more detail at
Kuhn's conception of the history of science, but it is worth bearing
in mind that part of Kuhn's main thesis concerning scientific knowledge is based on a perspective of the history of science that is in
marked contrast to a standard account of the gradual and progressive growth of scientific knowledge.

Kuhn took physics as his main subject matter, but subsequently
expanded his thesis to suggest that a similar case applied to all sciences. In *The Structure of Scientific Revolutions* Kuhn first described
what he saw as the everyday workings of science: *normal science*.
This was essentially *puzzle solving*. Scientific activity is a process of
applying theory to the natural world, usually by experimental procedures. All theories are born refuted: almost any theory of the world
will somewhere fail to mesh with the facts. This means that theories
are only rough descriptions of what is actually the case in the world.
When theories are actually tested against the world, they will throw
up problems, paradoxes – puzzles that call into question some aspect
of the theory. The role of the scientist is to solve these puzzles, to
explore why the theory does not mesh with the facts, and how one
can bring the facts into line with the theories through adjusting the
theory. This process of testing theories, looking at the results, and
adjusting the theory is the operation of normal science. The process

of normal science is to a large degree self-sustaining: theories predict what will be the case, are tested and found slightly wanting, are adjusted to fit the 'facts' and then make further predictions of what will be the case, which are then tested using experiments, and so on.

Normal science is not in the business of refuting theories and articulating new theories. It is in the business of fleshing out the way that a theory describes the world. Kuhn introduced the term *paradigm* to describe the theories that normal science uses: by this Kuhn meant the overarching form of knowledge that guides and legitimizes the activities of normal science. In physics he identifies a number of paradigms, and describes how, through scientific revolutions, paradigms replace one another. In almost all cases normal science works well, and usually some minor modifications to a theory can bring about the necessary adjustment such that theory and experimental results match up. However, there are times when this is not possible. These cases are referred to as 'anomalies'.

Sometimes the anomalies will not go away: they pile up, and some will come to appear to be especially pressing. They begin to attract the attention of the livelier members of the research community, who challenge the dominant paradigm. But the more people who work on the failures of the paradigm, the worse things get. Counter-examples accumulate. An entire theoretical perspective becomes clouded. The discipline is in crisis. A new hypothesis appears that can explain these counter-examples, and it attracts many converts – often the younger members of the profession. They articulate the new theory, and make rapid advancements in explaining the world. As the new theory makes this fast progress, the old theory is set aside. A *revolution* has occurred, and one paradigm is replaced by another. This paradigm contains the new theory which, like all others, is born refuted, and a new generation of workers gets down to the task of solving the puzzles that the new theory has brought with it. There is now a new normal science, which can then return scientific activity to its process of puzzle solving.

The idea of scientific revolutions is not a new one, and historians of science had used the term extensively prior to Kuhn. However, there is a difference here. Apart from refuting the idea that all science is involved in theory construction, Kuhn's analysis included two major new elements. First was the idea of *conversion*, like a Gestalt shift inside the scientific community. Conversion occurs when, following a crisis, one paradigm is replaced by another. The resolution of the crisis – the conversion – is achieved when a new narrative is constructed that allows the members of the scientific community to understand how they could have held their original beliefs and how they could have been so misled by them (MacIntyre 1977: 455). Scientific change is a social process, not a process that results from discovery. Scientific revolutions occur when a scientific community considers them to be necessary, not when facts don't match theories. As Kuhn puts it: 'Perhaps science does not develop by the accumulation of individual discoveries and inventions' (Kuhn 1970: 2).

Secondly, Kuhn brought to the analysis of scientific knowledge the idea of *incommensurability*: that one may not even be able to express the ideas of the old theory in the language of the new theory (this idea is similar to the general concept of relativism). This means that, whilst any normal science is cumulative, science as a project is not necessarily cumulative. Typically, after a revolution, a large chunk of the old science will be abandoned as it is incompatible with the new science. There are numerous examples from the history of science of former scientific 'truths' that were subsequently found to be not working and are quietly, or in some particularly controversial cases noisily, buried. For example, phlogiston theory (the idea that materials contained a component (phlogiston) that separated out when combustion occurred), the concept of the aether filling outer space (a theory that facilitated a wave theory of the propagation of light, as waves need a medium to travel through) and phrenology (the identification of character trends – particularly criminal characteristics – through the examination of bumps and other physical attributes of the surface of the skull), all highly respected scientific theories of their day, are now seen as being wrong, or in Kuhn's terms, *myths*:

> If these out-of-date beliefs are to be called myths, then myths can be produced by the same sorts of methods and held for the same sorts of reasons that now lead to scientific knowledge. If, on the other hand, they are to be called science, then science has included bodies of belief quite incompatible with the ones we hold today. Given these alternatives, the historian must choose the latter. Out-of-date theories are not in principle unscientific because they have been discarded. That choice, however, makes it difficult to see scientific development as a process of accretion. The same historical research that displays the difficulties in isolating individual inventions and discoveries gives ground for profound doubts about the cumulative process through which these individual contributions to science were thought to have been compounded. (Kuhn 1970: 3)

Science from this perspective is not the science that we thought we had. It has lost its cumulative character and is only really producing different versions of the same phenomena from different perspectives. The project of scientific rationality, the idea that scientific rationality could and should be applied to all areas of knowledge, was plunged into crisis. Kuhn's relativism suggests that scientific rationality is contingent, rather than universally valid. There are no external reference points, and we may not be achieving better and better descriptions of the world – just different ones. This poses a major challenge to the entire Enlightenment paradigm, and the notion that society and science are both progressive is questioned.

Incommensurability means that there may be no such thing as progress, just an idea that there is progress. Progress itself becomes difficult to measure if the knowledge inside paradigms is incommensurable, and hence not understandable outside that paradigm. There is simply no point where one can 'measure' progress taking place.

> Since successive stages of science may address different problems, there may be no common measure of their success – they may be incommensurable. Indeed since abstract concepts are often explained by the roles they play in theorizing, we may not be able to·match up the concepts of successive stages in science. Newton's term 'mass' may not even mean what it does in Einstein's relativistic physics. (Hacking 1981: 3)

Moreover, the idea that scientific experiments are producing 'truth' is called into question by the form of relative analysis. When Kuhn's analysis is applied to the practice of laboratory experimental science, it suggests that the results of experiments, although clearly being facts and having a fact-like character, are not necessarily 'true' for all time. After all, the experiments in phlogiston science in the eighteenth century were carried out just as rigorously as experiments today: it isn't the case that scientists are more honest, or less credulous, than they were in the past. What Kuhn is saying is that the results of experiments are considered to be true by a scientific community because that is what scientific communities do: they come together to agree on what will be considered to be the truth in their sphere of esoteric knowledge. This is a social process. Further, what counts as being 'true' is contingent on the paradigm under which scientists are labouring. In physics the current paradigm of knowledge is based on the work of Einstein, and only scientific knowledge that conforms to the strictures of Einstein's thought will in general be considered to be true.

Kuhn's work opened the doors to allowing a relativist understanding of scientific knowledge. Although Kuhn's work is by no means the first relativist account of knowledge, it was certainly the most influential in terms of scientific epistemology, and has become the basis for the critical appraisal of scientific activity that is now termed 'social constructionism'.

Feyerabend's challenge to scientific method

Feyerabend's work is firmly located in philosophy of science. However, unlike many other philosophers, he looked closely at how scientific knowledge was produced in real situations, challenging strongly the standard account that scientific method was a systematic tool that served to help us discover true facts about the natural world. He also challenged the idea that formal science is a superior way of looking at the world and that its knowledge is superior to other forms of knowledge. He introduces a large dose of relativism to philosophy of science by thinking about the social context of science.

Feyerabend uses examples from the history of science to show that progress made by science is often the result of accident, luck, argumentation and downright deception. For example, he shows that Galileo's theory of a solar system with the Sun at its centre (expounded in 1632: Oster 2002: 77–82) prevailed and prospered because Galileo wrote in a better style, had better tools of persuasion, and because in writing in Italian he appealed to a wider audience than his rivals who wrote in Latin (Feyerabend 1978a: 141). For Feyerabend, scientific progress is often a matter of social circumstances, rather than the emergence of discoveries. Many aspects of Feyerabend's theories of scientific progress are similar to those of Thomas Kuhn.

In terms of the status of science, Feyerabend dismisses the claims of the formal scientific institutions to produce knowledge that is superior to other forms of knowledge. Instead he holds that science is just another way of seeing the world. For example, in *Science in a Free Society* (Feyerabend 1978b) he compares current natural science with astrology. Historically, he notes, astrology was closely connected to what we now call astronomy and astrophysics, but since the eighteenth century it has become distanced and is now derided as non-science or nonsense. Yet the arguments that formal science presents against astrology are often inaccurate and themselves non-scientific. Feyerabend deconstructs in detail a statement made by 'leading scientists' against astrology in 1975:

> Now what surprises the reader whose image of science has been formed by the customary eulogies which emphasise rationality, objectivity, impartiality and so on is the religious tone of the document, the illiteracy of the 'arguments' and the authoritarian manner in which the arguments are being presented. (1978b: 91)

According to Feyerabend, formal scientists' vehement opposition to astrology is based largely upon prejudice, ignorance and a lack of proper research. That astrologers might have a similar attitude towards, say, astrophysics is no excuse, according to Feyerabend: 'It is interesting to see how closely both parties approach each other in ignorance, conceit and the wish for easy power over minds' (Feyerabend 1978b: 96).

In terms of scientific method, which is the bastion that underpins the status of formal scientific knowledge, Feyerabend finds a welter of different practices, approaches, inaccuracies, fuzzy descriptions and pragmatism instead of formal and fixed ways of doing things. By this account, there is no one scientific method: rather, there are a great many different scientific methods being constructed and enacted in the myriad different locations where science is performed. The concept of a unified scientific method is a dogma that serves to exclude non-scientists from science and to preserve the myth of the inevitable superiority of scientific knowledge. Feyerabend argues that we must recognize the moral character of this situation and challenge it at a moral level. The standard account of formal scientific knowledge is a construction that creates a picture of the human mind, where people are seen as being unified by rationality. By contrast, Feyerabend wants us to recognize that there is no unified rationalist framework to which we can all adhere: there are multiple rationalities, a myriad of ways of carrying out science, and there is always a possibility that science isn't the best thing ever. Indeed, we could even do without it and still have a good life.

Feyerabend is not 'anti-science', but he is anti-dogma. For Feyerabend, science has assumed a position of religion, and has taken on a mantle of invulnerability created out of an alleged ideal method, a history of progress and a superior rational method. Feyerabend challenges all these and proposes that we see science as being just one form of knowledge among many, neither necessarily better or worse. Feyerabend's relativism is embodied in many of the subsequent sociological approaches to the study of the creation of knowledge in scientific work-places.

In the work of Wittgenstein, Fleck, Kuhn and Feyerabend we see a strong challenge to the standard account of science emerging. Their work became increasingly influential through the 1960s and 1970s, and the intellectual climate they engendered prepared the ground for the current relativist, post-positivist trends in social studies of science. This is particularly clear in social-constructionist approaches to science and actor-network theory. The former became the dominant mode of analysis for sociology and social studies of science in the

1980s and 1990s; the latter is the dominant mode of analysis in the new field of science and technology studies (STS) that has emerged in the last decade. We will take a brief look at each of these orientations.

Social constructionism

As relativist analyses became more prominent, scientific knowledge gradually came to be seen as being contingent on a range of social factors; its progressive and cumulative character was challenged; and the dogma of science was placed in the spotlight. Crucially, the language of science and the language of the analysis of science came under sustained scrutiny. The shift from philosophical and institutional analysis to social analysis of science was completed as sociology of science began to consider the content of scientists' discourse and how it was constructed.

The emergence of sociology of scientific knowledge in the 1970s and 1980s started from some fairly basic, but radical, premises: perhaps science is just a practical activity – a form of social interaction and work that happens to have a rather special product (facts/truth). From this perspective we could treat scientists in much the same way as any other social group, and we can look at how such a social group is building social order and meaning around itself. But this is, potentially, a very threatening route for the project of science: from here it was only a small step to realizing that as well as creating order in terms of social interaction etc., scientists were also constructing the 'truth' and their 'facts'. These ideas are at the core of the social-constructionist approach to science.

Sociology of science, in the years following publication of Kuhn's *Structure of Scientific Revolutions*, gradually moved away from a concern with the institutions that scientists inhabit (e.g. scientific communities) to a concern with the activities and interpretations of scientists themselves. This meant a sharp change in methods. Whereas sociology of science had been able to 'look in' from the outside to make sense of scientific knowledge and its relation to institutions, this new approach required sociologists to observe the actual day-to-day processes of doing science to begin to construct accounts of what was happening inside science.

SSK allied itself to the Strong Programme. Harry Collins's 'Empirical Programme of Relativism' (Collins 1981) provided a formulation of how social-constructionist studies should be taken forward. Observation should be made of how it is that scientists themselves offer different interpretations of reality, or Nature: 'the truth or falsity of scientific findings is rendered as an achievement of scientists rather than of Nature' (Pinch 1986: 20). This is the basis of what is known as the Strong Programme of the sociology of science.

Trevor Pinch, a close collaborator of Collins for many years, offers a clear definition of what the Strong Programme in science studies entails.

> Let me first state the most important thesis which guides this work and other 'social constructivist' studies:
>   In providing an explanation of the development of scientific knowledge, the sociologist should attempt to explain adherence to all beliefs about the natural world, whether perceived to be true or false, in a similar way. This thesis, which is sometimes referred to as the principle of symmetry or equivalence within the so-called 'Strong Programme' in the sociology of knowledge, simply sets out the widest possible terrain for sociological explanation. (Pinch 1986: 3)

There are major implications from the Strong Programme. By adopting this frame of reference, investigators must treat all true and false beliefs in exactly the same way and use similar modes of explanation for them. This results in a situation where, inevitably, a number of different versions of knowledge will emerge, all of which will have validity:

> If true and false beliefs are to be treated in the same way, then we are not merely talking about distortions of the picture of knowledge which is painted. What is being claimed is that *many pictures* can be painted, and furthermore, that the sociologist cannot say that any picture is a better representation of Nature than any other. Scientists can socially construct many different versions of the natural world. (Pinch 1986: 8)

Science, even the formal science of the laboratory, becomes from this perspective relative, with meaning contingent upon how interactants in a laboratory are collectively 'making up' the reality that surrounds them. Scientific knowledge is relative. The Strong Programme assumes that truth and falsity are constructions with no necessary connection to 'reality': 'The importance of the philosophical arguments about relativism in the 1970s was, in retrospect, not that they showed that relativism was true but that it was tenable and therefore could be used as a methodology for the study of science' (Collins and Yearley 1992: 303).

The first major account to do this was Latour and Woolgar's *Laboratory Life* (1979), a meticulous ethnographic analysis of work, interactions, actions and meaning constructions in one biochemistry laboratory. *Laboratory Life*, although generating a certain amount of controversy, showed that it was possible for social researchers to produce accounts of the construction of scientific knowledge from a relativist perspective.

The relativist approach in the sociology of science suffered from a major problem: namely, that showing relativism is difficult and open to interpretation. Latour and Woolgar, who examined in detail what exactly was taking place *inside* a biochemistry laboratory, provided empirical data that showed relativism at work in a setting where it was not expected. Their work acted as a starting point for a great many other social-constructionist laboratory-based studies (Latour and Woolgar 1979).

Latour and Woolgar observed daily life in a high-profile, prestigious biochemistry laboratory (the experiments they observed were subsequently part of a Nobel Prize win) from an anthropological and highly sceptical perspective. They took nothing at face value, choosing, for example, not to see the laboratory as a work-place oriented towards the search for truth, but as a 'factory' designed to generate paper products (articles in scientific journals) from inputs of animals, chemicals and energy (Latour and Woolgar 1979: 46). They called into question the status of the humans and non-humans inside the laboratory, suggesting that non-humans could have a meaningful part to play in the generation of scientific knowledge. But, most crucially of all, they did not take at face value the core beliefs of the scientists, choosing to redescribe these in terms that implied a very different version of reality.

Rather than seeing scientists uncovering truths in nature through experiment and analysis of results, Latour and Woolgar found scientists constructing facts and generating a discourse of truth, through their practical activity, their interactions and actions. 'Scientific activity is not 'about nature', it is a fierce fight to *construct* reality. The *laboratory* is the workplace, and the set of productive forces, which makes construction possible' (Latour and Woolgar 1979: 243).

Categories of 'objective' and 'subjective' take on very different meanings here, and Latour and Woolgar imply that an 'objective' approach is simply not possible: this is a core tenet of the relativist position. Latour and Woolgar's perspective effectively abolishes the concept of 'nature', the substrate that scientists are supposedly working upon and the 'object' that the project of formal science is seeking to understand perfectly, and replaces it with a discursive construction. Nature simply doesn't exist. It is called into being by scientists acting, talking, interacting with non-human objects and writing, together:

> If facts are constructed through operations designed to effect the dropping of modalities which qualify a given statement, and, more importantly, if reality is the consequence rather than the cause of this construction, this means that a scientist's activity is directed, not toward 'reality', but toward these operations on statements. (Latour and Woolgar 1979: 237)

Collins expresses this idea even more succinctly: '[T]he natural world has a small or nonexistent role in the construction of scientific knowledge' (Collins 1981: 3).

Latour and Woolgar's work can be seen as a strong challenge to the standard account of the production of scientific knowledge. But it can also be read as an attempt to oppose technological determinism and cultural imperialism. Social constructionists in this mould argue that all discourses should be given equal weighting when social scientists encounter and analyse them, and that there is nothing essential in science that means that it is better than any other form of discourse. The social-constructionist line suggests that the things around us and the things we talk about are created by our speech, and thus we have power to change them.

This radical approach appears to present an entirely relativist version of science. Studies in the Strong Programme tradition often explain extremely well how it is that a group of laboratory workers will manage to achieve consensus on the objects that have emerged from experiments or that surround them. However, it is noteworthy that these studies of science largely confine themselves to looking at scientists' interpretations of science, or looking at direct relationships between scientists and non-scientists. Such social studies of science are themselves still involved in maintaining a separation between science and society, maintaining a boundary between where science 'really is' (in the laboratory or in the head of a scientific expert) and where science isn't (everywhere else, but notably in the minds of lay people and in popular culture). Although expressing a version of anti-essentialism with respect to concepts, social theories and methodologies, these social-constructionist accounts often end up reproducing an essentialist account of science through a kind of mimesis. They are taking the language and discourse that are creating one phenomenon (scientific knowledge) and translating them into the language of SSK to create another phenomenon (the social-constructionist account of scientific knowledge). This may be a process of clarification, of explaining what is happening; but it isn't a process that brings out key features of *why* things are happening in the way they are.

We can see from the preceding that challenges to the standard account have led to the emergence of a discourse of relativism. Science is decentred, and the essentialism implied by the standard account is refuted. In general these discourses become a post-positivist critique of science.

However, post-positivism is a diverse discourse, and although social studies of science have tended to adopt some aspects of post-positivism, what we see is a proliferation of different approaches to making sense of science and technology. The emergence of science and technology studies (STS) in recent years has been characterized by a range of attitudes, political and theoretical, and a range of sites for research. Simply looking inside laboratories and other sites of formal knowledge has ceased to be the main location for STS, and new imperatives, particularly concerning the relationship between human and non-human (in the form of technological objects) actors have come to the fore. This is particularly clear in the dominant orientation within STS, actor-network theory (ANT), which emerged in the 1980s and 1990s.

Actor-network theory

Originating in the work of Bruno Latour (1987, 1996, 1999), Michel Callon (1987) and John Law (1986, 1991, 1994), actor-network theory (ANT) is now a heterogeneous set of approaches that coalesce around a post-positivist, post-structuralist perspective that takes seriously the relationships between humans and non-humans. Actor-network theory's roots in SSK and social constructionism are clear. Actor-network theory is also the site from which a sustained analysis of technoscience has emerged, as it argues strongly that 'technology' and 'science' are inextricably linked and cannot be separated. Actor-network theory starts by challenging the general social theoretical idea that human social relations are 'simply unmediated relationships between naked human beings, rather than being made possible and stable by artefacts and technologies' (MacKenzie 1998: 14).

To achieve its aims, actor-network theory proceeds by identifying case studies of interest, and then investigating the network of relations that emerge from given situations. Case studies vary in size and subject matter – Maggie Mort's *Building the Trident Network*, as the title implies, is an actor-network-based analysis of the planning and emergence of the UK Trident nuclear submarine programme (Mort 2002). Covering the period from the early 1980s, when the Trident submarine and missile programme was first being discussed as a successor to Polaris, to the late 1990s, when the last Trident boat sailed from the VSEL shipyard and production ceased, Mort uses a range of sources from both inside and outside the shipbuilding community of the case study. Primary interview material with key actors in the Trident programme at the shipyard allows a range of voices other than senior managers and policy-makers to be heard. Mort focuses on key moments in the social and technical aspects of the Trident programme and illustrates the fluctuations of the fortunes of the shipyard with material garnered from local newspapers and campaigning groups. The result is a kind of map of the interconnections between different key actors – both human and non-human – who were central to the eventual outcomes of a piece of complex technology coming into being.

Similarly, Bruno Latour's examination of a failed transport initiative (project Aramis) in France from the 1960s to the 1990s identifies a complex of network relations, and relations between humans and non-humans (Latour 1996). Latour uses primary interview material coupled with original documents to chart the rise of project Aramis, noting who the key actors are and letting them speak. For Latour, non-human objects can also tell a story:

> [M]achines . . . are cultural objects worthy of . . . attention and respect. [Humanists will] find that if they add interpretation of machines to interpretation of texts, their culture will not fall to pieces; instead it will take on added density. I have sought to show technicians that they cannot even conceive of a technological object without taking into account the mass of human beings with all their passions and politics and pitiful calculations, and that by becoming good sociologists and good humanists they can become better engineers and better-informed decision makers. (Latour 1996: p. viii)

As the narrative progresses, it becomes clear that the engineering aspects of the project are intertwined with the human interests of the human actors – and are sometimes displaced by these. Latour argues that meetings of various spokespersons bring together the different worlds of interests:

> The highly placed official speaks in the name of developing the French infrastructure and supports the project of the transportation minister

– who speaks in the name of government, which speaks in the name
of voters. The transportation minister supports Matra's project, and
Matra speaks in the name of captive drivers, who support the project
of the engineer, who speaks in the name of cutting edge technology. It
is because these people translate all the divergent interests of their con-
stituents, and because they meet together nevertheless, that the Aramis
project can gain enough certainty, enough confidence, enough enthusiasm to be transformed from paper to prototype. (Latour 1996: 42–3)

Mort's and Latour's case studies focus on large-scale, and expensive, public engineering projects. However, the small-scale also admits
of actor-network analysis. John Law's early actor-network study of
a single physics research laboratory (Law 1994) identified the localized networks surrounding individuals and small groups of researchers involved in specific research projects and, in contrast to
Mort and Latour, not responsible for making tangible 'products' such
as trains or submarines. Law's theoretical and conceptual framework
has proved very influential on subsequent studies as he reconfigures
essentialist notions of what people are. Rather than maintaining a
version of people as single and bounded entities, Law notes that
'People are networks. We are all artful arrangements of bits and
pieces. . . . We are composed of, or *constituted* by our props, visible,
invisible, present and past' (Law 1994: 33).

In addition, Law notes that actor-network theory's basis in a post-
structuralist perspective means that social analysis is a process of
telling stories, and he foregrounds the contingent nature of the narratives we tell about the world:

> [ANT] tends to tell *stories*, stories that have to do with the processes
> of ordering that generate effects such as technologies, stories about
> how actor-networks elaborate themselves, and stories which erode the
> analytical status of the distinction between the macro and micro-social.
> (Law 1994: 18)

Actor-network theory cannot be faulted for its identification of the
complexity of relationships surrounding knowledges and technologies, and many ANT studies reveal aspects of the generation of scientific knowledge that had previously been hidden. However, the
trajectory of actor-network theory has been such that it has moved
away from considering the relationship between formal scientific
knowledge and the people who produce it, to focus on more proces-
sual aspects of the emergence of specific technologies. There is, of
course, nothing wrong with this *per se*: STS is an area of study that
is concerned with *technology*. Yet there is an issue here: formal

science and knowledge that emerge from formal science locations and that contribute to the construction of networks including technologies are objectified in a way that may not be entirely helpful. Whilst actor-network theory may show complexities of networks, it often does not challenge the power differentials and imbalances in such networks; nor does it consider science to be anything other than another object in a network.

Some STS writers have noted that there are considerations external to specific networks. David Hess, for example, notes that:

> Actors come to networks within cultures that provide them with biases about appropriate forms of knowledge, methodology and machinery. Thus, although an actor-network analysis brings to STS the helpful corrective that shows one way in which structural change is possible, discussions of actor-networks need to be framed by an analysis of culture and power. (Hess 1995: 53)

The stories that actor-network theory tells are plausible and illuminating, but they may not be telling us everything we need to know. They can be prone to getting bogged down in the minutiae of local networks, and this localized focus can lead to an exclusion of analysis of external factors, contexts, cultures and power. In addition, by putting 'science' back into a specific location that can be analysed through the identification of networks that pass knowledge around, STS and actor-network theory may actually be reinforcing the standard account of science, where science is bounded, separated and superior. Often STS remains a form of localized analysis, a new way of telling stories about technologies in specific places and times. Actor-network studies are prone to a number of criticisms and challenges, not least of which is their need to adopt realist positions as the non-human agents they encounter form part of the same network as humans (Sismondo 2004: 73). A further problem for actor-network theory, when analysed from a cultural studies perspective, is that its focus on discrete networks serves systematically to exclude from consideration exactly the same people who have been systematically excluded from consideration by proponents of the standard account. In other words, actor-network theory suffers from a problem similar to the SSK version of social constructionism: a tendency to reproduce, albeit in different words, the standard, essentialist understanding of what science is and where science resides.

SSK, STS and actor-network theory have common roots in a relativist project. Despite these shared roots, they have taken a path that serves to reinforce dominant accounts of science, and even though they challenge the standard account, they have been instrumental in strengthening the idea that science is separate and essential. In contrast, Wittgenstein's thought tells us that we need to have a much more complex and considered understanding of what science in society means, and Fleck's work suggests that to understand science fully we should look at scientific communities and the relationship between internal, esoteric knowledge and external, exoteric knowledge. As well as considering these relationships, we also have to consider the history of science, the 'back story' that constructs a significant part of the picture of science visible today. It is to this that we will now turn.

Further reading

Introductions to philosophy of science
All of the following provide good overviews to the main themes of philosophical analysis of science:

Chalmers, A. F. 1999: *What is this Thing called Science?* Buckingham: Open University Press.
Couvalis, G. 1997: *The Philosophy of Science: Science and Objectivity.* London: Sage.
Hacking, I. 1983: *Representing and Intervening: Introductory Topics in the Philosophy of Natural Science.* Cambridge: Cambridge University Press.
Trigg, R. 1993: *Rationality and Science.* Oxford: Blackwell.

Introductions to social studies of science
The field of science studies is rapidly proliferating and fragmenting. This means that finding single books to introduce key themes is difficult. The following all provide good introductions to specific areas.

Sociology of science
Fuller, S. 1997: *Science.* Buckingham: Open University Press.

Science and technology studies
Sismondo, S. 2004: *An Introduction to Science and Technology Studies.* Malden, Mass.: Blackwell Publishers.
Hess, D. J. 1997: *Science Studies: An Advanced Introduction.* New York: Columbia University Press.

Actor-network theory
Latour, B. 1987: *Science in Action.* Cambridge, Mass.: Harvard University Press.

Law, J. and Hassard, J. (eds) 1999: *Actor Network Theory and After.* Oxford: Blackwell.

Social constructionism
Social constructionism is a huge topic, and it extends much further than just analysis of science and technology. However, Ian Hacking's *The Social Construction of What?* (1999) contains a range of discussions about the STS, SSK and sociology of science usage of social constructionism. In addition, Sismondo's *An Introduction to Science and Technology Studies* (2004) analyses the origins and implications of social constructionism.

Paul Feyerabend
As with Kuhn, good introductions to sociology or philosophy of science will include discussion and analysis of Feyerabend's work. However, it is worth looking at his lively original writings, in particular:

Feyerabend, P. 1978a: *Against Method.* London: Verso
Feyerabend, P. 1978b: *Science in a Free Society.* London: New Left Books

Ludwik Fleck
The main sources for further readings on Fleck are, historically, the works of Wilhelm Baldamus, particularly his 1977 paper 'Ludwig Fleck and the development of sociology of science' (Baldamus 1977). More recently, a major collection of essays by and on Fleck has appeared:

R. S. Cohen, and T. Schnelle, (eds) 1986: *Cognition and Fact: Materials on Ludwik Fleck* (Dordrecht: D. Reidel).

There is also a useful general introduction in L. Fleck, 1979: *Genesis and Development of a Scientific Fact.* Chicago: University of Chicago Press.

Thomas Kuhn
Kuhn's main work is:

Kuhn, T. S. 1970: *The Structure of Scientific Revolutions.* Chicago: University of Chicago Press

There are a great many books and papers written on Kuhn. Among the more useful and influential are:

Barnes, B. 1982: *T. S. Kuhn and Social Science.* London: Macmillan
Fuller, S. 2000b: *Thomas Kuhn: A Philosophical History for our Times.* Chicago: University of Chicago Press
Fuller, S. 2003: *Kuhn vs Popper: The Struggle for the Soul of Science.* Cambridge: Ikon Books

Sardar, Z. 2000: *Thomas Kuhn and the Science Wars*. Cambridge: Icon Books

In addition to the above, almost all introductions to science studies or the sociology of science will include discussion and analysis of Kuhn.

Ludwig Wittgenstein

Most of the ideas of Wittgenstein used in this book are in:

Wittgenstein, L. 1958: *Philosophical Investigations*. Oxford: Blackwell.

Since his original writings can be hard to interpret, it helps to have a good introduction to Wittgenstein, and Peter Hacker's very short book will give you a good overview of key themes:

Hacker, P. M. S. 1997: *Wittgenstein*. London: Phoenix.

Hacker has also written some very detailed guides to reading Wittgenstein. Of particular use is:

Hacker, P. M. S. 1986: *Insight and Illusion: Themes in the Philosophy of Wittgenstein*. Oxford: Oxford University Press.

If you are interested in Wittgenstein's remarkable life, Ray Monk's biography is the most comprehensive and readable account:

Monk, R. 1991: *Ludwig Wittgenstein: The Duty of Genius*. London: Vintage.

4

History

Philosophy and sociology of scientific knowledge have changed perspective on science through examining what scientists are actually doing, and through considering what the status of scientific knowledge actually is. But they have also relied upon taking a broader perspective by looking at science and scientific knowledge in a historical context. This chapter explores some themes in the history of science with a view to providing a general overview of the trends in the historiography of science and the role that histories of science play in articulating a wider understanding of what science is. In the same way that we can identify a standard account of scientific knowledge that has been challenged more recently, so we can identify a standard account of the history of science which has also come to be contested and reworked.

The standard account of the history of science

The standard account of the history of science is a story of progress, accumulation of knowledge, and increasing discovery. It is a triumphal tale which starts with human ignorance of the workings of the natural world and presumably ends with total human understanding of nature. This history of discovery and invention is constructed with the benefit of hindsight, and obscures aspects of scientific history that do not conform to the ideal being promoted (for example, phrenology – a cornerstone of nineteenth-century sciences of the mind, but now wholly discredited – is usually omitted from contemporary histories of science). Such a history gives a generous role to 'scientific thinking', seeing it as the driving force behind all technical and technological development, and as a motor for much human social development. It implicitly defines science as being any human endeavours that have attempted to understand and control nature. Moreover, it frequently reinforces the myth of the creative power of the lone scientific genius.

Such an approach is taken by Isaac Asimov in his *Asimov's Chronology of Science and Discovery* (1989). From 4,000,000 BC to the late 1980s, Asimov presents a continuous thread of discovery and invention that begins with stone tools, passes through fire, agriculture and the windmill, and continues with the modern-age discoveries of the motion of the Sun (1783), pepsin (1836), psychoanalysis (1893), the Salk polio vaccine (1954), and ends with the discovery of the greenhouse effect (1988). The most notable feature of Asimov's account is the increase of pace that we can see in terms of specific discoveries being made. On his account, not much happened in terms of scientific discovery between 4,000,000 BC and about AD 1600. However, after that point, science really speeds up in terms of discovery and invention. We can display this graphically by counting how many pages of his book each slice of history is assigned and placing these on a histogram (see fig. 4.1).

Within this seamless narrative there is no pause to comment on the social causes and contexts of the emergence of these discoveries and achievements. Asimov's book is typical in its tone of many

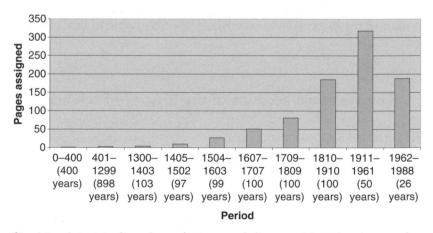

Fig. 4.1. Asimov's chronology of science and discovery. Note that dates BC have been omitted (Asimov covers 4,000,000 BC to AD 0 in 60 pages).

accounts of the history of science. For example, Brian L. Silver's *The Ascent of Science* (1998) gives away its orientation towards science in its title. The contents provide a story of the increase in rationalization and knowledge of the natural world – again, a standard version of the triumphal progress of science. Silver focuses on the role of lone scientific geniuses and their discoveries, reinforcing a popular stereotype of scientific work which is, arguably, a significant distortion of scientific experimental work. Like Asimov's, Silver's account provides much detail of specific inventions and theories. However, the representation of science as a remorseless accumulation of knowledge made by individuals working alone serves to reinforce the standard account of science as superior to other forms of knowledge, and to reinforce the idea that scientific knowledge provides a solid and almost complete account of the workings of the natural world. The history of science as triumphal progress shows the gradual, and then increasingly rapid, completion of the inventory of humankind's knowledge of the natural world. Such a history both inspires confidence and reassures, suggesting that if no specific knowledge of a particular natural phenomenon exists at the moment, the scientific method will be able to provide such knowledge through extension of experiment and theory in the future.

In the following sections we will focus on a single example which illustrates the standard history of science and more recent challenges to it. Throughout the following account we will see that the history of science and theories of scientific knowledge are closely linked.

A history of sunshine, I

'How does the Sun shine?' appears to be a simple and straightforward question that has a simple and straightforward answer: the Sun shines because a process of nuclear fusion is taking place inside it, releasing vast amounts of energy, and thus providing sunshine for our planet. This answer is part of the general societal knowledge of how the world works that is taught in school science classes and receives additional backing from the media. However, if all we can say is 'The Sun works by nuclear fusion', even if we could give a definition of nuclear fusion, we may not have a particularly sophisticated, or even 'scientific', understanding of how the Sun works. But again, many would agree that if we really had to, we could get more detail, either by looking at science textbooks, or by talking to someone with more knowledge than us – a physicist or an astronomer, for example. Our particular lack of knowledge of the detail of how the Sun works is not indicative of a general lack of knowledge: we know that somewhere some 'scientists' will know how the Sun works, and will be able to explain it. It is almost inconceivable that 'scientists' do not know how the Sun works, and most people are quite happy to leave it to them to possess the scientific knowledge that explains the fine detail. For most of us it is enough – perhaps even more than enough – to say that 'The Sun works by nuclear fusion'.

But is this correct, and is it a fair assumption? Can we be sure that this is how the Sun works? If we are to answer this question of the correctness (even truthfulness) of nuclear fusion being the cause of the Sun shining, then we need to actually appraise the elements that make up the statement 'Nuclear fusion makes the Sun shine'. This is not easy, not least because nuclear fusion is a complex process (see box 4.1).

Box 4.1   Nuclear fusion

Hydrogen and helium are the two main elements in the Sun. Nuclear fusion is the process by which hydrogen atoms fuse together to create helium atoms and release energy. In crude terms, four hydrogen nuclei fuse together to produce one helium nucleus. In the total reaction, for each helium nucleus created, two gamma ray of photons, two electrons and two neutrinos are produced.

> Overall, fusion in the Sun converts about 600 million tons of hydrogen into 596 million tons of helium every second: the 'missing' 4 million tons of matter becomes energy in accordance with Einstein's formula $E = mc^2$. About 2% of this energy is carried off by the neutrinos. (Bennett et al. 1999: 473)

When we begin to question the validity of this knowledge, what is it we are actually appraising? If we say that it is true that the Sun works by a process of nuclear fusion, are we admitting the validity of the theory of nuclear fusion, or that of the evidence that was used to compile that theory, or that of the data that physicists have collected when observing the Sun, or something else – perhaps the status of the person who is telling us the story (this list could go on and on)? Truth may not be the most appropriate thing to look for. Perhaps, rather than asking whether or not the story of nuclear fusion we are told is true or false, we should ask what makes up the story, what are its components, and how do they fit together? Arguments about truth are rarely productive: Wittgenstein tells us that usually our definitions of truth vary according to our circumstances. Rather than looking to appraise truth or otherwise, it would be better to look at what components are being used to construct statements that we subsequently accept as being true. So, we really need to ask, what is scientific knowledge? And, specifically, what scientific knowledge of the Sun do we have? Then we need to look at how that knowledge emerges from a scientific community and enters into our everyday world in a way that provides us with a very strong, secure story about how the Sun works.

It is necessary to note the parallel here to the examples of laboratory work: a group of workers carry out experiments, turn their results into scientific papers, and disseminate this knowledge to their scientific community. This knowledge doesn't simply stay in that location; it emerges in a range of forms and becomes what outside observers see as being formal science, or just 'science'. We are faced with a similar case here: there is a chain that extends from the theory and experiments of astronomers and physicists investigating how the Sun works that extends from localized thought communities to the 'lay' public, via a number of institutions and through a range of different media (e.g. scientific papers, university-level textbooks, school textbooks, reports in popular science journals such as *New Scientist* or *Scientific American*, documentaries on TV, newspaper reports and discussions held in informal, non-scientific settings, to name but a few). Very specific, detailed knowledge is transformed into generally held knowledge in society. In addition, all scientific knowledge comes with a 'history': the understanding that scientists have of particular phenomena is contingent to at least some degree upon what they knew in the past. Science often looks as if it is synchronic, as if the knowledge we have of the world has just emerged recently, but there is a strong diachronic component to all scientific knowledge: it has a history, a back story. This situation can be unpacked by looking at the example of studies of how the Sun works.

The Sun is the local star to the planet Earth, and the energy that comes from the Sun is responsible for *all* life on earth. Everything that lives on the Earth derives its energy, ultimately, from the Sun. Not only that, all the artefacts and objects that we see around us are a product of the energy of the Sun. (Actually, this is not strictly correct. Energy released by radioactive decay is not derived from the Sun. But you get the point – no Sun, no life as we know it. And no DVDs or mobile phones either.) For this reason, the Sun has been a major object of inquiry for scientists for centuries, and for mankind throughout history. Scientific studies of the Sun have also been an important object of inquiry for sociologists of scientific knowledge. Trevor Pinch's *Confronting Nature: The Sociology of Solar-Neutrino Detection* (1986) is a detailed sociological analysis of the physics of solar-neutrino detection from a social-constructionist perspective. A quick overview of the history of scientific investigations into how the Sun works reveals some interesting points.

Ancient formal thought saw the Sun as being a kind of fire – a lump of wood or coal, maybe a glowing rock. Suspended in the heavens, it would be lit in the morning and put out at night, carried across the sky by some supernatural being. This theory explained why the Sun was not visible at night, and why the Sun was warm. This is a pretty good explanation in scientific terms: it is based upon observation and experience and, probably, some hard evidence. Ancient scholars may have observed burning objects falling from the sky – meteorites – and may even have found examples on the ground and studied them. It would be plausible to assume that these pieces of 'fire from heaven' were a part of the Sun: a good empirical deduction, unfortunately leading to the wrong conclusion. From the first written records until the 1800s, not much changed in terms of explaining how the Sun worked. Of course, it was learnt that the Earth orbits the Sun, that it doesn't go out at night, that it is a long way away, and that it is very, very big. But gaining this knowledge about the Sun didn't help to explain how it worked. Some process of conventional burning was still assumed to be correct.

In nineteenth-century industrial societies there were two competing theories about how the Sun worked. The first, earlier one thought that it was a big cooling ember that worked in a similar way to burning coal or wood. This was another good theory in the sense of being plausible: it matched experiments that could be carried out on Earth, working out how long it would take for a burning object the size of the Sun to cool down. Experimental data collected from looking at incandescent substances in laboratories could be extrapolated to provide a 'guesstimate' for the age of the Sun. Results from this method were very promising: according to such experimental results, the Sun had only been burning for a few thousand years, which matched the current Christian-influenced thinking as to the age of the Earth. The theory of how the Sun worked was validated by experimental evidence that matched another theory that was not directly connected to the first theory, thus providing additional validation. However, it soon became obvious that there were flaws in this theory – chemical burning could not produce the required amount of radiation from the observed mass of the Sun, and if the Sun was actually a cooling ember, it must have been an awful lot hotter just recently, i.e. within the last few thousand years, too hot for life to survive on Earth. This theory had the advantage over previous theories in that, as well as using observation, both of the Sun and of meteorites, to collect evidence, it combined these with experiments to measure the rate of burning in the Sun. Its failure came from starting from a point that, whilst plausible, led to impossible conclusions. The theory itself was disproved, rather than the evidence being discredited.

The second, later theory of the nineteenth century was more robust. It focused on gravitational cooling, whereby the Sun generates energy by contracting in size. The Sun is a massive body that generates huge gravitational forces which pull material from the outside towards the centre, thus reducing it in size. According to this theory, as the Sun shrinks, it loses gravitational potential energy and converts it into thermal energy, which is emitted – hence the heat of the Sun's rays. Because it is so big, the Sun would need to contract by only a little each year to maintain its temperature, and by such a small amount that its shrinkage would have been imperceptible with nineteenth-century technology, i.e. unmeasurable. Calculations showed that the Sun could emit radiation from gravitational cooling at its present rate for about 25 million years (Bennett et al. 1999: 467). However, by the mid-nineteenth century, geologists already knew that the Earth was much older than that, so the theory must have been wrong (or the geologists had misinterpreted the fossil record – again, a plausible position to hold, particularly given the controversial implications of a 'very old' earth with respect to dominant religious thinking at the time). Again, there is a failure of theory, not of evidence or of measurement of data. All theories up to this point had used good scientific principles – observation, formulation of hypothesis, attempts to test the hypothesis – to try and validate the theory being tested. All had failed, yet we can see a key principle when analysing these failures: that as science proceeded through time, it became more and more unified – discoveries in one area, such as geology, could be used to confirm or reject theories in another area, e.g. astrophysics.

So what is the right theory? The 'correct' answer, the 'true' answer to why the Sun shines, was discovered only in the 1920s by the British physicist Eddington:

> Only after Einstein published his special theory of relativity, which included his discovery of $E = mc^2$, did the **true** energy-generation mechanism of the Sun become clear. Although it took several decades to work out the details, we now know that the Sun generates energy by *nuclear fusion*, a source so efficient that the Sun can shine for 10 billion years. (Bennett et al. 1999: 467, emphasis added in bold)

The above quotation from a current university-level textbook on astronomy and astrophysics is particularly interesting. First, it is quite triumphal – it says we now *know* the *truth*, and implies we were foolish in the past. It also explains the phenomenon of the Sun shining by reference to the paradigm of physics in contemporary scientific thought, i.e. Einstein's theory of relativity (for a detailed explanation of this see box 4.2). It implies that this problem has been solved and completed, pretty much by Einstein's work in the early part of the twentieth century. This account concurs with most other histories of science that describe gradual progress towards finally knowing the truth about phenomena, and being able to piece all these facts together under a single, overarching theory. It is useful to have a general understanding of this overarching theory, based on Einstein's theory of relativity and quantum mechanics, as it is the paradigm that currently underpins most scientific endeavour.

Box 4.2   Relativity and quantum physics: the new physics

Newton's unified physics, created in the seventeenth century, was used by physicists to describe the motion of all objects in the natural universe until the end of the nineteenth century. With the coming of a greater understanding of the size of the universe (much, much bigger than was previously thought) and the complexity of the microscopic level of the universe (much smaller and more complex than previously thought), and with the discovery of new natural phenomena (electromagnetic radiation), Newton's theory began to run into difficulties. James Clerk Maxwell's equations, describing the properties of electricity and magnetism solved some problems for a short time, but further discoveries in the realm of electromagnetism, radioactivity and atomic structure called these into question too. We now refer to the combination of Newton's and Maxwell's work as 'classical mechanics'. The breakthroughs made in the new physics were the result of anomalies arising – classical theory predicted one set of results, but experiments gave a different set of results – which could only be explained by moving beyond classical theory and adopting new theories.

We need to remember that classical mechanics was, and still is in most cases, very good at providing explanations of physical phenomena in the world around us. However, given that the new physics (that is, Einstein's theory of relativity and quantum physics) ultimately contradicts classical mechanics, we also need to think about how we could have been so wrong for so long. When we think about this, the reason for the difficulty and complexity of the new physics becomes obvious.

Bertrand Russell offers an explanation of why classical mechanics persisted for so long, only to be proved to be utterly incorrect by Einstein. 'Circumstances on the surface of the earth, for various more or less accidental reasons, suggest conceptions which turn out to be inaccurate, although they have come to seem like necessities of thought' (Russell 1985: 11). Basically, if we were an awful lot smaller and faster living creatures, or a lot bigger and slower living creatures, then we could not have used Newton's classical mechanics to explain phenomena as we saw them. Our perceptions of the world would be radically different, and we would need a different kind of physics to explain what we perceived. The visible objects that surround us can be accurately described in terms of classical mechanics, in that it provides a good account of how balls collide with each other, how roller-coasters work, and how satellites orbit the Earth. The new physics of relativity and quantum mechanics demands that we dispense with many common-sense notions of how the universe 'works' and adopt completely different frames of reference: we have to reconceptualize the natural world.

If we were much, much bigger and longer-lived – say, as Russell does, the size and age of stars – then the natural world that we see around us would be one of stars and other cosmological objects (e.g. galaxies, black holes, nebulae) coming into being, creating planets, attracting and repelling each other across truly cosmic distances. To correctly describe this reality, we need a theory that can take into account some key features of the observable universe, particularly the bending of light by gravity, the transformation of the size and weight of objects when travelling at very high speeds, and the lack of a single frame of reference from which to make reliable observations. Einstein's theory of relativity does this for us.

If we were much, much smaller, and we had senses that could work at very high resolutions, our world would likewise look very different. There would be no solid objects, or even individual atoms, visible to us. Instead, we would see a fuzzy haze of particles whizzing around each other, coming into existence and passing away before us, orbiting each other and bumping into each other. In this version of the natural universe we would need a theory that explains why it is that matter can assume different properties at

Continued

the same time: how it is that the units of matter that we can identify act as both particles of matter and waves at the same time.
Quantum physics provides us with the theory that can do this.

Quantum physics and relativity are complex theories that are
dependent on intricate mathematics for their proof. For our purposes here, we need to know roughly what these theories imply
and are used for, rather than how they work. If you want to know
more about them, and the new physics in general, consult the
works in the Further reading section.

Relativity is the term used to describe two theories (the special
theory and the general theory of relativity) developed by Albert
Einstein in the early part of the last century. The central tenet of
the special theory of relativity, which focuses on bodies in motion
at constant velocities, is that the speed of light is always the same,
and will be measured by any observer at any place and time,
whether the observer is stationary or in motion, as having the same
value, which is designated by the letter c and is approximately
300,000 km per sec. This accords with experimental data: the
speed of light is always the same, regardless of how, where, under
what conditions of motion or when an experiment is carried out.
By starting at this point, Einstein needed to reconstruct our understanding of space, time and motion in general, and arrived at a
very different conception of the universe from the mechanistic
image presented by Newton. The consequences of Einstein's theory
are that any observer who is stationary will find that a moving
object will shrink in the direction of its motion, a moving object
will gain mass and will gain more mass the faster it moves, and a
moving clock will record time more slowly than the stationary
clock that is with the stationary observer. The 'relativistic' aspect
of this theory comes from the need *not* to have different understandings of things like time, space and mass according to one's
speed relative to the object being observed. Effectively, Einstein's
theory shows that there is no one single frame of reference from
which absolute observations can be made.

This principle is central to Einstein's second, general theory of
relativity, which focuses on bodies that are accelerating, and shows
that it is impossible to distinguish between acceleration and the
effects of a universal gravitational field. This means that if you
were in a lift that was accelerating upwards, you would feel a force
attracting you to the floor of the lift, which would be identical to
the force you would feel if the lift was stationary (or moving
without acceleration) in a gravitational field of appropriate

strength. Even if you were trapped in a lift that was falling down a lift shaft (to take one of Einstein's famous examples), you would be unable to tell if you were accelerating towards the base of the shaft or floating freely in space, regardless of what measuring devices you had with you. The consequences of this are very important for understanding cosmology: light passing through the lift will appear to the observer inside the lift to be travelling in a straight line, but to an external observer would appear to be travelling in a curved line. This means that light is bent by gravity, and that space or, more accurately, spacetime is itself curved.

Quantum physics is the name used to describe the theories and techniques that physicists use to make sense of the natural world at the scale of atoms, molecules and subatomic particles. It may seem to us that this is a rather esoteric field of knowledge, but many of the everyday objects that surround us are a product of a quantum understanding of the world: the behaviour of silicon chips in computers, lasers in CD players, and the yellow/orange colour of sodium street lighting are all described by quantum theory. In addition, quantum physics and relativity are at the heart of the phenomenon of 'big science' (a contestable term, see Galison 1997: 553), the drive from the 1930s onwards to discover the hidden nature of atoms and subatomic phenomena, which led directly to the Manhattan Project and the creation and development of nuclear weapons.

Quantum physics, like relativity, requires us to dispense with many common-sense notions about the operation of the physical universe. At the scale of atoms, molecules and subatomic particles (such as neutrons, protons and electrons) all entities lose absolute characteristics. We cannot know both the exact position of a particle and its velocity at the same time, so end up having to make do with a degree of uncertainty and fuzziness in our descriptions of the world. But, because we are so much bigger than atoms or molecules, and our perceptions work at such a slow speed and low resolution, we see an illusion of solid objects around us all the time and an illusion of continuity. At the heart of quantum theory is a major paradox concerning the nature of light. According to experiments that can easily be carried out, light acts as both a wave – i.e. a continuous flow of energy – and particles – i.e. discrete packets of matter. Our traditional idea of matter as existing in discrete 'packets' must be modified to see matter as also existing as a wave. More disturbingly, light will 'change' its nature according

Continued

to how we choose to look at it. So, when physicists carry out experiments into the wave character of light, they get results that confirm this character, and when they investigate the particulate nature of light, they get results that confirm that character.

This paradoxical nature of light continues to manifest itself as more experiments into the nature of light are carried out. Perhaps strangest is the phenomenon of non-locality where two quantum entities (e.g. photons, 'packets' of light) interact with each other, are then separated, and a property of one of the entities is measured: the value of the corresponding property of the other is altered without any signal passing between them. Again, this seems to our common sense to be simply impossible, but experiments – in this case very difficult and complex experiments – can be carried out to show that this phenomenon does take place.

Overall, quantum physics implies that what we do as observers will affect the outcomes of the experiments that we do, that it is not possible to predict beyond statistical probabilities what the outcome of an experiment will be, and that the universe is a very strange place indeed. The philosophical implications of quantum physics are profound, and you may be familiar with some of the more famous thought experiments carried out in the name of quantum physics – Schrödinger's cat is probably the best known – to investigate these implications. However, it is worth noting that most physicists manage to carry out their experiments perfectly well without spending too much time contemplating these philosophical conundrums. John Gribbin calls this 'quantum cookery': using quantum equations as recipes to solve problems involving quantum entities without 'bothering to try to understand what is going on in the quantum realm and what the equations really mean' (Gribbin 1998: 307).

The 'new' physics?

The current paradigm of physics, that deployed by Stephen Hawking, for example, is dubbed 'new physics' to distinguish it from earlier, Newtonian physics, but it isn't particularly new. Einstein's theories, which underpin the whole of the new physics, have been almost universally accepted by the physics scientific community since the 1920s (the exception being Nazi Germany, where Einstein's theory was banned for its 'Jewish' character), so the 'new' physics is, at the very least, about 80 years old. It is interesting to note that there is still a good market in books explaining the 'new' physics: philosopher Betrand Russell's 1923 *The ABC of Atoms* included two chapters on 'The new physics'; popular science writer and physicist John Gribbin published a book in 1999 called *Get a Grip on the New Physics*.

On the standard account of history of science a clear progression can be constructed. Progress is made through theories being articulated, tested and either proved or disproved. In the case of how the Sun shines, there are a number of theories that are articulated and tested before the final 'correct' answer is arrived at. When the final answer is achieved, the previous theories look a bit foolish, although they appeared to be very plausible at the time.

Ancient wisdom actually provided quite a good explanation if one were to think in terms of the principles of formal scientific investigation: observations were made, a theory was formulated, and evidence collected to support the theory. The nineteenth-century theories that replaced this were perhaps slightly more 'scientific', but both were disproved. In the case of the 'glowing ember' theory, the disproof came from looking at the problem from a different direction, and using the same evidence that had supported the theory in a different way. The disproof of the 'gravitational cooling' theory came not from inside the community of scientists investigating the Sun, but from geological evidence: in this case we have a clear example of the co-ordination between different parts of the project of science bringing about a palpable change in the status of a scientific theory. At the end of the nineteenth century, and after a number of centuries of dramatic scientific progress and discovery, the question of how the Sun works was still a puzzle: the mass of the Sun was too small to explain its workings by conventional chemical burning, and the age of the Earth meant that the Sun must have been 'burning' at a constant rate for a very long time. The solution provided by the application of Einstein's theory successfully answered the questions that physicists were asking about the nature of the Sun – it could explain the puzzle of the mass of the Sun and the age of the Earth, and thus achieved general approval from the scientific community, and subsequently from everyone else.

What we see in this brief walk through the history of science is the gradual adoption of a scientific framework of analysis for dealing with a problem in explaining the world around us: from an explanation that could not be tested, to one that relied on an amalgamation of experimental evidence with theory, to an explanation that combined experimental evidence with theory and with further evidence from other theories of the world, to an end-point where a single theory – Einstein's theory – can explain all of the phenomena that surround us. We move from disparate explanations to a unified explanatory framework. But, interestingly, we have seen a decline in the amount of 'hard' evidence that is being brought to bear on the problem: ancient investigators used evidence in the form of meteorites. Although they were wrong, they did at least have some tangible objects to support their theory. Similarly, the nineteenth-century 'burning ember' theorists could use evidence from laboratory experiments investigating the rate of burning of various chemical substances as a way of supporting their theory. By contrast, the gravitational cooling theory admitted no experimental evidence, and the nuclear fusion theory – the current orthodoxy – would appear to have been adopted solely from the compelling evidence supplied by a theory, Einstein's, that had received universal assent. This state of affairs is unsatisfactory for a model of scientific knowledge, where the status of knowledge relies upon hard evidence being found to support a theory. Yet our astronomy textbook from 1999 clearly states that nuclear fusion is the 'true' theory. It will be necessary to return to this point. For the time being, we'll leave the question of how the Sun shines in favour of understanding just what this end-point explanation means and signifies.

Standard history of science

The account that we are presented with suggests that the history of science is best described as one of triumphal progress (see box 4.3). Scientific knowledge is cumulative and progressive: we used not to know very much, then we came to know a bit more and a bit more, until now we pretty much know most of the big things about the natural world. It's worth noting that some commentators who adhere to the standard account, far from seeing this as being a good thing, see it as being bad. John Horgan, for example, argues that science as a project of discovery is pretty much over, that we've found out everything there is to know, and now we are just tidying up the last few details (Horgan 1996).

To be more specific, if we think about a scientific discipline like physics, we can say that ancient wisdom was often wrong about the world, but did get some things right. This was added to by the work of medieval and Renaissance scholars such as Copernicus and Galileo, who extended our understanding of the nature of the physical world, and particularly the structure of the solar system. Then Isaac Newton came along and unified the laws of physics such that a great leap forward was made. Newton's theory produced a paradigm for physics with a set of theories that could be applied to all natural phenomena. In the nineteenth century, scientists such as Michael Faraday and James Clerk Maxwell extended our knowledge by building on previous work and applying it to new discoveries such as electricity and electromagnetic radiation. Then Einstein's work added and extended the work of previous physicists. This model suggests that we are gradually, and step-wise, moving closer and closer to a full and complete explanation of the natural world, and specifically that Einstein's theories are, if not the final steps, very close to the final steps to achieving a complete understanding of the natural world. Kurt Vonnegut summed this up neatly in describing his own attitude to science when working as a biochemist in the 1950s: 'I was sure that pretty soon we would be able to take photographs of God.' The standard account of scientific progress implies an end-point beyond which no further major discoveries can be made. Graphically we can display this on a Cartesian diagram, where we plot our knowledge of the world against time (fig. 4.2)

It isn't just scientific knowledge that fits this graph. A number of other ways of looking at the world, notably modernist social theories of the world, imply exactly the same step-wise progressive model. One example would be the Marxist theory of historical progression through successive epochs. Substitute 'rationality' for 'knowledge' on the graph, and the fit is perfect, although we should note that Karl Marx and Friedrich Engels did not argue that we were starting from a zero point, but rather that we fell to that point through the inven-

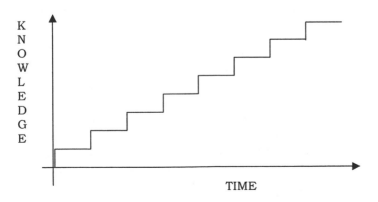

Fig. 4.2. The progressive growth of knowledge.

tion of private property. Equally, the Whig interpretation of history, the standard liberal account of historical progress, broadly fits this model. This isn't just a coincidence: the reason why these models match each other is because they all use a similar frame of reference for evaluating progress and for making sense of the world. Marx and Engels quite clearly describe and construct their historical materialism as a science which offers a rational analysis of the world. The project of science, when describing itself, is measuring only one thing – the amount of knowledge we have – and is using a rational method to measure this. The Whig interpretation of history is using a rational method to measure progress, and focuses only on clear progressive objects, such as human health, amount of technology available, and rationalization of everyday life through, say, urbanization.

It is difficult to argue with such an account: many people in Western industrial societies are, after all, a lot healthier and have much more technology to help them in their everyday lives; the world around them appears to be much more rational; and science has clearly advanced fantastically in the last two centuries. However, a serious challenge to this idea of triumphal progress in the sciences, and by implication

---

Box 4.3   Progress, I

Our received history of science is characterized by progress, and standard history of science validates its claims to progress in two ways.

First, it presents the history of science as a story of accumulation of skills in making sense of the world. The story runs something like this: we used not to know very much about the world, now we know a lot more, therefore there has been progress. This story can also be told not as accumulation but as loss – loss of mystical explanations of the world, or a process of disenchantment. The effect is the same: we move from being credulous humans to being rational humans who can make much better sense of the world about us.

Secondly, it presents the history of science as a story of accumulation of knowledge and facts, and supports this by pointing to the growth of different scientific disciplines, the growth in the number of scientific publications, and the increase in the amount of science being done in schools and universities.

triumphal progress of Western societies, has been made. The work of Thomas Kuhn (1970) is most closely associated with a critical assessment of progress in the sciences: we will also note that a number of other writers arrived at similar ideas independently of Kuhn.

T. S. Kuhn and scientific revolutions

The previous chapter discussed the key elements of Kuhn's challenge to the standard account of scientific knowledge. Kuhn's central idea – of paradigms replacing each other through scientific revolutions, and that paradigms are incommensurable – is based on a revised history of science.

The idea of scientific revolutions taking place periodically through history is not new, and certainly not original to Kuhn's work. Many historians have identified specific scientific revolutions that have taken place through history, and the standard account of the history of science relies upon seeing a significant scientific revolution occurring in the seventeenth century in Western Europe. Historians of science refer to 'The Scientific Revolution' as being the period in European history when the 'conceptual, methodological and institutional foundations of modern science were first established' (Henry 1997: 1). This account sees the discoveries of the sixteenth century as scene setting for the main phase of the scientific revolution in the seventeenth century, which culminated in the consolidation and founding of modern science in the eighteenth century. Henry notes that 'scientific revolution' is a term of convenience for historians of science, but also argues that it is a real thing, in that knowledge of the natural world was very different in 1700 from 1500. The standard history of science is an account of rational progress, and scientific revolutions – the revolutionary overthrowing of one way of seeing the world in favour of another way of seeing the world – are seen as rational developments that are progressive and lead to cumulative growth of scientific knowledge (Popper 1981).

Kuhn's version of scientific revolutions is quite different from this progressive account. Kuhn considered scientific revolutions to be social revolutions as well; they relied upon social interactions to provide a critical mass of dissenting voices to bring about the necessary upheaval. In addition, a scientific revolution may not result in the progressive growth of knowledge. Prior to Kuhn, scientific revolutions were seen as dramatic upheavals in the ideas of a specific sci-

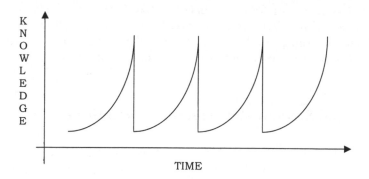

Fig. 4.3. Discontinuous history of knowledge.

entific discipline, where a great leap forward was made that was an extension of existing knowledge. Thus, in the standard account of scientific revolutions, Einstein's theory provided a new paradigm for physics that was a major step forward, but also a continuation of Newton's paradigm. In Kuhn's account a significant difference is noted: two paradigms can be incommensurable, and the language of the old theory may not be able to express the language of the new theory, and vice versa. This means that whilst any normal science will be cumulative, the science that takes place at the time of a scientific revolution – revolutionary science – is not necessarily cumulative. Quite the opposite: after a scientific revolution a huge chunk of the 'old' science will be abandoned as it is incompatible with the new science. A graphical display using a Cartesian diagram of scientific progress from the perspective of Kuhn's model is very different from that of the standard account (see fig. 4.3).

What becomes visible is a discontinuous history. Progress is made inside a time-frame which can be defined by the adoption of a paradigm, but then each subsequent scientific revolution knocks this progress back to a starting point similar to that of the previous paradigm. Kuhn's work is highly contentious, and argument still rages over whether his approach is correct. However, what is clear is that a significant challenge to the idea of progress in the sciences *and* progress in society had been made (see box 4.4).

Box 4.4 Progress, 2

Paul Feyerabend notes that the standard account of progress actually raises more problems than it solves. The story of progress and scientific progress tells us that we 'know more' about the world than did our predecessors:

> [W]ho is the 'we' the critic is talking about? Is he talking about himself? Then the statement is quite obviously false – there is no doubt that Aristotle, on many subjects, knew more than he does. . . . Is the 'we' educated laymen? Again the statement is false. Is the 'we' all modern scientists? Then there are many things which Aristotle knew but which modern scientists don't know and from the nature of their business can't possibly know. The same is true when we replace Aristotle by Indians, or by Pygmies, or by any 'primitive' tribe that has succeeded in surviving plagues, colonization and development. There are lots of things unknown to us Western intellectuals but known to other people. (Feyerabend 1988: 160)

Standard history of science tells us that the stock of facts and knowledge has increased, and Feyerabend has to agree that this point is probably correct: the sum total of the facts that now lie buried in scientific journals, textbooks, letters and hard discs does exceed the sum of knowledge from other traditions. 'But what counts is not number but usefulness and accessibility' (Feyerabend, 1988: 160). Many research papers are never read, and even scientists in a specialist field will have no time to read all the relevant material. Feyerabend goes on: 'Most of the "knowledge" that is sitting around is as unknown as were quarks around the turn of the century' (Feyerabend 1988: 161).

Progress is a concept that we need to be careful in ascribing, even to a venture like science which is avowedly about progressive accumulation of knowledge. Our society, and our science, relies on a story of progress to reassure itself that it is headed in the right direction. Yet the work of Kuhn and Foucault challenges not only the idea of progress in terms of the accumulation of knowledge, but also the idea of societal progress, i.e. the idea that our society is 'better' now than it has been in the past. Kuhn's work challenged the idea of progress in the natural sciences (see main text). In particular, the work of Foucault suggested that the idea of progress is simply not useful in making sense of our history. By showing that history is best understood as a series of discon-

Continued

tinuous episodes, or *epistemes*, Foucault replaced the idea of *progress* with the idea of *difference* (Foucault 1970). Rather than being able to say that societies are better or worse than each other, Foucault suggests that all we can do is identify how societies are *different* from one another: we simply do not have the criteria available to us to judge in absolute ways. The parallel to the work of Kuhn is clear: Kuhn's understanding of change through paradigm shifts has antecedents in Foucault's idea of change through epistemes replacing each other (Radnitzky 1973: 380). This *relativist* position is now closely associated with a postmodernist understanding of the world.

Many scientists disagree with such relativist understandings of science, and the 'standard' account of science still represents the project of science as an inexorable rise towards greater and greater knowledge. However, some scientists challenge this. John Horgan's best-selling *The End of Science* (1996) posits a different version of the end of progress. Rather than offering a relativist argument, Horgan suggests that science has been so effective in making sense of the natural world that there is simply very little left to find out. Science, on this account, has already pretty much run out of new large discoveries, and its task now is simply to work out some of the final details.

A history of sunshine, 2

It is time to rejoin the story of how the Sun shines, this time from a post-Kuhnian perspective. We are now at the point where a 'correct' answer has been arrived at: by the 1920s the currently favoured theory was in place, and our examination of science textbooks confirms that there is little doubt as to the veracity of this theory in our present time. Notably, there are no other competing theories. The current theory, based on Einstein's work, presents scientists with a range of puzzles that need to be solved to prove and validate the theory. Throughout the twentieth century we saw a range of experiments designed to solve the theoretical puzzles presented by the theory of solar nuclear fusion. This fits closely with the Kuhnian model: the theory presents us with puzzles to solve, and normal science is a process of solving such puzzles. Scientists design experiments to solve the puzzles. The puzzles either confirm or deny the theory. If they confirm it, then we extend the theory to the bit of the natural world we have just looked at. If not, we think again, decide that the results we obtained are an anomaly and ignore them, or decide that they constitute an anomaly and reappraise the theory.

In the case of the 'how does the Sun shine?' puzzle we have a pretty clear-cut case of what needs to be done to solve it. Einstein's theory predicts that the Sun works by a process of nuclear fusion, hydrogen atoms fusing together to produce helium, and a lot of energy is released in the process. We want to test this – solve the puzzle of how the Sun works – so we need to design experiments that do this.

We could just measure the energy that comes from the Sun. Doing this will confirm that the Sun radiates a certain amount of energy, and we can use our theoretical prediction of how much energy should be generated by that mass of gas to test the theory. If the two amounts match up, then we might want to say that we have solved the puzzle. But we wouldn't have, or would have done so only partly. It could just be coincidence that the two figures match up. Think back to the 'burning ember' theory – that may have matched the two figures (mass and energy released), but we know from other scientific interventions into other aspects of the phenomena of sunshine that it was not correct. Much better than just observing would be a process of testing the theory by designing an experiment.

To solve the puzzle, we need to look more closely at the specific aspects of the theory and find other points where we can match experimental results against theoretical predictions – and it is here that we get our experimental breakthrough. The process of fusion is, as noted above, quite complex, and involves three distinct steps, according to the current theory. Summarizing the whole process, four protons (hydrogen nuclei) fuse together to make a helium atom, and two gamma photons and two neutrinos are released. If we could count these reaction products (i.e. the gamma rays and the neutrinos), we could verify the theory. We can 'see' the gamma rays coming from the Sun, but they may not be the product of the reaction we are trying to test for – gamma rays come from lots of places and can be made in lots of different ways (e.g. by radioactive decay on Earth or from distant supernovas thousands of light years away). It will not do us much good to count gamma rays in a world that is saturated with them from many different sources – we probably would not be able to 'sort' the solar ones from the other kinds. That leaves the neutrinos: if we could count the neutrinos coming from the Sun, we could verify the theory, and this would tell us if the reaction is actually taking place. So, we need to set up an experiment to measure the solar neutrinos, and compare the results to the predictions of our theory. If they match up, bingo, we've proved that the Sun works by nuclear fusion, as predicted. If they don't match up, we need to reappraise our theory, or do the experiment again, perhaps in a more sophisticated way.

Neutrinos, being neutral particles that very rarely interact with other particles, are very difficult to detect. Nevertheless, in 1967 a detector was built – 400,000 litres of dry-cleaning fluid in an abandoned gold mine in South Dakota. The experiment, designed by Ray Davis of Brookhaven National Laboratory, was called 'Homestake', and it ran for about 20 years. The experiment needed a very long run time to collect a sufficient amount of data for robust conclusions to be drawn. Subsequently, a number of other solar neutrino detectors have been built to try and confirm or deny the Homestake results.

Given the predicted number of neutrinos coming from the Sun (many trillions per second), the Homestake experimenters calculated that their detector should locate an event about every day – which shows you just how non-interactive neutrinos are, and why the experiment took so long. However, in contrast to the prediction, neutrinos were captured only about once every 3 days on average. There were only one-third the number of neutrinos coming from the Sun as the theory predicted. This discrepancy between the actual and predicted number of observations is called the *solar neutrino problem*. (More details from Collins and Pinch 1993: ch. 7: 'Set the controls for the heart of the sun: the strange story of the missing solar neutrinos.' This chapter provides a comprehensive overview of the solar neutrino problem from the start of the Homestake experiment up to 1998. The chapter is based on Pinch's earlier book (1986), which is a very detailed social-constructionist account of the solar neutrino problem, based on interviews and observations of the scientists and laboratories involved.)

This bears some further investigation. The theory has made a prediction; it is tested, and it is found that the results don't match up – there is an anomaly. What should be done? Perhaps the detector isn't working? There have been a number of more recent attempts to build better detectors to try and find the lost neutrinos, but the Homestake results have been confirmed by these later detectors.

Perhaps it is the big theory that is wrong? To hold that the big theory is wrong is to enter dangerous territory – after all, the whole paradigm of physics is based on Einstein's equations, and knocking them down would have huge consequences. Einstein's theory does a good job of explaining many other natural phenomena in the universe. Yet the possibility that Einstein's theory is wrong must be considered. This is not a trivial point: the solar neutrino problem goes to the heart of the paradigm of physics. It isn't just the case that if the problem can't be solved, we would have to reappraise our understanding of how the Sun and, of course, all other stars in the universe, work. It would also suggest that a fundamental reappraisal of the main elements of particle physics is necessary; if fusion doesn't work like this, then what about all the other predicted interactions between non-observable particles? And what about all of Einstein's other predictions? However, this could be seen as the least likely outcome of the solar neutrino problem: finding another solution would be preferable for most observers.

Rather than challenging the whole paradigm, we could look at some of the smaller theoretical aspects of the process, such as the nature of neutrinos – maybe we've been looking for the wrong things, or looking in the wrong way? The problem is that if we do manage to make any progress here, it will probably only be at a theoretical level: our *experiments* for looking at neutrinos, how they work and where they come from, are already in difficulties. Changing our theory may make more sense, in that we can make neutrinos on paper fit our predictions better, but that doesn't alter the fact that our observations of neutrinos are giving results that need to be explained.

Note that at this point in the story we actually do not really know how the Sun works according to formal scientific methodology. There is a theory, but it is resistant to proof, which leaves us in the realm of speculation. Not only that, we actually have direct factual evidence from the Homestake experiment which suggests that the theory is wrong. How do scientists cope with this sort of uncertainty? 'For the moment, many physicists and astronomers are *betting* that we understand the Sun just fine and that the discrepancy has to do with the neutrinos themselves' (Bennett et al. 1999: 476, my emphasis). This quotation is from the same astronomy textbook quoted earlier. In that earlier quotation the authors noted: 'Only after Einstein published his special theory of relativity ... did the *true* energy-generation mechanism of the Sun become clear' (Bennett et al. 1999: 467, my emphasis). We've moved from triumphal certainty to betting. And the blame here is being placed firmly on the neutrinos, not on the big theory. No challenge to the main paradigm is proposed or discussed. The description in the textbook implies that astronomers are not overly concerned about this problem, and from the quotation here it would appear that they are exhibiting a high degree of *faith* in their theory of solar nuclear fusion.

So, we have now arrived at the paradoxical position in which the old discredited theories provided more certainty than the current theory. With the old theories it was 'obvious' that the Sun was a big ball of fire burning away in the sky, and there were even bits of hard material evidence (meteors and meteorites) at which people could point. We didn't have a situation where people were saying 'who knows?' With our twentieth-century situation, we simply couldn't prove how the Sun shines – we had less certainty. This provides a good example of Kuhn's theory of incommensurability, which we can plot on a graph similar to figure 4.3 (see fig. 4.4).

1   Ancient thought was confident that the Sun was a big ball of fire that moved around the fixed Earth: confirmation came from collecting evidence in the form of meteors that fell to the ground. But when it was realized that the Sun, not the Earth, was at the centre of the solar system, this theory was plunged into crisis and a new theory, eventually, emerged.
2   Early modern theories of how the Sun shines were based on analysis of how various substances combusted and remained incandescent. Evidence from other sources indicating the age of the Earth to be about 6,000 years coincided with this theory. However, dramatic results from fossil records put paid to this theory.
3   Late nineteenth-century theories focused on the new knowledge that the sun was made of hydrogen and helium, and was very large. The theory of gravitational contraction answered all the unsolved questions left by previous theories, but ultimately failed because it could not explain how the Sun could shine for so long.
4   Einstein's theory made predictions about energy released by nuclear fusion, and this became the next theory to be adopted. Again, the theory can answer all the questions left unanswered by previous theories, but is still lacking definitive proof.

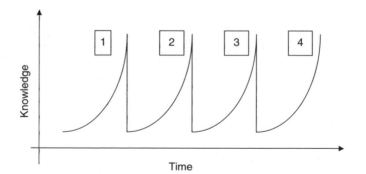

Fig. 4.4.   Discontinuous theories of how the Sun shines.

However, as I suggested earlier, it is almost inconceivable that most people in contemporary society would think that there is less certainty about how the Sun works now than in, say, 1850. Our techno-scientific society does not admit the possibility of there being major holes in our knowledge of large parts of the operation of the natural world.

Actually, the solar neutrino problem has been 'solved', but only recently (2001), and possibly in a way that many will not find particularly satisfying. As one would expect, the 'solution' confirms the paradigm-inspired theory of nuclear fusion:

> At last physicists have solved a problem that's been plaguing them for three decades. Why does the Sun seem to emit fewer neutrinos than it should? *It's simple.* Neutrinos can change from one form to another. Until now physicists had begun to think that either our understanding of the structure of the Sun was wrong, or that neutrino detectors did not work properly. But this week, a team of researchers from Canada, Britain and the US announced that neutrinos made in the Sun can change to other types en route to earth. The other kinds are harder to spot, and so fool the detectors. (*Cho* 2001, my emphasis)

A happy ending, and the story has an even happier ending for the scientists involved in the long, painstaking search for the elusive solar neutrinos. In 2002 the Nobel Prize for physics was awarded to Ray Davis and Masatoshi Koshiba for their work on the solar neutrino problem. Full details of the experiments, and a transcript of Davis's acceptance speech are available on the Nobel Prize website at <http://www.nobel.se/physics/laureates/2002/index.html> (see also Samuel 2003 and Franklin 2001 for further solar neutrino experimental outcomes).

Is this really the end of the story?

Exoteric and esoteric histories of science

So far the histories of science discussed have been general accounts of the growth of scientific knowledge as a whole. Accounts such as Asimov's and Silver's emphasize the cumulative aspect of scientific knowledge and development across a range of disciplines. The result is a picture of a triumphal science that is ever-expanding. However, an interesting facet of such historical descriptions of science is their lack of detail. As was shown in chapter 2, the scientific work that is carried out in laboratories is, almost always, operating at a level of great complexity and detail. The histories we have looked at so far have largely hidden this detail in favour of accounts that are manageable and comprehensible by the 'lay' public. In line with Fleck's terminology concerning thought communities and their dominant styles of thought, we could label these general histories of scientific progress and development 'exoteric histories of science': they are histories that are constructed *outside* the framework of meaning of the esoteric (*inside*) communities that are generating formal scientific knowledge. Such exoteric histories would, of course, be intelligible to those inside a specific scientific thought community, but would also be intelligible to those outside such a thought community. The exoteric historical account is thus a translation, and almost certainly a simplification, of the processes of formal knowledge generation that are taking place inside a specific scientific thought community.

Exoteric accounts will have a range of orientations. Some may be aimed at very general audiences (the 'lay' public in the case of very general overviews), others to more specialized audiences, all 'scientists' who are interested in science (the example used at the start of this section, Asimov's *Chronology of Science and Discovery* (1989), probably fits this category), others still to more specialized audiences – all physicists interested in history of science could be the audience for a book like George Trigg's *Landmark Experiments in Twentieth Century Physics* (1975). At this point in a continuum between exoteric and esoteric accounts texts will cross over into being esoteric accounts.

Esoteric accounts in the history of science can also be imagined as ranging across a continuum. At one extreme are quite general overviews of the production of formal knowledge: Trigg's compilation and analysis of a range of key experiments – from the discovery of X-rays to testing the reality of the neutrino – is an example of this. At the other end of this continuum can be found very complex and esoteric accounts of the development of single-topic specialisms in sub-disciplines of the natural sciences. For example, Hoddenson et al.'s *Out of the Crystal Maze: Chapters from the History of Solid-State Physics* (1992b) is a detailed and in-depth account of the development of experimental techniques in solid-state physics, and also a detailed account of theoretical developments in this field of physics. In approaching the text, the reader requires almost as much specialized knowledge as did the writer of the book. Audiences for this type of book are either members of the thought community within which the book is being written (these are, largely, internal accounts, as we shall see) or, perhaps ironically, historians of science.

The ironic aspect of this is that such esoteric histories hardly ever mention anyone outside the thought community being written about. Nor do they mention or discuss any social or political factors external to the thought community except where this is unavoidable for reasons of glaring historical precedent. For example, in the 697 pages of Hoddenson et al.'s book there are no references to any other histories of science, and there are few references to external factors that had an influence on the growth in the demand for semiconductors. The authors discuss the key players in twentieth-century theoretical physics – Dirac, Einstein, Fermi, Feynman, Fuchs. Fuchs? The same Klaus Fuchs (1911–88) who betrayed the atomic bomb secrets from the Manhattan Project at Los Alamos to the USSR, who was subsequently tried (in two hours!) for treason and imprisoned in the UK for 9 years (Moss 1987). In one footnote, Fuch's past is discussed: 'A few years later, at the start of the Second World War, Fuchs, as an "enemy alien" was interned and imprisoned in Canada, being subsequently released to take part in the atomic bomb project' (Hoch 1992: 229): rather missing the point of his very wide public fame. The second mention does note that 'Klaus Fuchs . . . some years later gaining notoriety as a spy for the Soviet Union' (Hoddenson et al. 1992a: 524–5). The point here, and for all esoteric histories of science, is that the real interest in Fuchs is in his scientific work: he is included in the history of solid-state physics because of his groundbreaking 1930s work on electrostatic calculation of elastic constants, *not* because of his notoriety as a spy. By contrast, Fuchs almost certainly would only appear in an exoteric history of science because of his spying for the USSR, i.e. not for his scientific work. Esoteric histories of science are written from an insider's perspective and do not include discussion of factors that originate outside the scientific community under discussion unless there is a very clear connection.

The distinction between exoteric and esoteric histories of science helps us to see how histories are received by audiences, and it helps us to see how histories of science are involved in constructing images of science. In both cases, histories of science produce accounts that serve to isolate and separate science from wider social, cultural and political issues. This is particularly acute in the esoteric histories, the internal accounts of science, and in the general exoteric accounts, such as Asimov's. Although using quite different content (very specialized formal knowledge versus general 'compiled' scientific narratives), both represent science as isolated through, on the one hand, a reinforcement of the 'specialness' and superiority of science due to its method, attitude and project and, on the other hand, emphasis on the role of the lone genius, the driven scientist who leaves society to create purer scientific knowledge. Both serve to present an account of science that can be misleading. As Fleck notes:

> The history of science also records cases of independent – one might say personal – exploits. But their independence is only characterized by an absence of collaborators and helpers, or possibly of pioneers; that is, it manifests itself in the personal and independent concentration of historical and contemporary collective influence. In a manner corresponding closely to personal exploits in other areas of society, such scientific exploits can prevail only if they have a seminal effect by being performed at a time when the social conditions are right.' (Fleck 1979: 45)

There are a number of accounts – generally more recent accounts – that have attempted to challenge these 'standard' histories. Rather than attempting to explain how a specific discipline emerged, or looking at the growth of knowledge of a specific phenomenon, some histories examine in great detail specific scientific practices and trends from perspectives inspired by philosophy and sociology of science. In *Image and Logic* (1997) Peter Galison presents a detailed account of the development of particle physics through the twentieth century, focusing not on the theories, objects or personalities associated with this discipline, but rather on the material cultures that scientists were involved in constructing to investigate subatomic particles.

Although this approach – focusing on the equipment rather than the theories – may appear to be marginal, the results are very useful for social investigators of science. For example, the identification of the emergence of 'big science' in the USA as a consequence of the Second World War's Allies' Manhattan Project to design and build the atomic bomb is already well known, but the identification of the adoption of modern management theory, modes of organization and attitudes is an interesting point to note. Such conjunctions of thought – between capitalist enterprise and the physics laboratory – could not be identified from an examination of the development of theory, or by focusing on the leading scientists in a specific area. Indeed, 'standard' history of science would obscure such points.

Pickering's *Constructing Quarks* (1984), a study of the history and sociology of high energy physics (HEP), also uses a more sociological frame of reference to make sense of a historical narrative. Pickering notes that, in general, histories of science represent 'scientist's accounts' and, notably, are written in such a way that the scientists involved in the production of the knowledge in question do not appear as genuine agents.

> In the scientist's account . . . [s]cientists are represented rather as passive observers of nature: the facts of natural reality are revealed through experiment; the experimenter's duty is simply to report what he sees; the theorist accepts such reports and supplies apparently unproblematic explanations of them. One gets little feeling that scientists actually *do* anything in their day-to-day practice. (Pickering 1984: 7–8)

Sociologically inflected histories, such as Pickering's and Galison's, are attempts to introduce the scientist as agent into the history being written. Without doing this, the history of science continues to replicate the dominant and standard account, where science is a triumphal progress, and is also a consolidation of the dominant scientistic attitude towards knowledge.

However, despite these efforts at producing 'alternative' histories of science, the micro-examination of the internal workings of a scientific sub-discipline, for all that it uses a sociologically inflected frame of reference, is still largely an esoteric account that does not challenge the fundamental assumptions of the project of science. Two issues – those of gender and colonialism – are embedded in standard histories of science, but simply reproducing the standard esoteric approach cannot begin to challenge these underlying assumptions.

Sardar notes that, despite much of Western science being based on fundamental discoveries made in non-Western societies, the history of science is written from a wholly Western perspective.

> The conventional (Western) history of science . . . does not recognise different types of civilization or cultural sciences. It has represented Western science as the apex of science, and maintained its monopoly in four basic ways. First, it denied the achievements of non-Western cultures and civilisations as real science, dismissing them as superstition, myth and folklore. Second, the histories of non-Western sciences were largely written out of the general history of science. Third, it rewrote the history of the origins of European civilisation to make it self-generating. . . . Fourth, through conquest and colonisation, Europe appropriated the sciences of other civilisations, suppressed the knowledge of their origins, and recycled them as Western. (Sardar 2000: 53–4)

The post-colonial challenge to the history of science has grown in strength in recent years. Post-colonial science and technology studies seeks to 'reclaim the history of non-Western science and expose the Eurocentrism of Western science' (Sardar 2000: 55). Such studies have revealed strong links between the development of Western science and the development of Western colonialism: science was used as a tool by the colonial powers to enforce their rule.

Conclusion

History of science takes a variety of forms, theoretical orientations and styles, and appears in a wide range of locations throughout society and culture. The formal science taught in schools will often make reference to a standard history of science describing progress and the accumulation of knowledge. In wider culture, scientific narratives are often structured around well-known vignettes: Newton's apple, Archimedes' bath, Einstein's genius. Contemporary cultural productions often use images and stories of famous scientists and their struggles as subject matter, or as inspiration for advertising. Scientific awards and prizes will make reference to the historical background of specific scientific problems and their successive resolution.

History of science is a story that is told by insiders, outsiders, supporters and opponents of science. The distinction between esoteric (insider) and exoteric (outsider) accounts of the history of science, or aspects of science, allows us to see how different audiences will be constructed by historians, and how common topics can be described in a number of ways. However, most standard histories of science serve to reinforce a dominant view of science as a heroic progression of discovery, of scientists as neutral and, often, passive discoverers of facts and truths, and scientific knowledge as a better kind of knowledge than other forms available. Post-colonial critiques of the history of science remind us that the standard account presents a history from a Western perspective and that this is a distortion, to say the least, of the contribution made by non-Western societies to the development of science across the globe.

The history of science has very little to do with what takes place in formal science environments such as laboratories. The history of science, the general account of progress and accumulation of knowledge, does contribute to formal scientists' understandings of what their 'project' is: that is, what the significance of their work is, and how it fits into a wider picture. However, historical features of the story of science do not impact on what is done in a laboratory except in a very limited way.

Experiments have histories: they have a past in the sense that they are a continuation of lines of thought that a group of researchers may have been working on for a long time. Experimenters need to be aware of what has occurred in the past with respect to their specific subject matter. This is no easy matter. As formal science increases in its extent, as more and more formal science is being carried out in laboratories around the globe, ensuring that one's work does not replicate someone else's is increasingly difficult. For example, when there are only a very small number of laboratories carrying out work on nuclear fission, as was the case in the 1930s, experimenters could be fairly sure they were not replicating others' work. Even under these conditions 'races' to publish discoveries of new phenomena and theories took place. Membership and activity in a scientific community is one way of ensuring that the work carried out in a laboratory is, usually, complementary to work in other laboratories (this will be discussed further in chapter 5). The exoteric history of science has little relevance in terms of day-to-day practices in a laboratory, but the esoteric history of science that is constructed by insiders in a scientific thought community will have significance in that it is a representation of the immediate past of the experiments that are central to the discipline. First, it will dictate what the members of that scientific community consider to be 'real' knowledge: that is, what objects and theories are significant in their work. Pickering makes this point very clearly in his discussion of the role of history and epistemology in the high energy physics community he studied for *Constructing Quarks*: '[b]y interpreting quarks and so on as real entities, the choice of quark models and gauge theories is made to seem unproblematic: if quarks really are the fundamental building blocks of the world, why should anyone want to exploit alternative theories?' (Pickering 1984: 7). The history that surrounds the scientists in a community is also a representation of the objects of knowledge for that community; that is, it is closely linked to epistemology.

The second point, of more use to social researchers, is that esoteric histories of science provide striking accounts of the meanings, motivations and attachments that are being generated inside a scientific community, and it is to this topic that we will now turn.

Further reading

Relativity and quantum mechanics
Introductory readers
Gribbin, J. 1999: *Get a Grip on the New Physics*. London: Weidenfeld & Nicolson.

Intermediate texts

Gribbin, J. 1998: *Q is for Quantum: Particle Physics from A–Z*. London: Weidenfeld & Nicolson.

Hawking, S. 1988: *A Brief History of Time: From the Big Bang to Black Holes*. New York: Bantam Books.

Rae, A. I. M. 1986: *Quantum Physics: Illusion or Reality?* Cambridge: Cambridge University Press.

Russell, B. 1985: *ABC of Relativity*. London: Unwin Paperbacks.

Textbooks

Brandsen, B. H. and Joachain, C. J. 2000: *Quantum Mechanics*, 2nd edn. London: Prentice-Hall.

Einstein, A. 2001: *Relativity*. London: Routledge.

Rae, A. I. M. 1981: *Quantum Mechanics*. Maidenhead: McGraw-Hill Book Co. (UK) Ltd.

Standard histories – exoteric

There are dozens of these, often written by well-known authors. Recent best-sellers include:

Hawking, S. W. 2003: *On the Shoulders of Giants*. London: Penguin.

Bragg, M. 1998: *On Giants' Shoulders: Great Scientists and their Discoveries from Archimedes to DNA*. London: Hodder & Stoughton.

Standard histories – esoteric

Historical accounts have been written of almost every discipline and sub-discipline in the natural sciences, and most of the main discoveries, processes and forms of experimental procedure. These are useful in terms of illuminating specific aspects of formal science, but also revealing in terms of how historians of science imagine their audiences. Using a good library catalogue or internet search engine, and using the sub-discipline, object or experiment you are interested in, you will be able to find a large number of these type of accounts. For example, typing 'napalm' into my university's library catalogue brought up:

Fieser, L. F. 1964: *The Scientific Method: A Personal Account of Unusual Projects in War and Peace*. New York: Reinhold Publishing Corporation.

Fieser invented napalm for the US government during the Second World War, and his story of the process is fascinating. The rest of the book is an account of how the scientific method and its application has dominated all aspects of his life, from fuel-air weapons to squirrel-proof bird-feeders. It is notable that Fieser avoids any discussion of the contestable aspects of his military work.

'Alternative' histories – challenging standard accounts
A number of these are mentioned in the main text, but the following are signal examples of this approach to history:

Fleck, L. 1979: *Genesis and Development of a Scientific Fact*. Chicago: University of Chicago Press.

Foucault, M. 1967: *Madness and Civilization: A History of Insanity in the Age of Reason*. London: Tavistock.

Foucault, M. 1973: *The Birth of the Clinic: An Archaeology of Medical Perception*. London: Tavistock.

Galison, P. 1997: *Image and Logic: A Material Culture of Microphysics*. Chicago: University of Chicago Press.

Pickering, A. 1984: *Constructing Quarks: A Sociological History of Particle Physics*. Edinburgh: Edinburgh University Press.

Rabinow, P. 1996: *Making PCR: A Story of Biotechnology*. Chicago: University of Chicago Press.

Books on the history of science
A good starting point to this huge topic is the following comprehensive reference book, which includes essays on historiography, theoretical orientations to the analysis of science, and chapters on key moments in the history of science:

Olby, R. C., Cantor, G. N., Christie, J. R. R. and Hodge, M. J. S. (eds) 1990: *Companion to the History of Modern Science*. London: Routledge.

5

Scientists and Scientific Communities

Sociological analysis of scientific communities was a strong theme in science studies of the 1960s and 1970s, but the emphasis on social analysis of scientific organization has changed in recent years. Cultural analysis of the scientific community, and of the cultural representations of 'scientists' has barely started. Yet science is central to many aspects of society and culture, and representations of science and scientists – from TV documentaries to adverts for cooking products – are very common.

The idea that scientists are all broadly similar, can be lumped together in a single category, and that this category can be seen as a single institution will be examined in this chapter. We'll see that the representations of scientists and standard modes of social analysis of scientific communities construct a 'picture' that is an essentialized understanding of science and scientists, an understanding that is not appropriate for making sense of scientists and science in contemporary society.

'Scientists should not be allowed to make food'

The general public – that is, those people who are not particularly familiar with the theory, methods and procedures of the formation of scientific knowledge – often refer to the practitioners of science as 'scientists'. This is an interesting term, one that immediately tells us something about the group being referred to and the individuals that it includes. It implies that we all know who scientists are, where we can find them, what they do, even what they look like, what their attitudes towards the world are, and what sort of cultural preferences they make. The Discovery Foods advertisement reproduced in illustration 5.1 from an advertising campaign of Summer 2002 is a good example of this. The advertisement, which is meant to be light-hearted and not an attack on scientists (who, after all, also buy cook-in sauces), starts from an assumption that scientists are all the same, are interchangeable, and that this similitude can be summed up by scientists' attitude towards the non-scientific, everyday world. Scientists, according to the advertisement, will always try to impose their technical and artificial skills and tools on all areas of life, however inappropriate this may be. The subtext here is that scientists think differently from non-scientists. The implication is that there is something essentially 'different' about scientists from the rest of us. The advertisement furthers this by including an illustration of a 'scientist' to remind the audience of what scientists are like. The stereotypical image of the scientist – male, bad hair, test-tubes full of noxious liquids – serves the purpose of reinforcing the negative perception of scientists. Just to make sure, the advertisement comments:

'We don't like scientists.'

There is an additional construction here – that scientists are concerned with efficiency, particularly with respect to cost:

'A scientist would have abandoned our two-step process in favour of something easier and cheaper to produce.'

The idea that 'scientists' are more concerned with making things cheaply and easily is, perhaps, challenged by the analysis of experiments that was presented in chapter 2. Of course, the Discovery Foods advertisement isn't referring to scientists who are working to provide new antibiotics, a cure for cancer, or more environmentally friendly transport solutions, just those 'scientists' who are responsible for imposing efficiency gains, whoever they may be. It may be that what the advertisement is really attacking is the rationalization of the work-place, and the alleged efficiency this has generated, which has been brought about, through modernity, by measures such as Taylorism and Fordism (Bradley et al. 2000: ch. 5). The point here is that the advertisement cannot distinguish the 'good' scientists from the 'bad' scientists: we have a societal image of scientists as a collective, and escaping that image will be difficult.

Illustration 5.1. Discovery Foods advertisement, summer 2002. © Discovery Foods. Published with permission of Discovery Foods from copy provided by Hooper Galton advertising agent.

From the advertisement it is clear that scientists should keep their techniques and knowledge away from some spheres of life – in this case the production of food. But, given that our technoscientific society relies on the work of scientists, and that science is generally seen in society as a 'good thing', why is it that there is a degree of hostility surrounding scientists, and why is it that scientists are often seen as being separate, different?

Perhaps the best starting point for us is to consider how and why it is that scientists are collectivized in the public imagination.

1 'A simple DIY tape can remove warts less painfully than traditional methods, scientists have proved': 'Duct tape kills warts', *The Mirror*, 17 October 2002.
2 'Doctor Peter Cotgreave, director of Save British Science, said the increasing arrogance of scientists after the Second World War meant that science had become removed from the public understanding, exacerbating the divide between the two cultures. Now the problem is being tackled with policies to increase public engagement in the sciences': Polly Curtis, 'Call to explode "mythical academic divide"', *Guardian Unlimited*, Friday, 5 July 2002, © Guardian Newspapers Limited 2002.
3 'Scientists should not be allowed to make food. All our chefs failed Chemistry O Level': From advertising copy for the Discovery Foods magazine campaign, summer 2002.

Three examples chosen from the many available that illustrate how the UK media deploy the term 'scientists'. There are, of course, other usages to be found, but the aim here is to give a flavour of the commonality of this usage, and some of the key features of the deployment of this term. First, we should note that what we are really seeing are two separate forms of usage. The first, usage 1, is a process of hiding, the removal of the specific disciplinary category that an individual would describe themselves as being in – for example, botanist, biochemist or palaeontologist – and its replacement with a generic term 'scientist'. This first usage of 'scientists' therefore designates a group of individuals involved in a common research effort or discipline-specific project, as in example 1: the *Mirror* article is, presumably, referring to research carried out by dermatologists. For such articles in the press, the identifier 'scientists' would appear to be sufficient to provide the reader with an idea of who is being talked about, and no further identification is usually provided. The accuracy or otherwise of this idea that the reader constructs is not the point here, for the moment at least. However, it is unlikely that we would do this with other occupational categories: describing both Eminem and Pavarotti as 'musicians' is accurate but misleading in the same way that describing palaeontologists and astrophysicists as 'scientists' is accurate but misleading.

Usage 2 is slightly different. Whereas usage 1 hides the specificity of the individual's work and research and replaces it with a generic term, usage 2 elides the specificity of the individual's social situation and replaces it with a construction of community and collective ethos. Examples 2 and 3 suggest that all scientists are part of a large grouping, a community that can have characteristics (e.g. arrogance or lack of cooking skills), leaders (e.g. 'leading scientists') and location (a single locus where scientists can be consulted by the media). As far as the media is concerned, scientists – by usage 1 – are pretty much interchangeable with each other, regardless of discipline or location, and, by usage 2, are all in one big grouping. Both of these forms of usage illustrate how society, via the media, is constructing an image of scientists and a community of scientists, a scientific community.

These two forms of usage suggest that there are two different ways of imagining scientists in wider groupings that are visible in society: as aggregated according to disciplinary boundaries, and aggregated as a single mass. It is notable that these two forms of definition, the general and the particular scientific communities, correspond broadly to the two main academic conceptions that have structured sociological studies of the scientific community. In addition, we can suggest that the prevalence of both usages in the media implies that the common-sense understanding of scientists and their collectives is that they can be part of small groupings and also part of a large, all-encompassing scientific community. This, too, has been a common analytical frame for sociology of science in the past.

Sociology of the scientific community

The first major conceptualization of scientific community comes from W. O. Hagstrom, who in his seminal work *The Scientific Community* (1965) presents an account of the relationship between individual scientists and the wider community they together form. It is this wider community that regulates their work, assigns status to individuals and groups, and articulates the commonly held values of scientists. Hagstrom's book is the first widely distributed account of the formation and structure of scientific communities, although Hagstrom did not invent the term 'scientific community'. The antecendents go back some years: Baldamus argues that it was Ludwik Fleck in *Genesis and Development of a Scientific Fact* (Fleck 1979) who first coined the phrase (Baldamus 1977: n. 1). Hagstrom's thesis describing the organizing principles and mechanisms of the scientific community is 'that social control in science is exercised in an exchange system, a system wherein gifts of information are exchanged for recognition from scientific colleagues. Because scientists desire recognition they conform to the goals and norms of the scientific community. Such control reinforces and complements the socialization process in science' (Hagstrom 1965: 52). Conformity is rewarded, and commitment to higher goals is also reinforced. These higher goals include a commitment to the scientific community itself – this extends beyond any specific collection of peers, and beyond any disciplinary boundary. In considering conformity and social control, Hagstrom does note that scientists are also employees, but here largely rejects any possibility that commitment to production inside science is a result of individuals' feeling bound by contractual obligations (Hagstrom 1965: 54). For Hagstrom, the productive nature of science stems from the open and egalitarian nature of the scientific community and its organization around gift-giving principles.

Hagstrom's thesis emerges from primary data collection he conducted, largely based on in-depth interviews with academic scientists in a range of disciplines working in US universities. Hagstrom's empirical work is an extension of the Mertonian theory of the institution of science (see box 5.1), an institution that is governed by imperatives that express the values of the members, and can be seen as an empirical 'testing' of Merton's theory.

Box 5.1 The institutional imperatives of science

In 1942 Merton identified four imperatives that characterize the ethos of science (Merton 1967: 550–61).

1 *Universalism*: truth claims are to be subjected to pre-established impersonal criteria. All claims are approached using similar methods (universal methods), and all claims are as likely as others until proved otherwise. For Merton, this expands to give the ethos of science a view of careers – these should be open to talents, not prejudice. Universalism rejects versions of science that are particular, such as the science of Nazi Germany, which was based on 'Aryan' science.

Continued

2 *Communism*: here Merton means the common ownership of goods. The substantive findings of science are a product of social collaboration and are assigned to the community. Property rights in science are whittled down to a bare minimum by the ethics of the scientific community. Secrecy is the antithesis of this norm – communication of findings is a must. The only things the scientist owns are the esteem and recognition due to him by the wider scientific community.

3 *Disinterestedness*: There is competition in the field of science, but this is not at a level of falsifying others' findings without good reason. Disinterestedness relates to the ways in which scientists scrutinize their peers such that the main winner is 'the truth'.

4 *Organized scepticism*: the suspension of judgement until the facts are at hand. The scientist suspends his or her common sense, thus allowing the hidden truth to appear.

Indeed, Hagstrom himself makes generous reference to the work of Merton as being a great influence on him, citing him frequently in the main text, and making special mention of the debt he owes him in the acknowledgements. Hagstrom, perhaps surprisingly, offers no clear definition of 'the scientific community', but as he makes no reference to the possibility of a range of different communities coexisting, we can assume that his scientific community is unitary and has a hierarchical structure of disciplines and individual members: both are ranked according to prestige awarded inside the community (with the discipline of physics and Nobel laureates at the apex). For Hagstrom, the scientific community is like any other functioning social institution in that we can scrutinize it from the outside to discover its structure, function and values. Significantly, with its shared ethos and shared values, Hagstrom's picture of the scientific community is devoutly essentialist. For him, the scientific community has an essence that is composed of shared norms and values.

The second major conceptualization of the scientific community comes from the work of Thomas Kuhn. *The Structure of Scientific Revolutions*, first published in 1962, was a sociological analysis of the construction and articulation of scientific theories (see chapters 3 and 4). The concept of 'paradigm' is central to Kuhn's thesis of change through scientific revolution, and central to the concept of paradigm is the scientific community: for Kuhn, it is through the sharing of a paradigm that we can identify a scientific community. In the first edition of *The Structure of Scientific Revolutions* Kuhn offered little by way of definition of scientific community (Jacobs

1987). Despite Kuhn's relativism, and his recognition of difference between different scientific disciplines, it looks as if he is talking about a general scientific community in much the same way as Hagstrom: 'Like the choice between competing political institutions, that between competing paradigms proves to be a choice between incompatible modes of community life' (Kuhn 1970: 93).

This loose form of definition by analogy can be seen as being, at least in part, responsible for generating an understanding of paradigms as being outlooks shared by very large groups of practitioners. Kuhn subsequently revised and refined his understanding of scientific communities in the Postscript to *The Structure of Scientific Revolutions*, included in the 1970 edition, and in an essay published in 1977:

> A scientific community consists, in this view, of the practitioners of a scientific specialty. Bound together by common elements in their education and apprenticeship, they see themselves and are seen by others as the men responsible for the pursuit of a set of shared goals, including the training of their successors. Such communities are characterized by the relative fullness of communication within the group and by the relative unanimity of the group's judgment in professional matters. (Kuhn 1977: 296)

This is quite different from the understanding of Hagstrom: for Kuhn a scientific community is a small group of practitioners, possibly as small as a few hundred members, who share a particular specialist area of research. Such a scientific community can be investigated through analysis of the works to which they ascribe, i.e. by analysis of the works that they cite in their publications. However, as well as a scientific community sharing key texts, it is interesting that Kuhn's definition includes reference to the shared values of such a community, and Kuhn does note the relevance of the work of Hagstrom in the second edition of *The Structure of Scientific Revolutions* (Kuhn, 1970: 176 n. 5).

Both Kuhn and Hagstrom are offering, albeit in different ways, an essentialist account of scientific community. The scientific community that they identify has an existence above and beyond that of the actions of its individual members, and it has a core set of values and orientations towards its actions. These two sociological analyses of scientific communities, which represent the standard and the relativist perspectives, both construct an essentialist picture of scientific communities and, by extension, scientists.

Summing up, our media usages correspond broadly to two key sociology of science definitions of scientific community. On the surface these sociological definitions appear to be in conflict with each other: we can either have a general scientific community that comprises all scientists working in all disciplines, or we can see scientific communities as being small, self-contained entities bounded by shared specialist subject matter, but independent of each other. However, many scientists consider themselves to be both members of specialist small-scale scientific communities that are centred on their specialist research, and members of a larger community that comprises all those involved in scientific endeavours.

Both major sociological conceptions of the scientific community have received significant criticism in recent years. Hagstrom's account, relying as it does on scientists sharing a value system that is normative and monolithic, has been attacked for its lack of consideration of variations inside the different specialities making up the scientific community (Crane 1972). Kuhn's account has received more sustained assault, particularly from ethnomethodology and social constructionism. In particular, the work of Knorr-Cetina has been used to show the flaws in both Kuhn's sociological understanding of scientists' organization – the community that Kuhn describes is not the group of individuals who are instrumental in producing scientific knowledge – and his understanding of change in science as a whole, in that without a scientific community being properly identified as sharing a paradigm there can be no paradigm shift taking place (Jacobs and Mooney 1997). More generally, Fuller identifies the very concept of 'scientific community' as being an artificial construct that emerged in the late 1950s and served a political purpose:

> It would seem that Kuhn managed to 'discover' that science flourishes in self-governing communities just at the time that the democratic instincts of American politicians and political commentators insisted on greater public accountability from scientists. As in so many other cases, a sense of 'community' emerges among disparate individuals as they face a common foe. To put the point in boldest relief, the construction of *science* as *social* served much the same purpose as earlier constructions of the *scientist* as *individual* – only now reflecting the potentially more widespread societal opposition that scientists faced. In both cases, the uniqueness of science is highlighted as demanding special treatment. (Fuller 2000b: 209)

Fuller goes on to note that the construction of scientific community that Kuhn put forward in *Structure of Scientific Revolutions* was so stilted and idealized in the way that it minimized observation of any form of disagreement that it deserves to be described as being 'oversocialized'. For Fuller, given this tarnished genesis, the use of the concept of scientific community is not helpful for sociologists of science. Fuller's critique can also be applied to the picture of the scientific community that Hagstrom presented. Hagstrom's identification of the values of science embodied in the scientific community produced a landscape that was pretty flat, in that almost all of his respondents conformed to the universally held ideals, and all expressed the commonality of values that Hagstrom ascribed to the scientific community.

These critiques, and the general shift towards a sociology of scientific knowledge (SSK) frame of analysis for sociology of science killed off the concept of scientific community as worthy of further examination, and as a category for analysis. It is notable that few studies specifically dedicated to examining the scientific community have appeared in recent years. This is not to say that the concept has disappeared. Far from it. A quick search through the *Social Sciences Citations Index* will find a huge number of mentions of 'scientific community'. However, such mentions are precisely that: the scientific community is seen as being an extant institution that needs no further analysis, and it is deployed in these journal articles without question. These are rarely studies of how scientific communities come together or examinations of their composition.

We could leave the matter there, simply noting that there is a common sense perception of a scientific community (as seen, for example, in contemporary media representations) which sociology of science can debunk or dismiss quite easily were it not for one further complicating factor. The problem here is that these descriptions of a united scientific community are not restricted to the media and the general public. If they were, we could explain their appearance as being due, perhaps, to a lack of knowledge of how scientific activity is structured. The problem is that scientists, too, present themselves in public and in private in this way, and a charge of lack of knowledge will not stick here. Here are some examples of scientists talking about their work in the media. All the examples have been taken from the *Guardian*, a UK broadsheet daily newspaper, and the *Observer* its sister, Sunday, publication:

1 'But fertility expert Lord Winston, of London's Imperial College, warned that talk of cloning risked bringing the whole science of assisted fertilisation "into disrepute". He told the Today programme: "Cloning is highly dangerous science. Every species that has been tried has resulted in massive embryo loss, high abnormality rates and all sorts of changes in the way genes are expressed. What worries me is that important reproductive work is endangered by the bombastic statements of people who would

like to clone human beings. I think that *the scientific community* should be unanimous in condemning these attempts"' ('Fertility expert gives cautious backing to human cloning', *Guardian Unlimited*, Monday, 10 June 2002, © Guardian Newspapers Limited 2002)

2 'The UK could be left behind in the race to develop new treatments for diseases, the Royal Society has warned. The society claims *the scientific community* is in danger of being drowned out by pressure groups in the public debate about GM animals' (Polly Curtis, 'UK "left behind" in GM debate', *Guardian Unlimited*, Monday, 10 June 2002, © Guardian Newspapers Limited 2002)

3 'Professor Edzard Ernst is director of complementary medicine at Exeter University. He studied medicine and psychology and has written 30 books, including *Homeopathy: A Critical Approach* (Butterworth Heinemann). He is a trained homeopath, a fact not acknowledged on his CV because, he says, "I'm not very proud of it." Fellow homeopaths see him as a Judas, but Professor Ernst says that he is "proud of being a good scientist, that is my only real love and homeopathy is treated with a great deal of derision by *the scientific community* because all its underpinnings openly fly in the face of science".' (Sally Beck, 'Natural selection', *Observer*, Sunday, 2 June 2002, © Guardian Newspapers Limited 2002)

What do these designations of scientific community mean? In a similar way to our deconstruction of the journalists' usage of the term 'scientist', we need to use a certain amount of inference to identify who is being referred to here. It would appear likely that in example 1 the 'scientific community' being referred to is that of embryologists, because a very specific procedure is being referred to (human cloning). However, it could be that Lord Winston does indeed mean 'all scientists': perhaps he feels that all scientists, from embryologists to astrophysicists, should collectively be opposed to attempts to clone human beings? This is not necessarily far-fetched: people involved in scientific research are often members, or adherents, of collective organizations, such as the British Association for the Advancement of Science, that do make pronouncements about specific areas of scientific interest on behalf of all their members.

Example 2 also uses the term 'scientific community' in an ambiguous way: many scientists are not involved in genetic modification of animals, and it seems unlikely that, say, palaeontologists' voices are being drowned out by pressure groups in the public debate about GM animals. Here, too, we must infer that the scientific community being referred to by the Royal Society spokesperson is a discipline-specific one, that of geneticists, although we could perhaps infer that these comments are directed at an unspecified anti-scientism?

Example 3 contains, perhaps, the clearest usage of 'scientific community'. By referring to the unscientific nature of homeopathy research – its lack of testable or verifiable results – Ernst's identification of a community in opposition to homeopathy is synonymous with those who do use testable and verifiable empirical procedures in their work – that is, all scientists.

Up to this point we have seen three different accounts of scientific community emerging. The first, the common-sense notion of a community of scientists, is seen clearly in media productions, particularly news media. The second, the sociological account of scientific community, is largely absent from contemporary sociology of science, but has a long tradition of identifying a community that is structured around shared values and goals. The third account, that of scientists themselves, is to be seen in the self-descriptions of scientists. Here elements of the 'common-sense' definition of the scientific community are mingled with personal experiences of working in collective ways to produce accounts that are personalized yet reflective of wider societal understandings of what science is. All three accounts promote an essentialist picture of science and scientists, but construct the idea of 'scientific community' in quite different ways. How can we begin to explain the existence of three different accounts, all of which seem plausible in their own right, all of which contradict each other at certain points?

Cultural studies and scientific communities

The problem we face is similar to that dealt with in cultural studies of nationalism and identity. How do we disentangle the threads of a national identity that is clearly constructed and artificial from a feeling of national identity that is held by individual members of a particular nation-state? On the one hand, we can clearly identify an 'ideology' of nationalism that is promulgated by the media, the government and by other social institutions (e.g. the idea that the English share certain national characteristics that contribute to defining their nation). It is not difficult to dismiss such discourses as propaganda that is often hollow or invokes stereotypical representations with few, if any, points of real contact with the members of a national community. On the other hand, we can identify personal discourses that clearly identify the speaker as a member of a national community, and clearly impute characteristics to that national community. Similarly, we can identify the construction of a nation as being an artifice, an 'imagined community' that has no real existence beyond the discourse of nationality and nationalism that is constructing it. However, we as members of a specific nation-state feel that we are a part of a larger entity that has a real existence for us.

In answering these questions of nationality and identity, Jorge Larrain, drawing on the work of Stuart Hall, presents us with a model for considering what the role and status of the scientific community is. Larrain's analysis of nationalism and national identity begins with an exploration of what we mean by identity. There are three elements to the construction of self-identity: the material, the other and the group. We define our identity with respect to the materiality of our existence – our bodies, our production and our consumption; with respect to others who are similar or dissimilar to us; and, crucially for the discussion here, in terms of some shared social categories:

> In forming personal identities most individuals share certain group allegiances or characteristics – such as religion, profession, gender, class, ethnicity, sexuality, nationality – which are culturally determined and contribute to specifying the subject and its sense of identity. In this sense it can be affirmed that culture is one of the determinants of personal identity. All personal identities are rooted in collective contexts culturally determined. This is how the idea of cultural identities emerges. (Larrain 2000: 24)

From this perspective we need to see scientists' identity and their membership of a professional community as closely linked. Scientists are constructing their own identities in the context of the wider social grouping with which they identify themselves. At the same time, this wider social grouping – the scientific community – is being constructed through the personal actions of individual scientists contained within it:

> [P]ersonal and collective identities are mutually necessary and interrelated. There cannot be personal identities without collective identities and vice versa. Which means that although there is certainly an analytical distinction between the two, they cannot be conceived apart and substantialized as entities to stand on their own without a reference to one another. This is because individuals cannot be conceived as isolated entities and opposed to the social world conceived as an external reality. Individuals are defined in their social relations and society reproduces itself and changes through individual actions. Personal identities are shaped by culturally defined collective identities, but these cannot exist separately from individuals. (Larrain 2000: 30)

There are two final points we need to make before we can fully understand the complexity of the relationship between individual scientist and scientific community. The first is that we cannot, on this theoretical schema, ascribe an independent existence to the scientific community. Whilst it is feasible and desirable to make sense of the identity of individual scientists, and to understand the process of identity formation of individual scientists to be taking place always with reference to the scientific community, it is not possible to speak of a collective identity that is manifested as a shared psychic structure or character which would be shared by all members of the collective:

> A collective identity has no character or psychic structure in the sense of a number of defined psychological traits. It cannot be said that a collective character manifests itself in the conjunction of individual characters, for instance that Chileans share a Chilean character structure which is different from the British character structure. (Larrain 2000: 31)

Finally, we need to remind ourselves that individual and collective identities are being constructed in relation to each other and in the context of a constructed culture. In this specific case, scientists construct their identity with reference to their membership of a collective of scientists, and the result is they feel that they are a part of 'the scientific community'. But, as Fleck (1979) and a great many other sociologists have reminded us over the years, scientists do not exist in, or emerge from, a vacuum, even though many cultural representations make it look as if they do. Here we must recognize that scientists' construction of collective identity is made not only by reference to other scientists, but also by reference to wider social and cultural representations of science, scientists and scientific communities. We can see this in formal scientists' descriptions of how other people see them: almost all of those interviewed in research for this book could clearly identify the social construction of 'scientists'. Here are some examples:

'White coat, frizzy hair, bubbling glasses full of green liquid. The true mad scientist. General populace think of scientists as being a person in a white coat working in a lab messing around with strange chemicals.' (Chemistry technician)

'Classic white lab coat, big scary hair and generally somebody dabbling in bits of nature where they shouldn't be dabbling. People have a negative view of them.' (Chemistry lecturer)

'What they see on the TV is people walking round in white coats with pipettes in their hands, coloured solutions and things going 'fizz', bang, exploding. They think it's exciting.' (Biochemistry postdoctoral research fellow)

It is not relevant to the point of this discussion that these images are stereotypes and largely inaccurate representations of scientists. What is relevant is that most scientists can define themselves in relation to the collective of which they feel they are a part, and are doing this defining in a cultural context that includes clear reference to their collective, and even has a clear construction of an archetype of identity for the members of that collective. Scientists, as an occupational group, are not unique in this respect, but are part of a very small minority in our society. Whilst we can find stereotypical descriptions of a range of distinct social groups, often pejorative ones, it is rare to find social constructions of occupational classifications as a whole. Journalists, politicians and estate agents spring to mind as being the victims of unfair negative stereotypes, but there are few others. We wouldn't, for example, find similar constructions concerning engineers, nurses, factory workers or call centre operatives. It could be argued that one reason for this is the morally contestable aspect of the work carried out by scientists (Bradley et al. 2000: 180). Many scientists are seen by the public as being involved in work that challenges their moral and ethical standpoint, or even threatens them personally. High-profile media coverage of contentious scientific research such as human cloning or genetic modification of organisms adds to these perceptions.

The collectivization of scientists by the public and by the scientific community itself, and the reinforcement of stereotypes in cultural representations, are not harmless. The Institute of Physics carried out a small-scale survey to investigate the prevalence of the 'boffin' stereotype. Showing shoppers in London the picture shown in illustration 5.2 and asking people to 'identify the physicist', the research found that 98 per cent of the public picked the wrong person from the line-up, usually opting for the middle-aged white man with a beard. The conflation here – of gender stereotypes and scientist stereotypes – is interesting: the reinforcement of these stereotypes with respect to science may lead to further reinforcement of the gendered aspects of the scientific community.

Scientists and their communities are gendered

A very important characteristic of the scientific community that the two main models – Hagstrom's and Kuhn's – fail to address at all is gender. Their omission of gender is a reflection of patriarchal attitudes in sociology of science and androcentric (male-oriented) science itself. That women are discriminated against inside scientific institutions is

Physicist - the usual suspects

Someone in this line up is a physicist . . . can you tell which one?

Illustration 5.2. Physicist – the usual suspects. Photo by Robin Chandra. © Institute of Physics 2003. Reproduced with permission.

well known – one need only think of the significant under-representation of women in senior (i.e. professorial) positions in UK university science faculties to confirm this. (In 1999, 11.6 per cent of science, engineering and technology subject professors in UK Higher Education were women; 18.3 per cent in Finland, 6.3 per cent in Germany, and 5.1 per cent in the Irish Republic (Peters et al. 2002: 39)). However, we need to take the analysis a bit further to begin to understand why there is so much gender discrimination in the sciences.

Zuckerman and Cole offered an explanation for the lack of representation of women in the higher echelons of the scientific community based on their concept of the 'triple penalty':

> First, science is culturally defined as an inappropriate career for women; the number of women recruited to science is thereby reduced below the level which would obtain were this definition not prevalent. Second, those women who have surmounted the first barrier and have become scientists, continue to be hampered by the belief that

women are less competent than men. Whatever the validity of this belief, it contributes to women's ambivalence towards their work and thereby reduces their motivation and commitment to scientific careers. And third . . . there is some evidence for actual discrimination against women in the scientific community. To the extent that women scientists suffer from these disadvantages, they are victims of one or more components of the triple penalty. (Zuckerman and Cole 1975: 84)

This is quite a tentative statement: Zuckerman and Cole are identifying some possible trends and tendencies, and are not in the business of apportioning blame. Indeed, Cole, writing four years later, notes that:

If women face these obstacles today, they were even more formidable in the first half of [the twentieth] century. By tracing over time several indicators of status, I will suggest that the status-sets of men and women scientists have moved increasingly from essentially heterogeneous to homogenous configurations. (Cole 1979: 187)

Cole's implication, that gender discrimination in formal science institutions is on the decline, is contentious (although there is good empirical evidence for his argument: in 1994, women received approximately 25 per cent of the science Ph.D.s awarded in the USA, compared to 6 per cent in 1970). In more recent studies, a much stronger critical tone has been struck, and specific factors – such as the connection between career and child-rearing – have been identified. For example, in the course of doing research for this book I found that almost all women in formal science who were interviewed identified that they had been asked, or could recognize the implicit question, at job interviews of whether they intended to take a career break to have children. None of the men interviewed reported the same. A major investigation into the participation of women in science in the UK, the Greenfield Report, commissioned by the UK government and published in 2002, found women reporting a wide range of problems in SET (science, engineering and technology) work-places, including:

few visible role models and mentors
lack of transparency for pay and promotion procedures
gender imbalance in the decision-making process
slow setting up and take-up of work – life balance policies
intangible cultural factors that seem to exclude them from the corridors of power
institutional sexism
stereotyping of careers advice

the research-based career is predicated around publishing in refereed
    journals and raising one's profile at key conferences, leaving little
    time for gaining broader management knowledge and skills that can
    add value to the professional skills of the scientist or engineer
the publication record is heavily compromised by a career break or a
    (more senior) partner relocating to a new institution
women having to work harder to convince and persuade their man-
    agers that they want and need more responsibility which they see
    being given to their male colleagues
(Peters et al. 2002: 29)

The triple penalty, however, does provide us with a useful starting
point for investigating the gendered aspects, and discriminatory
aspects, of scientific community and science in general. This starting
point is the same as that adopted by liberal feminists, who argue for
change in the structures of scientific institutions, and in the orientation towards the project of science, but not necessarily for a different form of scientific epistemology (Rose 1994 provides a good
overview of these different feminist camps, and Fuller 2000a notes
the differences between the political and ideological projects of feminist science). It is noteworthy that all of the factors identified by
Zuckerman and Cole are *external* to the content or operation of
formal science – that is, there is nothing about formal science itself
that necessarily excludes women; the liberal feminist project with
respect to science is about challenging these stereotypes and forms of
institutional discrimination. In addition to the sexist attitudes of
those in positions of authority in scientific institutions, the other
factor – science being an inappropriate career for women – is a cultural product which can be investigated through cultural analysis.
Challenging the cultural impediments to women entering scientific
communities entails challenging the essentialist conceptions of
science, scientist and scientific community and their embodiment of
patriarchal and androcentric preconceptions.

Conclusion

Sociology of science has shifted its focus with regard to the scientific
community. In one respect this is a good thing. The essentialist construction of a scientific community that has a life of its own beyond
that of its members, and embodies and expresses the values of its
members, is not helpful to us in making sense of scientists' work and

science in society. Such a construction, clearly visible in the work of Hagstrom and Kuhn, was a useful device for sociologists to characterize a social institution in the context of a form of sociological analysis that looked for systemic understandings of the world. It was also a useful device for scientists themselves, particularly at times when science was under attack or under public scrutiny: finding a self-regulating institution that embodies the core values of the society it is 'serving' is very useful in political terms. However, such understandings of the scientific community, if they ever were accurate, are inappropriate for us today. The scientific community that is visible in contemporary society is certainly not the monolithic version described by Kuhn and Hagstrom, although some elements of their descriptions, such as the idea that specific disciplines will form their own communities through sharing knowledge, are still visible. Formal scientific activity is now fragmented into sub-disciplines which are small in size and have a diminishing number of connections to other sub-disciplines.

However, this does not mean that we can dispense with the concept of scientific community. Sociology of science has shifted away from looking at collectives to looking at individuals involved in the production or construction of knowledge: SSK is in a hegemonic position with respect to sociology of science. Such studies are illuminating as regards local processes that occur in the research process in specific locations, and shed a great deal of light on the forms of interaction, negotiation and argumentation that are necessary for scientific knowledge to emerge. What they cannot show – indeed, what they occlude – are the external and collective factors that are significant in the everyday lives, work and careers of scientists. Using a conception of scientific community similar to that of Fleck could alter this.

Fleck's idea of 'thought communities', small groupings of people characterized by a particular style of thinking, is a useful model for making sense of the multiple scientific communities that exist. Fleck notes that people can be members of many exoteric thought communities (such as political parties, clubs and societies, social communities, families) but only a small number – maybe only one at a time – of esoteric thought communities. Fleck also notes that the exoteric and the esoteric will have an impact upon each other: the possibility of an exclusive, isolated thought community is simply not a possibility, in the same way that Wittgenstein considers a private language to be impossible.

Fleck's concept of thought communities allows us to explain why it is that scientists themselves identify membership of more than one grouping, but usually identify a strong affinity with an esoteric community (all microbial geneticists, all carbon chemists, etc.). This picture, of a scientific community that is fragmented and ordered around tight specialisms, concurs with the current organization of scientific research, and with the current state of wide-ranging generic scientific bodies that represent 'all scientists' such as The British Association for the Advancement of Science.

By looking at the entry of external styles of thought and ideas into esoteric thought communities, Fleck also provides us with at least a starting point for understanding the continued discrimination against women in the formal sciences. In addition, Fleck's schema allows us to consider how agendas inside formal science structures are set according to external, frequently androcentric priorities.

Why do we still need to investigate scientific communities? There are three main reasons.

1   SSK accounts of science are excellent at telling us what is happening in a particular scientific setting: what they do not and cannot address is *why* it is being done. By this I do not mean why choices concerning strategy or organization in a laboratory are made, but why, for example, decisions concerning applications for funding for particular experiments are made, why alliances between different institutions come about, why particular members of staff are chosen. Questions concerning the context within which particular studies are located, and the reasons why scientists are drawn to particular areas of study, can only be answered by reference to the collective that scientists feel they are a part of, for it is in this wider grouping that agendas are set and research programmes constructed. It may have been the case earlier in the history of science that lone scientists would decide on their own course of study, carry out all their experiments and observations in isolation, and subsequently produce sole-authored results for dissemination in the world – although such an account is probably apocryphal – but science in contemporary society is a collective effort, where decisions about what is funded and who gets funding are taken out of the hands of individual scientists and handed to collectives of scientists and networks of scientists and administrators.

2   Even from a SSK perspective we need to recognize that the production of scientific knowledge is something that is taking place at a collective level, and at a level outside that of the local environment inhabited by a group of researchers. Ziman argues this most clearly:

A scientific community is an agonistic field, where researchers cross verbal swords over the significance of each other's claims. This argumentation takes place in many different fora, ranging from research group coffee clubs to international congresses. It may involve face-to-face conversation, personal correspondence, electronic networking, public debate, or printed exchanges of opinion in a scholarly publication. . . . Scientific knowledge, then, is as much the product of argument as it is of observation or cerebration. (Ziman 2000: 248)

3   By failing to take into account the wider context in which science is located, by only looking inside a localized research situation, we run the risk of producing partial accounts of the production of scientific knowledge. It could be argued that if we discover, and describe in sociological terms, what is being done in a particular situation, then we are also addressing why it is being done. But this is not necessarily the case, for it depends upon what questions are being asked, and in what context we are locating our data. By removing external frames of reference, and by ignoring the effects that external conditions have upon the inward motivations of scientists (cf. Weber 1989), we end up producing a mimetic version of the production of knowledge: we translate the discourse of scientists into the discourse of sociologists, but we bring nothing additional to it. Crucially, we cannot begin to answer the question of why it is that the scientific knowledge that is produced at a particular time replicates key features and assumptions of a given society. Certainly, SSK can explain how experiments take place, even how results are constructed. But what it cannot do is explain why some scientific knowledge has a higher status than other knowledge.

We need to understand what it is that motivates scientists, how they think they are aiding a wider project, and how they feel about being associated with a wider project. That we can deconstruct the categories that scientists use to describe themselves, possibly even prove these to be erroneous constructions, is not the point here. We need to be able to understand scientists from their own perspective, and to do that we need to examine the values they ascribe to their activities, the source of these values, and the relationship that scientists have to others involved in similar enterprises. We need to analyse a scientific community on its own terms, and without such forms of analysis, sociology of science will fail to answer the crucial question of why it is that science takes place in the ways that it does. Achieving this aim means abandoning the essentialist versions of science, scientists and scientific community in favour of open-textured accounts that allow us to see the interpenetration of society, culture and science, and how scientists in specific thought communities bring external ideas into their communities, and export ideas from their scientific communities to the wider world. What is needed is a close examination of the cultural aspects of science in society. Science is being actively constructed both inside scientific communities and outside scientific communities in culture and society. These exoteric constructions of science play a role in shaping what scientists think of their work, their project and themselves.

Further reading

As noted in the text, sociological investigations of scientific communities have declined in recent years. Hagstrom's (1965) original study of the scientific community in America in the 1960s still provides some valuable insights into the structure of scientific institutions. His study influenced Cotgrove and Box's British-based study in the 1970s (1970). Both are worth consulting.

More recent analyses of scientific institutions have tended to focus on the relationship between institutions themselves and public understanding of science. Nowotny et al.'s *Re-thinking Science* (2001) and Fuller's *Governance of Science* (2000a) provide new ways of configuring the relationship between institutions and the wider public, and provide excellent overviews of the subject.

Part III

Representing Science

The progress of science shines through your hair. Because you're worth it.

L'Oréal advertisement, 2002

L'Oreal advertisement, 2002. Image courtesy of The Advertising Archives.

6

Popular Science

Popular science in contemporary culture

In his last major work, *The Demon-Haunted World: Science as a Candle in the Dark* (1996), Carl Sagan – America's most famous scientist of the late twentieth century – rails against the dumbing down of American culture and the increasing prevalence of pseudo-science, New Age mysticism and fundamentalist zealotry. Sagan's refrain is that we need to have a good understanding of, and a proper respect for, science in our contemporary society if we are to avoid being duped and fooled by charlatans who are waiting to fleece us, and if we are to protect ourselves and the world from spurious and specious claims being made by pseudo-scientists. Sagan presents a version of science as organized scepticism (cf. Robert K. Merton in chapter 5), where science, as well as providing specific knowledge about particular aspects of the natural world, also provides a way of thinking that is sceptical, always asks for evidence, and applies rationality to all problems in order to improve the world. Sagan's argument is typical of a contemporary genre that we can call 'popular science writing': texts produced by scientists or writers with strong scientific backgrounds for non-scientists. In this section we will examine how scientists themselves articulate a version of science, and actively encourage others to construct science in their image.

In previous chapters we have seen how scientists produce science, or explain science, in a formal scientific way. In this chapter, by contrast, what we will see is scientists explaining science in non-formal scientific ways and, often, promoting science in ways that could be construed as being anti-scientific. Many popular science books promote a version of science that is contrasted starkly with the 'other' of science – or at least the 'other' that popular science writers want to identify – namely, foolishness. Yet there is no necessity for one to accept this formulation; we do not need to accept the hypothesis that either we can be scientific in our outlook or we can be foolish. Let's take a quick example from Sagan to illustrate this use of a non-scientific approach to construct a dualism of science and foolishness.

After an extensive diatribe against the popularity and prevalence of books about Atlantis – the mythical continent of antiquity – Sagan draws the following conclusion: 'Spurious accounts that snare the gullible are readily available. Skeptical treatments are much harder to find. Skepticism does not sell well' (Sagan 1996: 5). This is a debatable point, and one that needs to be placed in some sort of context. If we were going to be 'scientific' about this, we would want to ask just how many 'spurious accounts' are currently available, who is reading them, and what are they making of the claims inside these books. Perhaps they are all being read by sceptics like Sagan for entertainment purposes only? The possibility of many people with Sagan's outlook existing in the world is very high, given Sagan's own claims for the power of the 'enormously influential' media to make up our minds for us. The potted biography of Sagan provided inside the back cover of *The Demon-Haunted World: Science as a Candle in the Dark* notes that:

> Dr Sagan is the author of many bestsellers, including *Cosmos*, which became the *most widely read science book ever published* in the English language. The accompanying Emmy and Peabody award-winning television series became the *most widely watched series in the history of public television* until then, and has now been seen by *500 million people in 60 countries*. (my emphasis)

I would suggest that this statement refutes Sagan's claim that 'skepticism does not sell well'. Rhetorically, Sagan constructs a version of popular culture that is awash with pseudo-science, New Age mysticism, and disrespect for genuine science. However, he does this from the vantage-point of the most popular and well-known scientist in America – possibly even the world – who has been read or seen by nearly a quarter of the world's population.

Sagan carries on his critique of popular culture:

> The dumbing down of America is most evident in the slow decay of substantive content in the enormously influential media, the 30-second sound bites (now down to 10 seconds or less), lowest common denom-

inator programming, credulous presentations on pseudo-science and superstition, but especially a kind of celebration of ignorance. As I write, the number-one videocassette rental in America is the movie *Dumb and Dumber*. 'Beavis and Butthead' remain popular (and influential) with young TV viewers. The plain lesson is that study and learning – not just of science, but of anything – are avoidable, even undesirable. (Sagan 1996: 25–6)

This is a familiar refrain from popular science writers and journalists and conservative cultural critics. Sagan is suggesting that people rent the movie *Dumb and Dumber* because they like ignorance and want to emulate it. Far from not being a scientific proposition, this is not even a sensible proposition. However, it does illustrate the hypothesis advanced above, that popular science writers will often place science in opposition to its 'other' and will, either directly or indirectly, identify the 'other' as being ignorance, foolishness, credulity or faith.

Popular science writing

The roots of this genre lie in the nineteenth century with writers such as Thomas Huxley, who wrote popular accounts and defences of Darwin's theory of evolution and was involved in significant public debates in the 1860s and 1870s, and John Tyndall, eminent physicist and discoverer of the Tyndall effect. Both men had work published by the newspapers of the day and in book form. However, from Tyndall's example we can trace back still further the genre of popular science writing. Tyndall's lectures were the source of his published writings, and the tradition of explaining scientific subjects to non-scientific publics begins in the early nineteenth century with the public lectures presented at the Royal Institution in London. Gregory and Miller, in their survey of the rise of popular science in the nineteenth century note that:

In its first 50 years, the Royal Institution transformed the presentation of science to the public from the cosy after-dinner exposition and discussion to the professional scientific lecture, with the lecturer-scientist separated from his audience not only by the increased distance but also by the laboratory bench groaning under the weight of specialist apparatus. The public lectures initiated at the Royal Institution by Sir Humphrey Davy and developed by Michael Faraday proved extremely popular: the middle and upper classes found excitement and entertainment in the latest science; and skilled workers entered the lecture theatre via a discrete, outside staircase, found a seat under the eaves, segregated from the gentlefolk, and drank in the knowledge that might improve their prospects in the new industries. (Gregory and Miller 1998: 21)

The Royal Institution still presents an annual lecture at Christmas, given by an eminent natural scientist for an audience of children.

The nineteenth and early twentieth centuries saw a proliferation of texts popularizing and explaining science to the lay public. The authors were often eminent scientists themselves – for example, James Watson wrote his idiosyncratic account of his discovery of DNA (with Francis Crick and Rosalind Franklin) in 1953 (Watson 1968). The emerging genre of science fiction (see chapter 7) provided another vehicle for explaining science; authors such as H. G. Wells saw themselves first and foremost as serious science writers. Film and radio provided new media where ideas and change in science could be explained in an entertaining way to the lay public. In the 1930s Joseph Jastrow's 'errorology' presented an analysis of the obstacles to scientific progress through history, directing this towards a non-scientific audience and those interested in the history of science (Jastrow 1967).

Popular science, particularly in book form, was in vogue throughout the twentieth century, and remains common in contemporary culture. Within the genre we can distinguish texts that seek to popularize science for a lay public and those that seek to 'save' the lay public from the dangers of pseudo-science, quackery and false scientific analysis. Whilst both forms of texts achieve a similar goal of re-inforcing the position of pre-eminence that science holds in terms of the status of knowledge in society, they achieve this in different ways. The genre of popular science books that specifically discuss the gullibility of the general public and seek to preserve them from 'false' science fully emerged only in the 1950s, but is still a very strong trend in today's popular science writing.

Many books, like Sagan's, debunk pseudo-science from the vantage-point of a scientific understanding. One of the first – Martin Gardner's *Fads and Fallacies in the Name of Science* (1957), first published in 1952, also provides a flavour of the immense optimism surrounding science in the 1950s. Gardner's targets are interesting, representing a snapshot of then current conspiracy theories and applied scientific nostrums: flying saucers, dianetics and creationism are still with us; orgone theory, Lysenkoism and Babson's anti-gravity material have largely passed out of the public gaze. However, his assaults on osteopathy (a 'medical cult'), chiropractice (another 'medical cult') and the Bates method for correcting eyesight would raise eyebrows amongst medical practitioners today, many of whom recognize considerable medical value in such approaches. Many of the scientists writing about pseudo-science and the abuse of science are also somewhat hostile towards social sciences in general. Clearly many authors do not consider it worthwhile exploring the history of their own genre, and this explains, in part, why the same book has been written so many times by so many eminent people. Gardner's list of pseudo-science is similar to Sagan's, which, in turn, is, similar to Robert Park's *Voodoo Science* (2000), Michael Friedlander's *At the Fringes of Science* (1998), and Michael Shermer's *The Border-lands of Science: Where Sense Meets Nonsense* (2001).

Looking at the construction and articulation of the discourse of popular science in contemporary texts shows us how scientists understand their own project, how they view their relationship to non-scientists, and what they consider to be 'dangerous' forms of 'spurious' knowledge abroad. Scientists and those associated with the project of science writing in this genre express an almost total faith in the project, method and goals of science; they rarely express any concerns about the application of science and consider the 'ignorance' of science that is expressed by 'non-scientific' media to be a major social ill. However, we also see a dramatic tension emerging from this form of writing: scientists writing for a popular audience will often generalize from their own specialist discipline to discuss the project of science as a whole. When they do this, they reinforce their own discipline's understanding of what science is, but also reinforce that there are significant disjunctures between the different sub-disciplines of science.

In addition to providing us with insights into how science looks at itself, popular science texts (and, of course, TV science documen-taries and popular science journals) constitute significant resources used in the social construction of science by the public. All of us are involved in constructing the meaning of 'science', and we do this with resources at hand, a significant one of which is popular science accounts. We can learn a lot from looking at and analysing popular science writing.

Contemporary popular science writing: enforcing the 'ideology' of science

An iconic example of the popularity, and persistence, of popular science writing is Stephen Hawking's *A Brief History of Time* (1988).

This topped the non-fiction bestseller lists in both the USA and the UK for many weeks following its publication, selling more than 9 million copies, was in the *Sunday Times* non-fiction bestseller list for over four years, and has been translated into thirty-five languages. Hawking's book, which is an account of recent breakthroughs in astrophysics and cosmology, is particularly significant, in that it was written for a general audience by a practising and very successful scientist (Hawking is Lucasian Professor of Mathematics at Cambridge University, a post that his publishers delight in pointing out was once held by Sir Isaac Newton). Hawking offers us a clear and unambiguous definition of his view of what the project of science is early on in *A Brief History of Time*: 'The eventual goal of science is to provide a single theory that describes the whole universe' (Hawking 1988: 10).

Hawking is a cosmologist: he produces theories of how the universe is constructed and what laws govern its behaviour. His understanding of what the project of science is, is predicated upon his desire to reconcile the two partial theories that dominate physics, astrophysics and cosmology at the present time: quantum mechanics and the theory of relativity (see box 4.2). Hawking's definition of the goal of science shows how theories that dominate the practice of science in a specific discipline will lead us to understand the project of science as a whole in a particular way; it also shows us how science makes sense of its own project. Hawking continues: 'Today scientists describe the universe in terms of two basic partial theories – the general theory of relativity and quantum mechanics' (Hawking 1988: 11).

As we saw in chapter 5, the conflation of all people working in formal science into a unified group of 'scientists' can be misleading, but is a move that the contemporary media make very frequently. Here, Hawking's use of the term 'scientists' is misleading in a similar way. It expresses a familiar – and not itself scientific – hierarchical analysis of the nature of science that is particularly common: science is great, but physics is the best (cf. Hacking 1983: 3). Hawking continues his account of what science is by subsuming all scientific disciplines into a unified project and set of perspectives:

> Now, if you believe that the universe is not arbitrary, but is governed by definite laws, you ultimately have to combine the partial theories into a complete unified theory that will describe everything in the universe. . . . Humanity's deepest desire for knowledge is justification for our continuing quest. And our goal is nothing less than a complete description of the universe we live in. (Hawking 1988: 12–13)

On this account, scientific understanding as a whole ultimately rests on how physics makes sense of the world, and understanding all the laws of the physical world will provide the explanatory framework for all branches of science. This may, of course, be true. It is incontrovertible, however, that at the present time no such framework could possibly provide us with an appropriate way of understanding, for example, the workings of the human mind, the complex operation of social structure, or the varied range of human social behaviour. All of these are aspects of the universe: whether we choose to see them as governed by definite laws is likely to be a product of, amongst other things, our gender, sexuality and cultural background. There is something deeply masculine about this account of the triumphal and progressive project of science.

In Hawking's account we see a restatement of the 'standard, formal' conception of the goal and aim of science. Science is an activity that will provide us with complete knowledge of the universe that we live in through constructing and testing theories. Science is comprised of a range of disciplines that are of varying degrees of 'hardness', with physics at the hardest, most rigorous end. Physics is the discipline that underpins all other scientific activities. It is also the discipline that has made the greatest impact on the twentieth century through its association with the creation of atomic and nuclear weapons. It is the most male-dominated and the most phallic of sciences.

Hawking's *A Brief History of Time* was not the first popular science book that sought to bring science from the highest level of achievement into the life of the non-scientist reader. Albert Einstein was encouraged to write a lay person's guide to the theory of relativity (Einstein 2001); Werner Heisenberg, inventor of the uncertainty principle, produced a number of accounts of quantum mechanics for a popular audience (Heisenberg 1958, 1959), and Richard Feynman, Nobel laureate 1965, was, by the time of his death in 1988, a well-known and popular commentator on a range of social and scientific matters (see box 6.1).

Box 6.1   Richard Feynman and the space shuttle

Richard Feynman, Nobel laureate for physics, was one of the most well-known and well-liked American scientists of the last century, and is still a major influence on scientists today (see chapter 8). Feynman's public renown was boosted in 1986 when he took a very prominent part in the NASA inquiry into the failure of the

Continued

space shuttle *Challenger* mission. Rumoured to have been selected by NASA as a potential ally, due to his commitment to science as a whole, Feynman showed, by the very simple method of dunking the crucial part in a glass of ice water, that *Challenger's* solid rocket booster O-ring seal was vulnerable to cold temperatures. The space shuttle was launched after a particularly cold spell, with disastrous consequences. Or so the story goes. But scientific actuality is much more complicated, and Collins and Pinch's examination of the *Challenger* inquiry (Collins and Pinch 1998: 30–56) reveals that both NASA and the manufacturers of the solid rocket boosters were very well aware of a range of malfunctions of the O-ring seals, and that the failure of the solid rocket booster on the launch of the *Challenger* is still not fully explained. Having examined the reports of the different teams of engineers involved in the decision to launch *Challenger* on that fateful day, Collins and Pinch conclude: 'We are also now in a better position to evaluate another misconception – the one spread, perhaps inadvertently, by Richard Feynman: that NASA were ignorant of the effect of cold on O-rings' (Collins and Pinch 1998: 55).

Unlike Einstein, Heisenberg and Hawking, Feynman's popular science publications deliberately enter the territory of the world outside physics. Feynman enters into debate on a range of social and cultural topics, but does so from the perspective of a scientist who is looking in on the social and cultural world to offer an 'external' critique. In a series of public lectures entitled 'A Scientist Looks at Society' delivered in 1963 (Feynman 1999), Feynman discussed how society was dependent upon science in many ways, but profoundly ignorant of science at the same time – a familiar theme today, as we have seen in the work of Sagan. In keeping with the style of this genre, he provides us with an initial definition of science:

> What is science? The word is usually used to mean one of three things, or a mixture of them. I do not think we need to be precise – it is not always a good idea to be too precise. Science means, sometimes, a special method of finding things out. Sometimes it means the body of knowledge arising from the things found out. It may also mean the new things you can do when you have found something out, or the actual doing of new things. This last field is usually called technology. (Feynman 1999: 4–5)

This is a deceptively simple definition, and one that makes of technology a cornerstone of the project of science. Feynman may be slightly misleading here: he is, after all, giving us a popular definition of what science is for use in a popular science context. Unlike other authors, Feynman is writing about how science can be applied to aspects of the social world not normally considered 'scientific'. Thus his definition of science has to be open-textured, rather than the tightly and rigidly defined versions of science that, say, physicists present to their lay audiences when explaining physics. B. K. Ridley's book *On Science* (2001) is a general overview of the scope and limits of science in contemporary society, written from the perspective of a physicist (Ridley is Professor of Physics at the University of Essex, UK). Ridley presents an in-depth and critical account of scientific thinking and, unlike some other contemporary commentators on science, avoids the temptation to present science as the best form of thought available, and the most suitable solution to all problems. However, like Hawking, he sees science as essentially reducible to the paradigm of physics: 'Science is essentially a description of the motion of matter' (Ridley 2001: 31). This description of the 'essence' of science is certainly debatable, and for our purposes as social investigators of science we would want to challenge it in a number of ways. However, Ridley is expressing his own thought community's understanding of what science is: the science that physicists do is, ultimately, a science of describing the motion of matter. In Ridley's case, his thought community of physicists reduces phenomena to fundamental units and forces, and his definition of science (Ridley is talking about science *as a whole*, not simply the science that he and his colleagues carry out) thus becomes an atomistic, reductionist definition.

The reductionist view of science is the current dominant model for the project of science as a whole (Lewontin 1993; Midgley 2001). Scientific explanations look for ultimate causes at the level of fundamental and discrete units: the cause of cancer is our genes; the structure of matter is ultimately caused by fundamental particles. The correctness or otherwise of such perspectives is not at issue here, although, particularly in the case of the dominant genetic reductionism in contemporary biological science, there are some significant dissenting voices. However, such reductionism does, quite neatly, match up to the understanding of the social world as being the manifestation of the properties of individual human beings (Lewontin 1993: 107ff). Inside the genre of popular science we can see a similar form of reductionism in terms of the topics and titles produced by authors. Of course, there are still some general texts that analyse science as a whole – as we have noted above – but many of these do this from a specific disciplinary perspective. Indeed, in the past decade the expansion of 'atomized' popular science texts has been quite remarkable:

the single-word book title is very popular in popular science. Just looking across the shelves of the 'popular science' section in my local bookshop produced the following list from authors between A and H: *Impossibility, Fingerprints, Randomness, Robot, e = mc², The Calendar, Fly, The Brain, Superforce, Trilobite, Life, Phosphorous, Creation, Faster, Chaos, Genius, Aeons, Diamond*. Chopping the natural world up into discrete units for consumption is a strategy that appeals to publishers.

But is Ridley's science the same science as the palaeontology (the discipline that deals with the life of previous geological periods as found in fossil remains) that palaeontologists are carrying out? Palaeontologist Stephen Jay Gould, author of a significant number of popular science books (see box 6.2), as well as a distinguished naturalist in his own right, expresses concerns about some forms of popular science writing.

> I have fiercely maintained one personal rule in all my so-called 'popular' writing. (The word is admirable in its literal sense, but has been debased to mean simplified or adulterated for easy listening without effort in return.) I believe . . . that we can still have a genre of scientific books suitable for and accessible alike to professionals and interested laypeople. The concepts of science, in all their richness and ambiguity, can be presented without any compromise, without any simplification counting as distortion, in language accessible to all intelligent people. (Gould 2000: 16)

Box 6.2 Stephen Jay Gould

Stephen Jay Gould (1941–2002) was a highly respected palaeontologist, inventor of the punctuated equilibrium interpretation of Darwin's theory of evolution. He was also a prominent representative of the scientific community in the USA, writing more than 20 books, 300 columns in *Natural History*, and 1,000 scientific papers. Gould was a robust defender of evolutionary theory, a campaigner against creationism, and a tireless opponent of sociobiology and evolutionary psychology, both of which he saw as being distortions and inappropriate applications of Darwin's theory of evolution.

Gould sticks to his own strictures, producing dense, hard texts that can be used to inform the lay public as well as undergraduate palaeontology students. However, unlike other scientists writing for a popular audience, Gould uses analysis of cultural representations of evolution as a resource in his critique of scientific discussions of evolution. The term 'evolution' has entered popular consciousness in powerful ways, and the accepted lay definition can be summed up as 'progressive change', or even 'survival of the fittest'. The lay definition of evolution thus includes a value judgement: something that has evolved is better than something that preceded it. Yet evolution, for biologists and palaeontologists, has a strict meaning: descent through modification, the gradual transformation of one form into another (Jones 2000). In Darwin's original work no such judgement is made, and biologists and palaeontologists agree that evolution, in their sense, does not include such a value judgement. Gould shows the proliferation of images in contemporary culture that exemplify this use of the term, particularly the use of the image of a 'ladder' of 'progressive' evolutionary forms, often starting with a chimpanzee and ending with a human being. In its late-nineteenth-century form such images often had racist overtones, purporting to show the 'superiority' of the white 'race':

> [T]he false equation of evolution with progress records a sociocultural bias, not a biological conclusion, and one hardly needs great insight · to locate the primary source of this bias in our human desire to view ourselves as the apex of life's history, ruling the earth by right and biological necessity. This fundamental misconception of evolution is strongly abetted by one of the most pervasive of all canonical icons for any scientific concept – the march or ladder of evolutionary progress. (Gould 1997: 44)

Gould notes that it is also in the exact sciences, in biology and his own discipline of palaeontology, that the misleading iconography of the 'ladder of progress' and the 'cone of diversity' appear frequently in undergraduate textbooks (Gould 1997), illustrating just how pervasive this iconography is. His suggestion for a replacement pictorial representation of evolution, that of a 'grass field with most stems mowed and just a few flowering profusely' (Gould 1997: 67) circumvents the canonical cone, but still does not adequately represent the radical perspective on evolution that contemporary biology and palaeontology have arrived at: '[M]ost losses occurred by luck of the draw rather than by the predictable superiority of a few founding lineages, and that any particular lineage still alive today (including our own) owes its existence to the contingency of good fortune' (Gould 1997: 67).

Gould's writings on science tend to focus on his own disciplinary specialism: his concern is to defend his perspective on the concepts and main tendencies of his discipline and to promote how they are understood by participants in that project, and by the wider general public. He, too, is also talking about science as a whole, but only in the sense that palaeontology and biology are a part of that wider project. Gould is a subject-specific scientist writing about his own small area of science: his presentation of science begins from his own position inside the research project of science as a whole, hence the emphasis on the explication of evolution as a concept, rather than an emphasis on the nature of, for example, empirical work in general. Despite this, there are consequences emanating from his writing about his discipline for our understanding of science as a whole.

This is in marked contrast to another group of writers in this genre of popular science writing. Here, writers with a science background but with an experience of general discussion of a range of different disciplines of science write about science as a whole. These writers are often journalists working in specialist areas of science writing. Once again, we find a strong thread of opposition to 'anti-science' (which encompasses religion, social science and imputed ignorance) in these texts, and a very strong validation of science as the single best form of knowledge available.

John Horgan's 1996 book *The End of Science* is a good example. In this text Horgan, a science writer who worked mainly for the US general science monthly *Scientific American*, discusses the limits facing science as a whole, and presents a range of examples from physics to biology. Horgan also discusses a number of social-scientific critiques of science, and these are universally presented in an unfavourable light. Horgan's animosity towards social scientists investigating science is perhaps revealed by his attitude towards Paul Feyerabend, whom he interviewed to discuss his view that science is relative and expresses no more 'truth' than any other discourse. Following Feyerabend's death from cancer, Horgan phoned Feyerabend's distraught wife to offer his condolences: 'Recalling Feyerabend's excoriation of the medical profession, I could not resist asking, did her husband seek medical treatment for his tumor?' (Horgan 1996: 56).

Horgan's thesis is that the main discoveries of the natural sciences have already been made, and that all that remains for scientists today is tidying up the loose ends of the main paradigms of science, or engaging in the practice of 'ironic science', a post-empirical quest to overturn current theories by a deliberate misreading of those theories. In all, this is a very strong defence of the triumphal project of science, albeit a pessimistic one in terms of future activities. For Horgan, the most exciting scientific activities took place in the past:

the age of scientific discovery may be over now that we've found out pretty much all there is to know about the natural world: 'Further research may yield no more great revelations or revolutions, but only incremental, diminishing returns' (Horgan 1996: 6).

Once again we are presented with a version of 'science is great and physics is the best', a common theme in contemporary science journalism. We can speculate as to why this may be the case, and an obvious explanation comes from even a cursory reading of journals such as *New Scientist*, *Scientific American*, *Nature* or *Science*. Here we see science being presented to a knowledgeable audience, although readership, particularly of the first two, extends beyond the boundaries of what we would normally describe as being the 'scientific community' if we define it as those working in formal science. Science does not need to be justified or explained for this audience, but this audience does not want to see science being depreciated or even strongly questioned: these journals are 'doing a job' of defending science from irrationality and prejudice, and fulfilling a 'necessary' function of presenting science in the strongest possible light to ensure the continued adherence of states, corporations, educators and the general public to the project of science. The feeling, when reading such journals, can often be one of an excluded and somewhat foolish person who does not understand the principles of the most important aspect of contemporary industrial societies. The perspective expressed in the pages of such journals is never intentionally a patronizing one, and if it seems so, it is more likely to be the result of the need for economic use of language, leading to journalists making quite large assumptions about the knowledge base and capabilities of the readers. Undergraduate students on my Science in Society course at Birmingham University analysed a wide range of formal science journals and concluded that these were not deliberately patronizing or excluding, but did assume a vast stock of prior knowledge which can produce an effect in readers of feeling either patronized or excluded. The result is a reinforcement of the 'separateness' and 'difficulty' of science for those not familiar with the discourse being presented.

It is not only in the semi-specialist press that we can see this expression of the superiority of science; there are notable examples of this 'lay people are ignorant and scientists are clever' attitude in popular science books intended for a lay audience. Robert Park's *Voodoo Science: The Road from Foolishness to Fraud* (2000) reveals just such a prejudice against ignorant and foolish non-scientists, and exemplifies a view that sees science as being strongly separated from society or, at the very least, scientists being strongly distinguishable from non-scientists. Park's book is, on the surface, an attack on 'bad science' – pseudo-science, junk science, pathological science and voodoo science. However, Park carries out his assault on these bad forms of science through the construction and defence of a strong version of 'good' science, a reiteration of the 'standard' account of science discussed earlier in this book. Park is firmly convinced of the benefits of a scientific world-view, seeing it as more important for the general public than simple scientific literacy: 'It is not so much knowledge of science that the public needs as a scientific worldview – an understanding that we live in an orderly universe, governed by physical laws that cannot be circumvented' (Park 2000: 40).

Park may be right to point to the credulity of non-scientists, and he provides numerous examples of fraudulent claims made by scientists (cold fusion is the example Park focuses upon), ludicrous pseudo-scientific claims made by pseudo-scientists (faith healing, ESP), and distortions of scientific principles to justify claims made by junk scientists (such as the healing properties of homeopathic drugs couched in scientific language). Realizing that we are being ripped off by such distortions of science may be a good thing. However, Park seems to be oblivious to his own distortions of science, and his own pseudo-scientific claims. Park wants to be able to explain why it is that we are susceptible to superstition, fake science claims, faith healing nostrums, etc. His mechanism for explanation is a predictable one: evolutionary psychology. By his account, our brains are programmed by our out-of-date Pleistocene genes, designed to make us efficient hunter gatherers, but not designed to make us efficient discriminators of claims made by the media. He claims that: 'Behavioral traits are just as much a part of our genetic inheritance as physical characteristics. We respond to external stimuli in ways that conferred some sort of survival advantage on our distant human and prehuman ancestors' (Park 2000: 35). Yet many eminent scientists would disagree very strongly with Park's reductionist and crude evolutionary psychology (see Hilary and Stephen Rose's *Alas, Poor Darwin* (2001) for a comprehensive survey of such positions). Park's account displays the hubris of some members of a self-nominating scientific elite that can provide answers for all the questions we can ask about the world.

Park concludes that we can overcome our own foolishness and credulity through science: for him, science is the strategy that humans created to overcome our genetic propensity to believe what is placed in front of us. Science is, of course, also a product of our genes, but only in an indirect way, in that it is a consequence of our genetic inheritance providing us with higher centres of the brain that can consciously construct such strategies as science.

So, to recap, for Park we are largely credulous mammals who will believe what is put in front of us due to our genetic inheritance. Fortunately, we have created a superb object called science, and this provides us with a scientific world-view that allows us to see through nonsense and lies and enables us to identify how the world really is, and what correct knowledge actually is.

The problems with this account are manifold. It will not be possible to falsify such an account, as Park is not presenting a scientific theory (cf. Popper in chapter 3). However, it is possible to present a myriad of examples that show that Park should, at the very least, think again about the strength he assigns his argument. Here is one such example, as reported in *New Scientist* (and a great many other journals and newspapers) on 5 October 2002:

> Hendrik Schön, who worked at Bell Laboratories for 4 years, has just been exposed for fabricating much of his data. Working in nanotechnology, specifically buckyballs, molecular transistors and other conductors, Schön's work promised revolutions in plastic electronics, high-temperature superconductivity and nanotechnology. '[N]ow no one knows where the frontiers in these fields really lie.' ('Conduct Unbecoming', Editorial, p. 3)

And, given the prominence of Schön's work, we should not forget the many researchers around the world who wasted time trying to replicate his findings. Schön was producing scientific papers at the rate of one every eight days in 2001: surely the peer review process (a method of selecting papers where one's peers – in this case other researchers working in a similar field of science, read a paper prior to publication and recommend it to a journal) should have noticed that there was something wrong? Molecular-scale transistors made by Schön worked far better than anyone expected. When asked to substantiate his claims by showing his raw data, he said he had deleted the relevant files after running out of space on his computer. Such poor record keeping constitutes scientific misconduct. In some of his papers to *Nature* and *Science* the anomalies in his work were:

> hardly subtle: in one, he used the same curve to represent the behaviours of different materials, in another he presented results that had no errors whatsoever. Both journals stress that papers are chosen on technical merit and reviewers for their technical skills. Should not the manuscript editors or reviewers have remarked on these discrepancies? These papers were, after all, of huge importance to industry and academia. Ultimately, Schön was unmasked by scientists not engaged in formal peer review. (Ibid., p. 3)

Dr Schön apologized for any mistakes he had made, but is sticking by his work: 'I truly believe that the reported scientific results are real, exciting and worth working for' (Samuel 2002: 5). However, the independent panel of experts called in to look at his work (25 recent papers, many published in highly prestigious journals), after exonerating all others involved in his work, said: 'the evidence that misrepresentation and manipulation of data occurred is compelling' (Samuel 2002: 4).

The point for us here is not whether or not Schön fabricated his results. Rather, it is that scientists themselves could be so easily fooled by specious scientific work. Social investigators of science can suggest some lines of inquiry that might help us to understand why this may have been the case. For example, it is interesting that many of Schön's papers were co-authored but, of course, none of the co-authors had ever witnessed Schön's most stupendous discoveries. Surely this calls into question the practice of being named as an author of formal scientific papers. We might want to begin to look at the *social* conventions that allow scientists not involved in a particular experiment to have their name placed on a scientific paper as author. We would want to look inside the lab space used by scientists to investigate how experiments are actually carried out. We know from previous studies that scientific experiments are almost always carried out by a group of experimenters who are involved in most phases of the process. It is very rare that a lone scientist will be carrying out all parts of an experiment, from construction of equipment to measurement of results and data analysis. Surely someone in Schön's laboratory must have noticed that he was the only person who ever saw his results or made measurements? As critical social scientists, we would also want to investigate the pressures that researchers are put under to produce results and publications, and whether such pressures themselves lead to scientists feeling that it may be worth the risk of falsifying results, or selecting data that makes their work look stronger than it actually is. What we would not do in explaining such occurrences is have recourse to the genetic make-up of the scientists themselves. Yet Park, as well as many of his fellow writers in this genre, is almost entirely dismissive of social-scientific analyses of science.

Are these popular accounts of science educational, entertaining, or both? In some accounts, such as Robert Youngson's *Scientific Blunders: A Brief History of How Wrong Scientists can Sometimes Be* (1998), the aim is much more to entertain, this being done through a compilation of anecdotes showing that the great scientists of history occasionally had feet of clay:

'X-rays will prove to be a hoax' (Lord Kelvin).
'Anyone who expects a source of power from the transformation of the atom is talking moonshine' (Ernest Rutherford).
'There is not the slightest indication that energy will ever be obtainable from the atom' (Albert Einstein).

However, Youngson's book also reiterates the standard account of the unitary and triumphal nature of science. Despite (or perhaps because of) his somewhat light-hearted approach and his technique of quoting scientists out of context, Youngson, along with all the other popular science writers we have discussed here, offers a very robust defence of science:

> Science is the supreme expression of rationality. Fully established scientific facts have been subjected to a process of scrutiny and testing that is far more rigorous than, for instance, those applied to political opinions or economic 'principles'. When scientific research throws up seemingly irrational facts – such as some of those of quantum mechanics – this is not a breakdown of rationality. It is a reflection of the fact that there has been an important gap in our prior knowledge or experience, so that our rationality, which was based on that limited experience, has to be extended to include the new facts. (Youngson 1998: 323)

Other popular science accounts take the entertainment even further, whilst still maintaining the status of science as the best mode of explanation and analysis. The cover blurb for Len Fisher's *How to Dunk a Doughnut: The Science of Everyday Life* (2002) says: 'Science is all around us, and this brilliant book shows you where to find it and how to put it to good use.' Amongst the chapters included in the book are 'How Does a Scientist Boil an Egg?', 'How to Add Up your Supermarket Bill', 'How to Throw a Boomerang', and, rather predictably, 'The Physics of Sex'. Certainly entertaining, but also educational. Regardless of the authors' intentions, throughout these popular science texts one message is inescapable: that ignorance of science is a bad thing because science itself is a good thing; in fact, it is the best thing that there is. The subtext is clear: we should avoid ignorance at all costs.

What does it mean to be ignorant about science?

Park, and the host of other writers in this genre, from Gardner to Sagan, is upset that people in modern Western industrial societies are ignorant about science. He feels that they need a scientific world-view so as to be able to understand the regularity of the world, the law-like behaviour of the natural world, and the possibility of rational analysis of issues and problems.

Similarly, Philip Plait in his book *Bad Astronomy: Misconceptions and Misuses Revealed, from Astrology to the Moon Landing 'hoax'* rails against the TV journalists who laughed at their own ignorance in science (Plait 2002: 3). He points out that it is unthinkable that TV journalists would joke about their ignorance in other areas, such as geopolitics, and goes on:

> It *isn't* okay. In fact, it's *dangerous* to be ignorant about science. Our lives and our livelihoods depend on it. No one can doubt the power of computers in today's world, computers that rely on physics to operate and improve their performance. Science is what makes our houses warm, our cars go, and our cell phones ring. Medical science progresses very rapidly, with new medicines, treatments, and preventions coming out almost daily. We *must* understand the science of medicine to be able to make informed decisions about our health. In the United States, hundreds of billions of dollars are spent every year on science and technology, disciplines with which the typical voting citizen has not even a passing familiarity. *That's your money.* You should understand not only how it is being spent but also why. (Plait 2002: 4)

Plait and Park and all those other popular science writers are missing a major point here. Many scientists I spoke to in the course of carrying out research for this book were themselves profoundly ignorant about science, and in the following way. They had a deep understanding of their particular specialism, and also had a good knowledge of general scientific principles, but the biochemists were hard pressed to explain the workings of a mobile telephone, the physicists openly admitted to being uncertain as to the benefits or otherwise of genetically modified food, the chemists knew very little about automotive engineering, and so on. Plait is right in that science does make our world work (although we can argue about the differences between science and technology). The problem is that we simply cannot know it all, or even a good chunk of it. Michael Polanyi pointed this out some time ago in *Personal Knowledge* (1958). He estimated that any single scientist would only be competent to judge at first hand about one hundredth of the total current output of science. Given the dramatic growth in scientific output in recent years, we should probably adjust that figure downwards.

When we need to make decisions about, to take Plait's example, medical funding, we rely on experts and politicians. This is not an expression of 'anti-science' hostility, just a recognition that we need to be pragmatic and use societal resources to make societal decisions. What writers like Plait, Park and most of the other popular science writers are doing is expressing the 'ideology' of science – that science is the best mode of explanation available to us, and we need to apply it in all situations. Further, when we do this, we need to consider the 'scientific' answer to be the best answer and should privilege it above other answers. This in itself is dangerous, and we need to guard against it. Privileging such forms of explanation and analysis hides the need for ethical and moral analysis of particular issues. To take Plait's medical funding example again: as members of a society that is providing health care for its members, what is it more important to have:

- knowledge of the scientific principles behind the ways that particular drugs and treatments work?
- knowledge of the operation of capitalism and the health care industries that will promote, possibly in a corrupt way, their products at the expense of other companies' products?
- knowledge of the relationship between health care in general, political decision making, and how politicians will describe their efforts to secure maximum health benefits for the good of society in an attempt to be re-elected?
- knowledge of the costs and benefits of selecting one expensive treatment that will help a small number of people as opposed to another cheaper treatment that will benefit a much larger number of people?
- knowledge of how scientific medical research is funded by large drug companies, and that further funding from such drug companies may depend on previous results? (See e.g., Matthews 2003)

The complexities of such issues are not confined to simple scientific questions (and, compared to ethical questions, those scientific questions really are simple) about how gene therapy works, or the advantages of using one antibiotic as opposed to another to treat TB. To claim that providing greater scientific knowledge of medical treatments would help us to make decisions about medical care as a whole is specious, but telling. Such claims show the prevalence and persistence of a scientism that promotes scientific explanation above all others.

What do popular accounts of science show us?

First, simply by their number and proliferation, such popular accounts of science show us that science is a hugely popular topic in contemporary culture. The sheer weight of numbers of such books being sold shows a great capacity on the part of the general public to know more about science. Secondly, popular science accounts serve to restate the triumphal status of science in contemporary society. These accounts rarely admit that science cannot explain everything. Frequently, where such failings are alluded to, as in Stephen Hawking's refusal to answer questions about God, science is seen as being the method by which such answers will be available in the future. Thirdly, science is presented as being a unitary phenomenon: many branches of science will be shown and discussed, but all are ultimately connected by a common purpose and method according to these accounts. Of course, individuals writing inside their own disciplines will often express their opinion that, say, physics or biology is the 'supreme' science, but, ultimately, science is represented as being a unified whole, a restatement of the essentialist picture of science.

Finally, these accounts allow us to see the prevalence of a scientific world-view, an 'ideology' – scientism – that is a commonly shared perspective on the world around us (Midgley 2001). The public are presented with and assimilate a range of resources in constructing their understanding of science, and, given the composition of much of this material, it is unsurprising that we see a societal understanding of science that reflects aspects of popular science accounts. Scientism suggests that explanations of the world around us should be based on scientific principles rather than religion, superstition or sheer guesswork. Advocates of scientism are prone to express these sentiments in even stronger ways. For example:

> Scientism is a scientific worldview that encompasses natural explanations for all phenomena, eschews supernatural and paranormal explanations, and embraces empiricism and reason as the twin pillars of a philosophy of life appropriate for an Age of Science. (Shermer 2002: 25)

It is this scientistic world-view that is both cause and consequence of the status of science in Western industrial societies. Yet there is complexity in this: whilst the popularity of popular science texts suggests that the public want to be informed, they also want to be entertained, and science is entertaining, particularly in its guise of science fiction.

Further reading

There is no shortage of popular science books available in bookstores and libraries, but there are few analyses of the significance of this mode of representing science. Those that do look at popular science, be it texts, TV documentaries or education programmes, tend to focus on the theme of public understanding of science. Two texts stand out as being particularly useful:

Gregory, J. and Miller, S. 1998: *Science in Public: Communication, Culture, and Credibility*. New York: Plenum Trade.
Nelkin, D. 1987: *Selling Science: How the Press Covers Science and Technology*. New York: W. H. Freeman & Co.

7

Science Fiction

Cultural studies and science fiction

Science fiction is a product of time and place, and as such is a modern creation: a society in which science was hidden or confined to a very small sphere of influence would not create these types of narratives. It is only in the very late nineteenth century that we see the emergence of speculative tales of the future with a focus on science and technology and people's relationship to these. Much science fiction film, television and writing is specifically located in a particular time and place. To see this, we need only think of the sci-fi B-movies of the 1950s with their narratives describing invasions of evil aliens (which can be seen as metaphors for the Cold War threats faced by the USA (Seed 1999)), or the 1990s cyberpunk movement with its emphasis on the transformative power of the internet, personal computers and biotechnology (which can be seen as presaging a transformation of identity and society (Cavallaro 2000)).

There is a paradox at the heart of science fiction, one that reflects a tension between science and the society of which it is a part. 'Science fiction' is a contradictory term: our common-sense understanding of science is that it is a form of knowledge that describes what is the case, whilst our societal understanding of fiction is that it describes what is not the case. Fiction and science do not sit easily with one another. However, as we shall see, much science fiction is reliant on themes and theories taken directly from contemporary scientific research, and some texts make an ostentatious display of their scientific and technical accuracy and credentials.

Science fiction is a popular topic for cultural theorists and cultural studies in general (A. Kuhn 1990; Penley 1989, 1997; Bukatman 1993; Jancovich 1996). As a genre that is firmly embedded in popular culture, this is unsurprising: the discipline of cultural studies has long been concerned with popular, as opposed to high, culture, and in particular with the emergence of new genres and new forms of expression that are specific to time and place. However, almost all cultural studies analysis of science fiction ignores an important facet of this genre: that some science fiction texts are about science itself, and that all science fiction depicts, if only in part or only obliquely, social attitudes towards science, scientists and scientific institutions. This becomes particularly clear if we consider the role of gender in science fiction narratives. Most mainstream science fiction writers are men, most of the main characters in these stories are men, and their plots often hinge on the tension between emotions (often represented by female characters) and rationality (embodied in male characters). *The X-Files*, where the credulous male Mulder and the rational female Scully investigate stories of the paranormal, relies in part on this gender reversal for its success. Similarly, scientific activity in contemporary society is a largely male-dominated sphere, where most leading scientists are men and the ideals of scientific endeavour are seen as the expression of pure rationality and the avoidance and rejection of subjective and emotional analyses. Our male-dominated science is represented by our male dominated science fiction. The politics of representation visible here describes our androcentric science and culture. Science fiction, reliant as it is upon perceptions of the science that exists in our society, becomes a vehicle for the attitudes and experiences of people inside the institutions of science, and also those on the outside who form their opinions and construct their meaning of science from consuming cultural representations of science.

Many cultural studies of science fiction do consider in some depth what these narratives of futurity are saying about technology, and identify some link between technology and scientific knowledge. For example, Peter Hutchings's essay on science fiction narratives that use the device of super-powerful microbial pathogens that threaten civilization does consider the relationship between such fictional objects and real attempts to create new biological warfare agents. However, this is done only in passing. The main point of the essay is a discussion of how novels and films that use the device of lethal pathogens escaping into the environment – such as *Outbreak* and *The Andromeda Strain* – are concerned with constructing other cultures and other countries as 'alien', threats to the 'integrity of the (implicitly white)

Western self' (Hutchings 1999: 28). Such an analysis is powerful in identifying a strong trend in Western fictional narratives, with a pedigree that goes back to at least the nineteenth century (Lindqvist 2001). We must recognize the importance of locating these sci-fi narratives in wider cultural contexts that allow us to see the implicit (hidden?) orientalism of Western culture. Annette Kuhn's seminal collection of essays on contemporary science fiction cinema (1990) provides a range of perspectives on what science fiction cinema in contemporary society is about. The essays focus on, variously, the changing relationships between humans and non-humans, our use and understanding of technology, the transformation of humans by technology, the possible form that future societies may take (and, by implication, the critique by science fiction of the present state of affairs), and the adoption by this genre of more widespread narratives such as that of eventual redemption, the monstrous feminine (the example used is the film *Alien*), and the primal scene fantasy. In addition, commentators focus on the audiences for science fiction narratives, considering how audiences use sci-fi to understand and articulate their desires and construct identities (Penley 1997), or how the technology that is represented in science fiction is also the medium that we are using to access the representation. In these studies we can see that science fiction is, amongst other things, about technology, the self, identity, sexuality, politics and the environment.

These analytical approaches to the genre of science fiction – as well as noting that the concept of 'genre' itself is problematic – construct the text in different ways, focusing on different features and producing a wide range of results. However, what we don't see is that science fiction is also about science. Cultural studies can identify a large number of facets of science fiction narratives, but rarely does cultural studies focus on one of the core sets of beliefs that underpin science fiction narratives: namely, 'faith' in the power of science. This is by no means a failing on the part of cultural studies. The analysis of science fiction narratives as indicative of unconscious desires, as expressions of gender relations, as examples of latent or hidden orientalism, are all important outcomes of cultural analysis: using an avowedly popular culture genre such as sci-fi to show that our society is actively involved in constructing others and ordering social divisions through cultural production is a profoundly important task, and it is not the aim of this chapter to detract from it in any way. Yet it remains that such approaches avoid discussion of what we are learning from science fiction about science and its role in our society. It may be obvious, but science fiction is also about science.

In the rest of this chapter we will look at what science fiction tells us about science. At a very general level, science fiction narratives reinforce some of our societal attitudes towards science, although this happens in conflicting ways, and at a specific level there are some sub-genres of science fiction that deliberately locate themselves inside a scientific world-view and celebrate science, scientists and scientific knowledge. Overall this chapter will argue that science fiction becomes a resource in the social construction of shared ideas about science, but representations of science are also a consequence of shared meanings and understandings of science in society. There is a dynamic relationship between the cultural productions and the social meanings attached to knowledge, people and institutions, in this case science. Because of this dynamic and changing relationship, it is difficult to provide hard-and-fast definitions of the phenomena we are looking at, so we will start by trying to place some boundaries around the phenomena we are discussing. A starting point is to ask, What is science fiction?

What is science fiction?

It is interesting to look at how science fiction is being defined. At the outset we need to be cautious about assigning cultural productions to genres: as we shall see, such categories often have very fuzzy boundaries and can change dramatically with time. The idea of genre itself becomes contested, as definition becomes ever more difficult. Indeed, as Annette Kuhn notes, genre studies declined and all but disappeared in the 1970s (A. Kuhn 1990: 3). In this section we will make the assumption that genres can be identified, but will also note that such identification will always be problematical for reasons of contestability and problems of closing boundaries. The sub-genres of science fiction identified here suffer from similar problems of indeterminacy.

Most people are able to identify texts they would consider to be science fiction, and will have a good idea of what it is that makes these texts science fiction. However, as with most genres, providing hard and fast definitions of where the boundaries lie is difficult (A. Kuhn 1990: 1). The process of definition itself is significant: why are cultural productions placed in genres? The ease with which science fiction texts in contemporary culture can be identified is no doubt facilitated by the prevalence of categorized cultural productions, and we must be aware that such categorizations are made, at least in part, by the organizations that have a vested interest in ensuring maximum profits through maximizing audiences, or through constructing new, niche markets. Similarly, audiences and authors may deliberately choose to locate themselves inside a genre category for reasons of identity construction or community formation. Constance Penley's study of 'trekkies' (*Star Trek* fans) identifies the strength of feeling inside this fan group to construct identities and relationships around a set of cultural productions: fans felt that they had a personal investment in being 'different' from non-trekkies (Penley 1997).

Science fiction, in the form of movies, is a major income earner, and science fiction stories are embedded in our culture. For example, 2003's major movie releases from Hollywood included the blockbuster science fiction movies *Matrix Reloaded, Matrix Revolutions, The Hulk* and *Terminator 3*. Each of these has been a major commercial, if not critical, success. Notably, three of them (*Terminator 3, Matrix Reloaded* and *Matrix Revolutions*) are sequels to previous major successes. Science fiction is perhaps the most widely distributed fictional genre in terms of the media that it appears in: novels, movies, television are obvious locations, but science fiction also has a medium that it has colonized almost exclusively (at least in the US and UK versions) – the comic book. In addition, we can see science fiction elements appearing in graphic design and advertising, in contemporary popular music (particularly 1980s performers like Gary Numan and Kraftwerk, and 1990s techno bands, e.g. Eat Static), in architecture (the new Bull Ring shopping centre in Birmingham, designed by Future Systems, has been widely described as futuristic and sci-fi inspired (see illustration 7.1), and in contemporary art (the work of Eduardo Paolozzi is again appropriate here – much of his 'pop art' works combine elements of science fiction popular culture such as model space ships and toy robots). At times, science fiction becomes a way of making sense of the world of science: the use of the term 'Frankenstein foods' to describe GM crops is now firmly embedded in contemporary culture, and NASA's use of *Star Trek* themes and actors to popularize and promote its mission is discussed in some depth by Penley (1997).

Despite, or perhaps because of, this popularity, science fiction is often seen as a form of fiction that is not as good or as legitimate as other forms of fictional writing. Whilst this is almost certainly changing with time, allowing science fiction a much more central role in popular culture today, science fiction was for a long time a marginalized genre whose position allowed it a much greater degree of latitude in terms of what it could include. An example of this is the first

Illustration 7.1.   The Bull Ring shopping centre, Birmingham, 2004. Photo by Bec Chalkley.

on-screen TV kiss between a black and a white character: this took place in an episode of the 1960s TV sci-fi *Star Trek*, a programme that represents a fantasy future.

This disparity and ubiquity make it difficult to produce a unitary definition of science fiction. However, we can point to some general trends in science fiction narrative, particularly the themes of the future, technology and space. Often it is science fiction authors who would identify such themes as being their preoccupations:

> Now – contrary to a general belief – prediction is not the main purpose of science-fiction writers; few, if any, have ever claimed 'this is how it will be'. Most of them are concerned with the play of ideas, and the exploration of novel concepts in science and discovery. 'What if . . . ?' is the thought underlying all writing in this field. What if a man could become invisible? What if we could travel into the future? What if there is intelligent life elsewhere in the Universe? These are the initial grains around which the writer secretes his modest pearl. No one is more surprised than he is, if it turns out that he has indeed forecast the pattern of future events. (Clarke 1977: 3)

Arthur C. Clarke is one of the most influential sci-fi authors alive today, and with a career spanning seven decades, his work is an interesting 'barometer' of the course of sci-fi writing. We will return to Clarke's work later in this chapter. For the time being we should simply note that Clarke's definition of science fiction deals with speculation about possible futures. Sci-fi, by this definition, can be about just about anything, as long as it is looking at the future and answering a 'what if?' question. But this is not a sufficient working definition of sci-fi: clearly asking and answering a 'what if?' question of the form 'what if a woman were to fall in love with her best friend's partner?' could be the start of a romance, a sci-fi, a murder mystery, a screwball comedy, etc. We need additional components to discriminate what sci-fi is:

> Years ago I was working in Schenectady for General Electric, completely surrounded by machines and ideas for machines, so I wrote a novel about people and machines, and machines frequently got the best of it, as machines will. (It was called *Player Piano*, and it was brought out again in both hard cover and paperback.) And I learned from the reviewers that I was a science-fiction writer. I didn't know that. I supposed I was writing a novel about life, about things I could not avoid seeing and hearing in Schenectady, a very real town, awkwardly set in the gruesome now. I have been a soreheaded occupant of a file drawer labelled 'science fiction' ever since, and I would like out, particularly since so many serious critics regularly mistake the drawer for a urinal. The way a person gets into this drawer, apparently, is to notice technology. The feeling persists that no one can simultaneously be a respectable writer and understand how a refrigerator works, just as no gentleman wears a brown suit in the city. (Vonnegut 1976: 25)

Vonnegut identifies the second point of our starting definition of sci-fi: it is about technology and, by inference – as technology is seen as a product of science – science. But Vonnegut also reminds us of the 'lower' status of sci-fi as a genre, at least at the time of his writing: indeed, a central character in many of Vonnegut's books is Kilgore Trout, a failed but incredibly prolific science fiction writer, whose works – which appear as filler in cheap pornographic magazines and are largely unread – contain the answers to most of life's mysteries.

These two quotations from prominent sci-fi authors (albeit in Vonnegut's case a reluctant one) provide us with a good starting-point definition: sci-fi is about the future and has a focus on technology. Most sci-fi will conform to this definition. However, science fiction is a very complex genre that has fuzzy edges and a great many subdivisions. Clearly a film like *Terminator* is science fiction: it is about the future and our relationship to technology (robots and computers), and presents humans in conflict with technological forces. How about Orwell's *1984*? It is about the future (or at least, it was when it was written), has a strong focus on technology (telescreens, memory holes, etc.) and presents humans in conflict with technological forces (the attempts of Julia and Winston to escape their constant surveillance). *Terminator* has a 'happy' ending, with humans defeating the technology that is trying to destroy them, whereas *1984* has an unhappy ending with the humanity of the heroes being destroyed by the technocracy and dictatorship that surround them. Would you describe *1984* as science fiction? The context in which a text emerges clearly plays some role in how we define a text. The novel based on James Cameron's screenplay of *Terminator* (Frakes and Wisher 1991, long out of print despite the huge popularity of this film) would have been located in the sci-fi section of your local bookstore, but George Orwell's *1984* would be in the literature section of the same shop: you may have been encouraged to read *1984* as part of an English literature course at school, but *Terminator* was probably not on the syllabus. Yet *1984* displays the characteristics we look for and closely identify with sci-fi: future orientation and a focus on new forms of technology (Orwell 1954). These two characteristics are clearly visible in most sci-fi that we consider: we could, of course, add a huge number of other common themes (such as space exploration or contact with alien species), but not all sci-fi texts will contain these, and it is often sci-fi by women writers that departs from these standard themes. All, however, look to the future and make technology a key issue to be utilized in the text, and we can use this as a starting-point definition. (And yet, even with such a broad definition, we find exceptions. For example, William Gibson and Bruce Sterling's *The Difference Engine* is an examination of a fictional mid-Victorian society that has been transformed by the introduction of information technology – clearly science fiction, but set in the past, not the future.)

Problems in producing hard-and-fast definitions of sci-fi notwithstanding, we can look at a range of sci-fi texts to provide examples of our relationship to science and technology in contemporary society, and an indication of our attitude towards what the future will hold for us. Taking such an approach reveals a wide range of meanings inside sci-fi texts, and we will look at some of these below. But the main focus here is on what mainstream sci-fi, and subsequently what a number of sub-genres of sci-fi, tell us about science. We will use sci-fi representations of science as a means of understanding general societal concerns about science and general societal images of science.

Mainstream science fiction – definitions and its relation to science

Notwithstanding the difficulties of defining science fiction, and the problems associated with analysing genres, there is something we can identify as being 'mainstream' science fiction: that is, science fictions that receive widespread public attention through their promotion in a range of media. Again, boundaries surrounding this definition will be fuzzy: the *Star Trek* TV series could clearly be defined as mainstream science fiction, as could *The X-Files*: both have extensive exposure, and would be clearly defined as science fiction by audiences (although it is notable that both of these texts have significant soap opera elements). However, we will encounter more difficulties in categorizing a film like *2001: A Space Odyssey*, which is certainly one of the most famous science fiction films of the twentieth century, and arguably one of the best – but mainstream? Stanley Kubrick's 1968 film, with its strict realism, hard-to-follow story and often silent soundtrack, diverges considerably from what is expected in a sci-fi movie; yet it is frequently shown on television, and in the year 2001 was re-released to nationwide cinemas in the UK. Suffice it to say that the construction of a category such as 'mainstream' science fiction is problematical if we try and sustain a form of categorization in a systematic way. That is not the intention here: rather, I want us to be able to distinguish science fiction that a large part of the general public will have an opportunity to encounter from more marginal, specialized forms of sci-fi. In the case of science fiction films, I will describe the main blockbuster sci-fi movies released in 2003 – namely, *The Hulk*, *Terminator 3* and *The Matrix Reloaded* – as being 'mainstream'.

Mainstream science fiction movies

Do movies like *Terminator 3*, *The Matrix Reloaded* and *The Hulk* tell us anything about science? This is not a straightforward question. All three feature technological futures as principal plot themes, and all three present futures where technology has escaped from control. In contemporary society science and technology are seen as inseparable. Aspects of these movies may reinforce our general societal understanding of science. These movies articulate a strong form of technological determinism, where the technology engendered by scientific knowledge takes on a momentum that is hard or impossible for humans to stop. These films also present scientists in roles that are very familiar: in particular, *The Hulk*'s scientists are seen as being remote from society, cold, calculating, unethical and beyond control. Finally, the institution of science itself is located very firmly in conjunction with, or within, structures of power. In *Terminator 3*, SkyNet (the capitalist corporation) engineers the fabrication of the terminator robots and the destruction of human civilization; in *Matrix Reloaded* the state is fused with technology to produce a simulacrum of the social world that enslaves the human population of the planet; in *The Hulk* the experimenters who create Hulk are working for a military-industrial corporation that exists in the background of a near-future American society.

These themes – knowledge leads to technology that will threaten us; scientists are cold and emotionless; scientific institutions are part of the structure of power in society – are common to a great many mainstream science fiction narratives that describe contemporary society or near-future alternatives. Science, scientists and scientific institutions are not the only themes of the films, but these movies present a consistent and fairly coherent image of science as a dangerous and hard-to-understand entity that has inherent power. Mainstream science fiction films rely upon general societal attitudes and cultural representations of science for their effect and impact, but also to allow the audience to position the film. The opening credits of *The Hulk* (Ang Lee 2003) contain just about every single visual cliché from the pantheon of stereotyped images of biological science laboratories: test-tubes, centrifuges, experiments on animals, graphical representations of DNA molecules, animations of bacterial reproduction, and so on. The first 30 minutes of *The Hulk* are almost entirely located inside a laboratory, with experimenters carrying out dubious and unpleasant experiments on animals (including a graphic scene of an exploding frog) and themselves, surrounded by ultra-high-tech equipment, and overseen by shadowy military-industrial complex figures. These images provide a *mise en scène* within which to locate the film's protagonists: science is hard, calculating, obscure and asks us to do things which are unpleasant and best kept hidden. The film taps into the general popular culture images of science, scientists and scientific institutions that are already extant. Some representations in the film are quite knowing: at one point the hero's (Bruce Banner) laboratory assistant points out that his form of dress is geeky even by the standards of scientists. However, most of the film sticks rigidly to the norms of the Hollywood blockbuster. For example, the heroine (Betsy Ross) conforms closely to the stereotype of feminine beauty that is current in Hollywood movies, despite her membership of the same laboratory. These are images of science that we have seen for decades, and tropes that can be traced back to the early days of movie making and science fiction writing. It is difficult to note any 'postmodern' or ironic take in these images and stereotypes, and we could perhaps explain this by reference to a desire on the part of Ang Lee to remain as close as possible to Stan Lee's original 1960s conception of *The Hulk* character. However, this did not stop Ang Lee from changing the 'cause' of *The Hulk*'s transformed state from being a nuclear accident to being a biotechnology accident. Clearly some aspects of *The Hulk* story needed updating in Lee's reworking.

Contemporary mainstream science fiction trends and tendencies

Science fiction, even 'mainstream' science fiction, encompasses a huge range of different types of narratives, appears in a range of media, and appeals to a diverse audience. The following sections explore three trends and tendencies of science fiction books, all currently popular: space opera, cyberpunk and hard science fiction. These three are the main categories that contemporary science fiction books fall into – although we should note that a fourth, fantasy, is also very popular. The exclusion of fantasy here is quite deliberate: unlike space opera, cyberpunk and hard science fiction, fantasy quite deliberately ignores science and replaces it with some version of magic, spirituality or religion as a mechanism for bringing about change. It retains a connection to science fiction in general by, often, locating its narratives in the future and in alternative worlds. By contrast, the books we focus on below all use science, to varying degrees, as a way of explaining the world as depicted in the text.

Once again we face problems in closing boundaries around our definitions. In a number of cases, science fiction texts fall quite easily into more than one category, and others do not admit of categorization at all. As with our discussion of mainstream science fiction, the aim here is not to produce rigid, systematic classifications, but rather to locate trends and tendencies in this area of cultural production.

Space opera

'Space operas' describes 'galaxy-spinning tales of battling starships, exploding planets and questions on the nature of good and evil and the evolution of man' (from the blurb on the jacket of Hamilton 1999a). This definition of space opera holds for a range of science fiction productions. The roots of space opera go back to, at least, the 1930s, when Hollywood produced serials such as *Flash Gordon*. In terms of books, the most important early space opera was Isaac Asimov's *Foundation* trilogy, written in the 1950s and subsequently expanded in the 1970s and 1980s (Asimov 1979a, 1979b, 1982, 1983a, 1983b, 1985, 1986, 1988, 1993). The sequential aspect of Asimov's work was new and was subsequently copied by many other science fiction writers. In television, the clearest example is the *Star Trek* series of the late 1960s and early 1970s, again expanded and extended in the 1980s and 1990s with the sequel series *Star Trek the Next Generation* and spin-off series *Babylon 5* and *Deep Space 9*. Space opera movies are legion, typified by the *Star Wars* series of films and the *Star Trek* film series. All share the characteristics of inter-galactic travel, encounters with aliens and conflict-based plots. Here we will focus on one author's space operas to identify key features of the uptake and articulation of a vision of science by science fiction.

Iain M. Banks's 'Culture' series of novels (Banks 1987, 1988, 1990, 1996, 1998, 2000) are set in another part of our galaxy, include actors who are human and non-human, feature sentient super-massive spaceships, and are replete with startling technological devices: thinking weapons, constructed orbital environments that house billions of people, 'displacers' that can transmit matter instantaneously through space, faster-than-light travel through hyperspace, etc. However, Banks wastes little time in his novels 'explaining' how such devices could come into being, doesn't use technical jargon, and avoids discussions of the sorts of paradoxes that must inevitably arise when a vast civilization is engaged in huge amounts of faster-than-light travel (e.g. meeting your unborn children, or your self; for a good popular science introduction to issues surrounding faster-than-light travel and the paradoxes this would create see Davies 2001). Banks's novels can be read in a variety of ways, one of which is as a criticism of contemporary UK society and world geopolitics. Banks's utopian civilization, the Culture, is based on a form of libertarian anarchism that relies upon advanced technology to free people from any kind of material want. Banks can be seen to be offering a critique of Western capitalism, in which acquisition, especially of money, is promoted by culture, and his 'Culture' is posited as a future alternative that we should aspire to. Indeed, in the short story *The State of the Art* (Banks 1991), agents of the Culture visit planet Earth in the 1970s, are mostly appalled at what they see, but decide not to intervene or change the course of events on Earth, despite many of the spaceship crew identifying that Earth will probably destroy itself through nuclear Armageddon in the near future. Sma, the Culture agent, discusses the problem of 'contacting' Earth with the ship's artificial intelligence:

> *Ready* for it? What does that matter? What does it even *mean*? Of course they aren't ready for it, of course we'll spoil the place. Are they any more ready for World War Three? You seriously think we could mess the place up more than they're doing at the moment? When they're not actually out slaughtering each other they're inventing ingenious new ways to massacre each other more efficiently in the future, and when they're not doing *that* they're committing specieside, from the Amazon to Borneo . . . or filling the seas with shit, or the air, or the land. They could hardly make a better job of vandalizing their own planet if we gave them lessons. (Banks, Iain M., *The State of the Art*, London, Orbit (an imprint of the Time Warner Book Group UK), 1991: 111)

Banks uses the Culture as a cipher for human possibility and as an idealized position from which to criticize contemporary politics, morality and capitalism. He does not discuss science or scientific knowledge: for him, the technological marvels and miracles of the Culture need description but no explanation. Familiarity with the genre conventions of science fiction in general, such as faster-than-light travel and artificial intelligence, means that explanations do not need to be included in the text for the audience to understand the main narrative, or to believe in its plausibility. For the most part, the plausibility of Banks's novels is provided by skilled writing and by locating the narrative inside a genre where the audience are already aware of the parameters that construct and constrain the possibilities being described. *Consider Phlebas*, Banks's first science fiction novel, tells the story of a galactic war between the Culture and the Idirans from the perspective of Horza, a mercenary 'changer' who can adopt any humanoid form, and who has allied himself to the Idiran cause. Captured on a mission to subvert a neutral government and persuade them to join in against the Culture, Horza is rescued by his Idiran controllers on their spaceship *The Hand of God 137*.

Banks's choice of names for his fictional Culture spaceships is commented on by Horza:

> By their names you could know them, Horza thought as he showered. The Culture's General Contact Units, which until now had borne the brunt of the first four years of the war in space, had always chosen jokey, facetious names. Even the new warships they were starting to produce, as their factory craft completed gearing up their war production, favoured either jocular, sombre or downright unpleasant names, as though the Culture could not take entirely seriously the vast conflict in which it had embroiled itself.
>
> The Idirans looked at things differently. To them a ship name ought to reflect the serious nature of its purpose, duties and resolute use. In the huge Idiran navy there were hundreds of craft named after the same heroes, planets, battles, religious concepts and impressive adjectives. The light cruiser which had rescued Horza was the 137th vessel to be called *The Hand of God*, and it existed concurrently with over a hundred other craft in the navy using the same title, so its full name was *The Hand of God 137*. (Banks, Iain M. *Consider Phlebas* London: Orbit Books (an imprint of the Time Warner Book Group UK, 1987: 19–20)

This simple device, early in the narrative, provides us with a quick overview of the two competing civilizations in this war and, whilst not providing us with any details of why such a galactic war is taking place (and the reasons remain very much a secondary part of the novel), at least gives us an idea of who is going to win (the Culture) and why (they have a sense of humour). Ironically, it is the ultra-intelligent and rational artificial intelligence machines of the Culture that express the most humour in Banks's novels, often through their choice of names or personas to represent themselves: in *Use of Weapons* (Banks 1990) the Culture 'Special Circumstances' agent Diziet Sma, accompanied by her drone colleague Skaffen-Amtiskaw, has joined the crew of a demilitarized Culture warship, the *Xenophobe*, which will transport her to her assignment. Here is her first meeting with the ship and its crew:

> One of the people in the group held a little bundle of brown and yellow fur, cradled against one shoulder rather as one might hold a baby. 'Here,' the man said, presenting the tiny furry creature to Sma. She took it reluctantly. It was warm, had four limbs arranged conventionally, smelled attractive and wasn't any sort of animal she'd ever seen before; it had large ears on a large head, and as she held it, it opened its huge eyes and looked at her. 'That's the ship,' the man who'd handed her the animal said.
>
> 'Hello,' the tiny being squeaked.
>
> Sma looked it up and down. 'You're the *Xenophobe*?'

'Its representative. The bit you can talk to. You can call me Xeny.' It smiled. It had little round teeth. 'I know most ships just use a drone, but,' it glanced at Skaffen-Amtiskaw, 'they can be a bit boring, don't you think?'

Sma smiled, and sensed Skaffen-Amtiskaw's aura flicker out of the corner of her eye. 'Well, sometimes,' she agreed.

'Oh yes,' the little creature said, nodding. 'I'm *much* cuter.' It wriggled in her hands, looking happy. 'If you like,' it giggled, 'I'll show you to your cabin, yes?'

'Yes, good idea,' nodded Sma, and put the thing over her shoulder. The crewpeople called out to say they'd see her later as she, the ship's bizarre remote drone and Skaffen-Amtiskaw headed for the accommodation section.

'Ooh, you're nice and warm,' the little brown and yellow creature mumbled sleepily, snuggling into Sma's neck as they headed down a deeply carpeted corridor for Sma's quarters. . . .

'Can I cuddle up with you when you sleep?'

Sma stopped, detached the creature from her shoulder with one hand and stared it in the face. 'What?'

'Just for chumminess' sake,' the little thing said, yawning wide and blinking. 'I'm not being rude; it's a good bonding procedure.' . . .

'Listen *Xenophobe* ——'

'Xeny.'

'Xeny; you are a million-tonne starship; a Torturer class Rapid Offensive Unit. Even ——'

'But I'm demilitarised!'

'Even without your principal armament, I bet you could waste planets if you wanted to ——'

'Aw, come on; any silly GCU can do *that*!'

'So what's all this shit for?' She shook the furry little remote drone, quite hard. Its teeth chattered.

'It's for a laugh!' it cried. 'Sma; don't you appreciate a joke?'

(Banks, Iain M. *Use of Weapons*, London: Orbit Books (an imprint of the Time Warner Book Group UK), 1990: 55–6)

That we know that an artificial intelligence of great intellect is a current impossibility is not to deny that we have encountered a great many science fiction narratives that describe just such a possibility: locating a narrative within the conventions of the sub-genre makes it unnecessary to explain every technological detail. This doesn't, of course, stop some writers from doing just that, and, as Penley notes, science fiction audiences will often become closely engaged in projects that provide just such details in the artificial universes they enjoy exploring (Penley 1997).

Banks's novels present new characters, such as his enhanced capability humans and sentient spaceships, in familiar science fiction environments – interstellar travel, hedonistic societies, space warfare, etc. Readers know how to read Banks's novels because, as an audience, they are so used to these conventional environments and don't need much explanation for the emergence of scenarios.

Yet it is their association with similar texts that allows us to identify how Banks's novels present a picture of science. His fictions present super-technological societies that have advanced through the application of science and technology to problem solving. Human (or alien) want is eradicated by having better technology, and the good life is provided to people through technologies of awesome power. Banks's faith in technology is a form of faith in science: if our contemporary governments would put as much time and money into scientific research directed towards curing disease and feeding the population as they do into making newer and bigger weapons or prosecuting wars, then society would be a much better place. Banks sees science as a neutral force which can be harnessed for good or for evil: his text is that in future science will be harnessed for good; his subtext is that now science is being harnessed for evil or, at the very least, is not being used properly.

Banks's science fiction books are very popular, all featuring on UK bestseller lists on publication. In many ways Banks's work revitalized UK science fiction in the 1990s, although we should note that two further factors are significant here: the emergence of cyberpunk and the move towards a 'hard' science fiction.

Cyberpunk

Cyberpunk fuses science fiction, the hard-boiled detective genre and dystopian visions of the future. The first cyberpunk novel to be recognized as such was William Gibson's *Neuromancer* (1984), and the first cyberpunk movie was *Blade Runner* (James Cameron, 1982). *Blade Runner* offers a vision of Los Angeles in 2019 where replicants – machines in the likeness of humans – are hunted down and destroyed by government agents (blade runners). *Neuromancer* describes a near future world in which cyberspace is a virtual reality environment that individuals can access and interact within. This world is dominated by multinational corporations of supreme power, and nation-states are no longer significant entities. Into this environment the lone hero Case, the cyber cowboy and computer hacker, and his assassin accomplice Molly (an enhanced human) are set tasks to be completed by an artificial intelligence. The mood of the novel is consistently dark; the characters are in a permanent state of uncertainty, surrounded by or involved in acts of violence (both real and virtual), and there is no appeal to external sources of help, advice, morality or even knowledge. This is a world of relativism, fluctuating and shifting identities, uncertainty, loneliness, transience and fear: a technoculture in which individuals must understand the operation of cyberspace, or must have supreme fighting skills to survive. And survival is not a particularly pleasant option here: Case can access the virtual cyber world for pleasure and excitement, but his everyday 'meat' existence is lonely, brutish, dirty and manageable only through the use of powerful drugs. Gibson's hard-boiled authorial voice describes Case's neighbourhood:

> Night City was like a deranged experiment in social Darwinism, designed by a bored researcher who kept one thumb permanently on the fast-forward button. Stop hustling and you sank without a trace, but move a little too slowly and you'd break the fragile surface tension of the black market; either way, you were gone, with nothing left but some vague memory in the mind of a fixture like Ratz, though heart or lungs or kidneys might survive in the service of some stranger with New Yen for the clinic tanks. (Gibson, William, *Neuromancer*, London: HarperCollins, 1984: 14. Reprinted by permission of Harper-Collins Ltd © 1984, William Gibson)

Given this everyday existence, it is not surprising that Case chooses to spend hours at a time jacked into the matrix, living in the cyber-world. Being jacked in allows Case to live out his fantasies and also, through his hacking and programming skills, assume much more power than is available to him in the 'meat' world.

Neuromancer's prescience is striking. Written before the internet had been conceived, its vision of a world of infinite electronic data, where information would be the prime factor in power struggles, predicts the technoculture that now predominates in Western industrial societies. Central to *Neuromancer* and other cyberpunk novels (notably those of Bruce Sterling, Neal Stephenson and Peter F. Hamilton) is the relationship between technology and identity, a theme that has become crucial in current cultural analyses of technology. However, there is a tension over whether cultural studies 'adopts' texts and genres for analysis because they are popular or because they are fertile for particular forms of theoretical exploration.

Cyberpunk novels, despite their general rejection of space opera conventions of starships, aliens and space battles, are clearly science fiction: they describe worlds that are unimaginable without extensive technological development, and recognize that major advances in scientific knowledge are necessary to achieve such transformations. Some have recently homed in on the central thematics of two key areas of current scientific research: nanotechnology and genetic engineering. For example, Neal Stephenson's *The Diamond Age* (1995) describes a familiar cyberpunk near future of immensely powerful corporations that have built their power on control of information and application of nanotechnology to produce a society of plenty, but a society that is even more deeply divided than our own. The application of nanotechnology, specifically the invention of nano-machines that can assemble products from individual atoms and molecules (thus making diamond an everyday commodity) borrows research themes and discussions in which the physics community is engaging concerning the possibilities of such research. Many of the inventions Stephenson posits are mentioned in Eric Drexler's influential, if perhaps sometimes implausible, *Engines of Creation* (1990) and his *Nanosystems* (1992). Similarly, the use by cyberpunk authors of themes from genetic engineering research reminds us of a growing concern in public discourse about the benefits or otherwise of genetic modification.

The possible worlds being described by cyberpunk authors have at least a foothold in reality, unlike those of space opera: we can imagine extensions of current scientific knowledge that may allow nano-machines to be created, or may allow human beings to receive considerable genetic modification to enhance senses or interface directly with machines. However, cyberpunk novels do not become involved in discussions of the development, or even the workings, of such systems. As with Banks's 'Culture' novels, explanation is not seen as necessary: audiences already *know* that contemporary science may deliver such wonders in the future. We are familiar with the ideas being expressed in cyberpunk because our lives and our media are already in contact with such ideas. Cyberpunk deliberately uses contemporary debates in the public sphere to construct its narratives and plots, and relies on the audience to bring the wider context and detail of such debates to the texts.

There is another reason for this lack of explanation of 'magical' technology. Cyberpunk novels are plot-driven, moving at a pace that is similar to that of the hard-boiled detective novels of Dashiell Hammett or Raymond Chandler. Maintaining the plot, moving it constantly forward, would be disrupted by detailed explanations of the technical details of devices being deployed, or by disquisitions on the factual roots of the fictional technology being described. Gibson himself notes that his use of 'jacking in' to a virtual reality cyber-space, and 'flipping' between states of reality are a result of his 'impatience with figuring out how to write physical transitions; I wanted to be able to channel-zap' (Gibson 1984: 319).

Cyberpunk's dystopian futures are often, if not always, the result of huge technologically induced change. In Gibson's work it is the ever present 'net' that brings about the social changes and new social divisions; in Hamilton's near future UK society it is environmental collapse as a result of human technological change that has altered the world (Hamilton 1993, 1997a, 1998). Technology is ubiquitous in both groups of fictions: for Gibson, our interactions will be increasingly mediated by the net; whereas for Hamilton, our bodies themselves will be invaded by neural implants that enhance our abilities and connect us to artificial intelligences. Both groups of novels make much of the possibilities of artificial intelligences, and often make references to historical figures significant in the development of computing, like Alan Turing and John von Neumann. Like space operas, these fictions are not necessarily focused closely on science itself, but make great use of the deployment and application of science, and imply that scientific progress is threatening and exciting at the same time. Again, cyberpunk novels are not overly concerned with providing watertight plots that withstand all scrutiny concerning their plausibility, but they often make attempts to stay within what we might consider to be the bounds of possibility: those traditional science fiction themes of 'what if?', technology and space are still at the core of most cyberpunk novels.

Yet, also at the core of most cyberpunk are some very traditional gender roles. *Neuromancer* may have characters like Molly, the physically enhanced female assassin who is tough, independent and virtually invulnerable, but as Sarah Kember points out, cyberpunk novels are really just rewritings of some very old narratives – cowboy stories – that display a traditional range of patriarchal gender stereotypes (Kember 2003: 177). However, the core of *science*-based ideas inside cyberpunk – extensions and modifications of the self, the net and cyberspace, the breakdown of 'modern' institutions – provided women with a new discourse of cyberfeminism, and a new set of possibilities for cultural productions.

Feminism, science and science fiction

Feminism and cyborgs

A number of recent versions of feminism have been concerned with showing how formal science, and scientism in society, is inimical to the interests of women. Science and technology has been seen by many feminists as a means of domination and not of liberation. Much of this argument stems from the 'attitude' of science to control and dominate nature, and the approach by feminists towards science in the 1960s, 1970s, 1980s and onwards has often been one of anger and opposition. Formal science has excluded women from its institutions, discriminated against those admitted, made objects of women's bodies, and experimented on them. It has also harmed the environment and contributed to the militarization of society. Not surprisingly, many feminists have seen science as irredeemable, although many have also attempted to improve existing science institutions. Those who see science as being salvageable, as being in need of reformation rather than radical restructuring, can be described as liberal feminists – Rose gives a good account of such approaches in *Love, Power and Knowledge* (1994). Liberal feminists seek to redress imbalances in the structures of scientific institutions by promoting women's careers, protecting women from discrimination in the workplace and ensuring fair treatment for all. However, there are some feminists who see science as irredeemable, as being in need of radical change or even abandonment. There are two broad approaches: those who propose a return to nature and a more holistic, less technical approach to the study of the natural world (ecofeminists), and those who propose an embracing of the technicity of contemporary science and society (cyberfeminists).

Although these two approaches produce very different consequences, they both start from a position that suggests that people and industrial societies need to construct a different version of our relationship with nature.

Ecofeminism and goddesses

Ecofeminism proposes that, rather than attempt to apply rationality to the control and domination of nature for our own ends, we can identify a movement towards a spiritual and ecologically sensitive approach to nature. The reconstruction of debates in this movement between the 'good' organic world and the 'bad' technological world has resonances in many of the anti-material and political counter-culture movements of the late 1960s and onwards. In the debates of the 1990s the metaphor of the goddess was used to indicate the altered relationship to nature that should be aimed for.

Although appearing to offer an opposition to science, through opposing technological interventions, the ecofeminist perspective often takes on aspects of the foundational scientific approach. This it does through constructing arguments about the nature of 'woman' as being a superordinate being – a 'goddess'. This is essentialism – it relies upon the identification of transhistorical and transcendent character-istics of organic beings. The shift of emphasis, from women as objects of the (male) scientists' gaze to women as objects of the ecofeminists' gaze is profound in terms of how women are viewed, but the repro-duction of the form of rationality and investigation is quite obvious. This is not an alternative to science, but a reworking of it.

Cyberfeminism and cyborgs

Cyberfeminism presents a contrast to ecofeminism. Rather than seeing the goddess as the state to be achieved, cyberfeminists argue that we should recognize that we are now all cyborgs: women should welcome the unreal and the artefacts (artifices?) of technological change. American feminist STS researcher Donna Haraway's cyborg approach takes a different line on nature from that of ecofeminists. Rather than seeing nature as a given, external object that nurtures us, cyborgs see nature as an artefact, as something that is made as both fiction and fact.

'A cyborg is a cybernetic organism, a hybrid of machine and organ-ism, a creature of social reality as well as a creature of fiction' (Haraway 1991: 149). For Haraway, as a second-generation feminist, it is not enough simply to challenge the social inequalities experienced by women. It is also necessary to construct new languages, law and mythology through challenging the gender bias in existing language, law and mythology. Haraway clearly challenges the gender bias in scientific discourse, but also constructs a new mythology, one that is not dependent upon the past or upon transcendental, essentialist cat-egories, in her construction of the cyborg. For Haraway, a way to reappropriate and reconstruct science so that it loses its androcentric character and oppressive practices is to begin to understand that human beings no longer exist, having been replaced in technoscience by cyborgs.

> If organisms are natural objects, it is crucial for us to remember that organisms are not born; they are made in world-changing techno-scientific practices by particular collective actors in particular times and places. In the belly of the local/global monster in which I am ges-tating, often called the postmodern world, global technology appears to *denature* everything, to make everything a malleable matter of strategic decisions and mobile production and reproduction processes. (Haraway 1992: 297)

Haraway's cyborg is a playful, blasphemous creature inhabiting the networks of high-tech culture.

> The figure of the cyborg is of one who moves playfully, ironically, non-innocently beyond the old identities of human, animal or machine, deconstructing the phallocentric definitions of 'selfhood', 'woman' or 'nature' among many others. It is a fascinating approach, useful not only for its affirmation that feminists cannot afford to create 'science' as an enemy, but also for the way it enables us to see our contemporary practice as feminist researchers: fax, computer, photocopier, car, telephone, aeroplane have all contributed to writing this paper – where is the 'me' that is separate? (Martin 1996: 103)

The cyborg represents a networking life that is polymorphous, changing, potentially more liberating than our old human lives. Thus it opposes concepts of unitary identity and self and recognizes ideas of difference and differentiation. It opposes the idea of a self in opposition to nature. It is a reflection of the fragmentation of 'modern' culture and society and its replacement by 'postmodern' forms.

Haraway is recognizing the importance of science and technology, and the inescapability of the technological in our lives. We are part of a 'machine' of technological social structures, overlapping social structures that lead to the articulation of identities that have no organic or transcendental form. Identities are technologized and constructed. Haraway's approach, like that of Latour, is to identify the stories that science tells about itself and identify the things that science makes up to justify its stories. The cyborg story is a story to challenge and replace existing science stories – it gives power to its user and allows us to identify the technoscientific world in a new way. Unlike the goddess story, the cyborg story allows us to celebrate the invasion of our lives by technology – allows us to use technology in ways that releases us from drudgery, oppression or stereotyping.

Hard science fiction

There is a group of science fiction writers who deliberately embrace formal scientific knowledge in their texts, and attempt to provide scientifically accurate – if speculative – accounts of the technology that they use in their texts. This trend, which has come to be known as 'hard science fiction', has a long pedigree, which dates back to the early phase of the popularization of science fiction in the 1940s and

1950s. Hard science fiction texts will often incorporate quite extensive discussions of scientific research and scientific principles: as such, it is unsurprising that few mainstream films or TV programmes are part of this sub-genre, although a notable exception is Stanley Kubrick and Arthur C. Clarke's *2001: A Space Odyssey* (book and film 1968).

Hard science fiction attempts to be accurate according to scientific principles: it doesn't 'take liberties' with the laws of physics, extrapolates from current trends in scientific research (often in consultation with scientific researchers), and tries to suggest genuine possibilities that may appear in the future. The best example of this form of writing, and the most consistent exponent of this sub-genre, is Arthur C. Clarke, but contemporaneous with Clarke is the work of Isaac Asimov and in the contemporary UK science fiction field that of Stephen Baxter, Alastair Reynolds and Ken MacLeod.

Hard science fiction, like cyberpunk, relies on an 'ideology' of science for its narratives to achieve their plausibility. Throughout the sub-genre there is a constant assumption that science is progressive, generates technology, and will continue to do so without end. This assumption is a reminder of the lay public's attitude towards science: we may not understand it, and possibly even fear it, but we know that it will produce material change through generating new technology. No explanation in hard science fiction need be provided for plots that describe the development of nanotechnology, genetic modification, automation and robotics, space flight and interstellar travel. Hard science fiction sees all of these things coming about because science is working towards solving these puzzles. Indeed, hard science fiction can lay claim to having made accurate predictions of a range of future technologies. Arthur C. Clarke predicted, and was involved in, the invention of orbiting communication satellites a decade before Sputnik, the first man-made satellite, was launched, and followed that up with further predictions concerning space flight, personal computing and transport systems. Clarke's *Profiles of the Future* (1973) was first published in 1962, and remained in print for many years, with revisions in 1973 and 1984. Clarke produced a new collection of future predictions in 1984 with *1984, Spring: A Choice of Futures*. Interestingly, Stephen Baxter, who could be seen as the heir to Clarke's sci-fi vision (and collaborated with Clarke on the novel *The Light of Other Days* (Clarke and Baxter 2000)), has also recently published a similar non-fiction collection of futurology essays (Baxter 2002).

Clarke's scientific training – he was a government scientist during the Second World War, working on radar systems – is doubtless a significant factor in terms of the 'plausibility' of the narratives produced.

Indeed, many of the 'hard' sci-fi writers have extensive scientific backgrounds: Isaac Asimov graduated with a degree in biochemistry, Stephen Baxter is a maths and engineering graduate (and his bio. on all of his books notes that he applied to become an astronaut in 1991), Ken MacLeod has a B.Sc. in zoology from Glasgow University, and Alastair Reynolds works as an astrophysicist for the European Space Agency. This information is prominently incorporated into the marketing of these authors: such credentials are important.

These texts share an attitude towards science and an affection for science that is clear to the audience. Frequently the heroes of these texts will be scientists: a mathematician (Hari Seldon in Asimov's *Foundation* series), biologists and computer programmers (Clarke's family of heroes in the *Rama* cycle of novels (Clarke and Lee 1991, 1992, 1994)), an astronautical engineer (Baxter's Reid Malenfant in his *Manifold* cycle of novels (Baxter 2000a, 2000b, 2001)), or a marine biologist and a cosmonaut (MacLeod's Gregor Cairns and Grigory Volkov in the *Engines of Light* trilogy (MacLeod 2000, 2002, 2003)). The tasks and adventures in which they become involved often require the application of technical skills and scientific knowledge rather than force, emotion or cunning to ensure success. By contrast, the lead characters in space operas are often starship captains (e.g. Hamilton's heroes in the *Night's Dawn* trilogy (Hamilton 1996, 1997b, 1999b), or soldiers and mercenaries (e.g. in Banks's 'Culture' novels), and the main protagonists of cyberpunk novels, are computer hackers, streetwise cycle couriers, assassins and culture industry stars. In hard sci-fi novels having technical knowledge is often as important as having more traditional heroic qualities. However, other 'traditional' heroic characteristics are visible in the main characters in these hard sci-fi novels: they are, almost invariably, all men, and their expression of scientific rationality as the best way of coping with problems and crises is a strong validation of the 'standard' account of science.

The valorization of science that takes place in these texts is quite palpable: hard science fiction has a didactic quality that space opera avoids in favour of character development and description of new landscapes and environments. Here is an example from Stephen Baxter's *Moonseed* (1998). Henry, a geologist working at Edinburgh University on samples of Moon rock collected by the Apollo missions, is explaining his work to his new friend Jane, also a geologist:

> 'Jane leaned forward and inspected the Moon samples, where they nestled in the slit-open bags. 'I'm not sure what I was expecting,' she said. 'Something – primordial. More glamorous. This looks like – '
> 'What?'

'Like jacket potatoes that got left too long on the barbecue.'

He laughed. 'The Moon is a dark world, Jane; it only looks bright in the sky for lack of competition.'

She pointed to an empty bag. It was numbered '86047'. 'What happened to that one?'

'That's the most important rock in this box. The focus of the study. It's lunar bedrock. Possibly . . .'

The work on the Moon rock was actually picking up quickly – although Henry hadn't much time for any real science yet, as so much of his time was being taken up with organizational stuff. He had to ensure the lab assigned the right facilities for the preliminary studies he wanted to run – emission spectrometry, X-ray crystallography, mass spectrometry, X-ray fluorescence and neutron activation. He wanted to push for a scanning tunnelling microscope study, but there was no STM here, and Dan McDiarmid made it clear exactly where the boundary of his budget lay, as if every STM in the world had been transported to the Moon itself. . . .

He told Jane, 'I'm interested in finding fragments of the Moon's primordial crust, the first that formed after the Moon turned into a molten ball, after it accreted. *Global melting*: if it happened to the Moon, it must have happened to Earth, and other large bodies like Venus and Mars. But we have to know how it all happened. And the Moon is a natural place to study the process, the evidence is all buried deep on earth, by the continuing geology of the planet.' (Baxter, Stephen, *Moonseed*, London, HarperCollins, 1998: 101–2. Reprinted by permission of HarperCollins Ltd © 1998, Stephen Baxter)

The gender dynamics in this interchange are fascinating. The plot tells us that we are about to overhear a conversation between two professional geologists. But it is structured as a conversation between an informer and a learner, and a learner whose grasp of the scientific issues is so basic that all she can manage when encountering a Moon rock is to make a reference to a more familiar object from her domestic realm (burnt potatoes). Presumably Jane has forgotten all of the basic geology that she learned, and needs Henry to explain these pretty basic details to her (even *I* know what Moon rock samples look like just from casual investigation of the Apollo programme). She has also forgotten that her brother put a sample of Moon rock (actually taken from the same rock she is now encountering in Henry's lab) into her hand on page 63 of the book. The gender dynamics here are a reflection of many people's experience of science: it is male-dominated, is often explained in a patronizing way, and is characterized by an uncompromising technical discourse that can be fully understood only by assuming a new 'scientific' persona. The quotation shows a classic piece of boundary defence by scientists against outsiders. Given the gender bias of scientific careers, more often than not, outsiders are women.

Baxter is (probably) not trying to teach his readers basic geological theory, or even about chemical analysis of geological samples. It is the level of detail here that is interesting: the information about the STM or the actual look of Moon rocks is unimportant to the subsequent plot developments, but these details locate the text in a context that isn't simply that of the 'fantastic literature' that sci-fi usually inhabits.

Margaret Atwood, whose work both exhibits facets of hard sci-fi and also breaks with the conventions of hard sci-fi (her recent *Oryx and Crake* (2003) uses hard sci-fi, cyberpunk and political satire), says:

> A lot of science fiction is fantasy. It's people flying around on dragons, other worlds of strange life forms. Some of them are quite well thought through. They know what the strange creatures eat, they know that life could be sustainable. Others are just having fun.
>
> *Oryx and Crake* (2003) is not science fiction. It is fact within fiction. *Science fiction is when you have rockets and chemicals. Speculative fiction is when you have all the materials to actually do it.* We've taken a path that is already visible to us. In *1984* and *Brave New World*, you could see all the elements that were farther down that particular path. I don't like science fiction except for the science fiction of the 1930s, the bug-eyed monster genre in full bloom. (Case and McDonald 2003: 40, my emphasis)

Perhaps we should follow Atwood's convention and adopt the term 'speculative fiction' for these 'hard' science fiction narratives. Readers 'learn' from texts such as this, not specifically about scientific knowledge, but about scientific environments, attitudes and procedures for generating knowledge. Hard science fiction tells us stories about the future, about possible outcomes for humanity, about heroic struggles against adversity – in that sense it is little different from other forms of science fiction. However, it also tells us about science itself, often focusing on what it means to be a scientist, how scientific knowledge and procedures can be applied, and the tensions that exist between the rational, technical, scientific aspects of characters and their emotional, romantic sides. Hard sci-fi is about science, and is actively involved in constructing a vision of what science means to scientists, and how scientists make sense of the world around them. It is, in many ways, a simulation of the attitudes and experiences of scientists and scientific communities. Yet, as we saw when we examined how scientific communities come together and how scientific knowledge is produced, the science of hard sci-fi is still very much a fictional form of science: an enhanced science in which projects are more intense, scientists have more influence, and knowledge is much clearer and less contested.

Conclusion

Science fiction is a complex, contradictory genre. We can identify clear points of contact in the relationship between science and science fiction: science fiction is reliant on science for plots and ideas, and we can track changes in plots and ideas as the cutting edge of science has shifted through the twentieth century (Hulk's genesis changing from a nuclear accident to genetic engineering is a good example of this). But science fiction is not simply a sponge that picks up the themes of scientific research. Cyberpunk and space opera represent a version of science that will concur, at least to some extent, with audiences' hopes and fears for the future. The space opera vision of limitless, technologically driven human expansion and the cyberpunk vision of a dystopic, technocratic and soulless future both emerge from societies with ambivalent attitudes towards scientists, scientific institutions and scientific knowledge. Even the hard sci-fi narratives of avowed cheerleaders for science as activity, and as project, see, at the very least, challenges emerging from the continuation of scientific research into areas such as nanotechnology, genetic engineering and quantum physics. In hard sci-fi texts we learn about science as activity and as attitude, but also discover that scientific progress may be harmful to humanity – although this harm almost invariably comes from the 'corruption' of science by politics or big business. All three types of science fiction show us that we have a complex, contested relationship to science – a mixture of positive, negative and unknown. Sci-fi tends to reconfirm existing notions of the project of science, but does not disabuse us of our distorted knowledge of what actually takes place inside scientific work-places. The science of science fiction remains, even in hard science fiction, an occluded set of processes, a black box, out of which emerges technology, sometimes dangerous, that transforms our world, scientists who retain control of crucial knowledge, institutions that exclude most members of society, and a project that has a momentum of its own and an inexorable drive towards 'progress'.

This version of science is not simply a product of the content of sci-fi narratives. As we have seen, such narratives rely to a large extent on our pre-existing knowledge of science and science fiction. Much more important is the context within which these narratives are located: it is the context of the narrative that provides the meaning of science that we see in science fiction. Our narratives of futurity have changed, because our social understanding of the future has changed, not because we decided to construct new stories of space exploration.

Further reading

Cultural studies has, in recent years, taken a close look at some aspects of science fiction, particularly film, although there are very few texts that focus specifically on science in science fiction. However, the following provide good general introductions to cultural analysis of science fiction:

Bukatman, S. 1993: *Terminal Identity: The Virtual Subject in Post-modern Science Fiction*. Durham, NC, and London: Duke University Press.
Cartmell, D., Hunter, I. Q., Kaye, H. and Whelehan, I. (eds) 1999: *Alien Identities: Exploring Difference in Film and Fiction*. London: Pluto Press.
Hunter, I. Q. (ed.) 1999: *British Science Fiction Cinema*. London: Routledge.
Jancovich, M. 1996: *Rational Fears: American Horror in the 1950s*. Manchester: Manchester University Press.
Kuhn, A. (ed.) 1990: *Alien Zone: Cultural Theory and Contemporary Science Fiction Cinema*. London: Verso.
McCaffery, L. (ed.) 1991: *Storming the Reality Studio: A Casebook of Cyberpunk and Postmodern Science Fiction*. Durham, NC: Duke University Press.
Seed, D. 1999: *American Science Fiction and the Cold War: Literature and Film*. Edinburgh: Edinburgh University Press.
Tudor, A. 1989: *Monsters and Mad Scientists: A Cultural History of the Horror Movie*. Oxford: Blackwell.

The following audience studies focus on science fiction:

Barker, M. and Brook, K. 1998: *Knowing Audiences: Judge Dredd, its Friends, Fans and Foes*. Luton: University of Luton Press.
Penley, C. 1997: *NASA/Trek*. London: Verso.
Tulloch, J. and Jenkins, H. 1995: *Science Fiction Audiences: Doctor Who, Star Trek, and their Fans*. London: Routledge.

Feminist approaches to science studies
Mayberry, M., Subramaniam, B. and Weasel, L. H. (eds) 2001: *Feminist Science Studies: A New Generation*. London: Routledge.

Cyborg theory and cyberfeminism
Haraway, D. J. 1991: *Simians, Cyborgs and Women: The Reinvention of Nature*. London: Free Association Books.
Haraway, D. J. 1997: *Modest_Witness@Second_Millennium: FemaleMan©_ Meets_OncoMouse™: Feminism and Technoscience*. New York and London: Routledge.
Kember, S. 2003: *Cyberfeminism and Artificial Life*. London: Routledge.

Part IV

Living with Science

The strength and creativity of our science base is a key national asset as we move into the 21st century.

UK Prime Minister Tony Blair, 23 May 2002

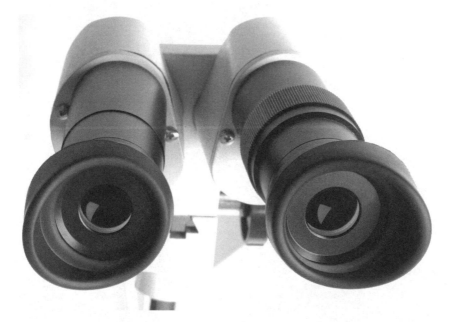

8

Investigating Science in a Cultural Framework

At the start of this book I said that there is no simple and straight-forward answer to the 'What is science?' question, and I hope that this short review of some of the sites and descriptions of science in contemporary society has reinforced that point. Science is too complex, too varied and too embedded in so many different parts of the social and cultural world to allow a simple set of definitions.

This complexity, however, should not deter us from trying to make sense of science in our society, and this book provides some initial steps to doing just that. In this chapter I will recap the main themes and suggest some future strategies for looking at science. I will focus on a specific example, nanotechnology. Nanotechnology has often been described as 'the next big thing', the emerging field of science and technology that will transform the world around us. (Similar claims were, of course, made for nuclear power in the 1950s and 1960s, and are now being made for genetically modified organisms (GMOs).) My aim is to provide a general understanding of the inter-relationships of science by taking an anti-essentialist, culturally oriented approach, by suggesting how you might carry out a short research project investigating what nanotechnology means in society. This research is characterized as a process of questioning, where each different site of representation of science can be not only interrogated to reveal more detail of its connections to other sites, but also questioned to understand how a particular representation of science is emerging from that site. Understanding what science is in contemporary society involves connecting and piecing together these different pictures. The approach adopted here is similar to that of Dorothy

Nelkin and Susan Lindee in *The DNA Mystique* (1995). They looked in detail at the relationship between genetic knowledge, cultural representations of genes and DNA, and the interconnections between the two, and found that the findings of scientific genetics became a resource in culture, because they complemented existing cultural beliefs such as the 'naturalness' of gender differences and social inequalities. In addition, the promises made by scientists reflect these beliefs (Nelkin and Lindee 1995: 197). Their eclectic approach encompasses analyses of formal scientific knowledge, government reports, popular science texts, science fiction texts, cartoons, TV sitcoms, movies and newspaper reports.

This book started by focusing on the emergence of scientific knowledge from formal scientific institutions. It then went on to look at the structure and history of that knowledge. Scientific knowledge emerges into esoteric scientific communities, and these are the primary audience. Science is represented in many ways to many external (exoteric) communities, and we focused on popular science and science fiction. We will look at nanotechnology in broadly similar ways, from the production of formal scientific knowledge to the representation of nanotechnology in contemporary culture, and will then look for connections operating in the reverse direction – that is, from esoteric to exoteric and back to esoteric. What is being proposed is a process of questioning in which we interrogate each different facet of science both as a way of finding connections and as a way of exploring each specific aspect.

The process of investigation proposed here involves looking at different thought communities, interrogating them and developing an empathetic understanding of each such that one can identify the meanings that are being attached to nanotechnology (see box 8.1) and, by extension, science. Central to this is getting a feel for the different forms of description and rhetoric being used by different thought communities. This is not the only process of analysis that may be necessary, but it is a good starting point that allows the voices of different agents (be they human or non-human) in different thought communities to be heard.

BOX 8.1   What is nanotechnology?

Nanotechnology is technology that operates at the 'nano' scale. A basic definition can be made by focusing on the size implications of nanotechnology: the prefix 'nano' comes from a unit of measurement, the nanometre, which is one billionth of a metre (10^{-9} metre). To provide a sense of scale, ten hydrogen atoms side by side would measure about 1 nanometre, most simple organic molecules are a few nanometres in diameter, and a human hair is about 80,000 nanometres thick. 'Technology' means making tools that carry out specific functions. So, nanotechnology is about designing things to work at extremely small scales. 'Nanotechnology' has many definitions, but most commentators would identify the ability to control or manipulate matter at the atomic scale as being its main feature.

The origins of nanotechnology research and theorizing are often traced back to two key thinkers. Richard Feynman, US physicist and Nobel laureate, issued a challenge to the scientific community in the late 1950s: 'What I want to talk about is the problem of manipulating and controlling things on a small scale. . . . It is a staggeringly small world that is below. In the year 2000, when they look back at this age, they will wonder why it was not until the year 1960 that anybody seriously began to move in this direction' (Feynman 2000: 118; also available at <www.zyvex.com/nanotech/feynman.html>)

Feynman pointed out that it would be perfectly possible to write the information from the page of a book on an area 1/25,000 smaller in scale, or to make a working electric motor that is smaller than a 1/64 inch cube. He even offered a $1,000 prize for 'the first guy' who did this. Feynman went on to suggest applications for extreme miniaturization such as tiny writing, the surgeon that you can swallow to effect repairs inside your body, and the ultimate chemical synthesizer that compiles molecules atom by atom. The miniature writing and electric motor challenge were both won, in 1986 and 1960 respectively. The other predictions are still taxing the minds of researchers, although there has been extensive speculation about the possibilities of ultra-miniaturization.

This speculation has been prompted by an influential book, *Engines of Creation* by K. Eric Drexler (1990; also available at <www.foresight.com>). This became a major source of ideas for future possibilities of nanotechnology. Drexler's work has been very influential, if highly controversial. His Foresight Institute brings together a range of scientific disciplines to promote the ideas of nanotechnology, in particular Drexler's vision for 'machine-phase nanotechnology' which would involve tiny robots revolutionizing manufacturing, transforming society and even solving the problem of global warming. (He has remarked that: 'Today most

Continued

people believe that global warming will be hard to correct – with nanotechnology, excess greenhouse gases could be inexpensively removed from the atmosphere' (Drexler 2001: 67).)

The problem here is that nanotechnology does not exist, or rather, does not exist in the form that the definition suggests. There is a huge amount of research taking place *trying* to construct nanotechnology devices, and there are a number of products that are consequences of research at the nanoscale (new coatings for glass, nano-particles that enhance cosmetics, improved hard drives in computers that exploit giant magnetoresistance (GMR) technology, to name just three); but the idea of miniature machines and devices that operate at the nanoscale, the visions of Feynman and Drexler, remains a matter for speculation and conjecture.

This means that we need to be careful in using the term 'nanotechnology', and it will often be prudent to use the word *nanoscale* to describe research taking place in formal science that attempts to manipulate and control matter on an atomic scale. What is uncontestable is that there is a significant public debate about what nanotechnology will mean for us.

Formal science, formal knowledge and nanotechnology

Formal science is a set of practices and a form of knowledge that emerges from the collective activity of people engaged in scientific research. Understanding the production of formal science can be an important step to making sense of science as a whole, since formal science is often the substrate upon which other representations of science work. Chapter 1 of this book suggested imagining science as a complex, multi-faceted object where each face had relevance and validity, but no one facet expressed all of science, and no one facet could be understood without investigating how it is connected to other sites and meanings of science.

Formal science is largely restricted to recognized institutional locations such as universities and commercial research and development facilities. Formal science activities produce formal scientific knowledge that is generally confined to quite specific locations. This means that representations of formal science are specific to scientific journals and academic text books.

We are faced with a number of significant problems when it comes to constructing an overview of formal science relating to nanotechnology. The first is a problem of definition. Although nanotechnology would appear to have a fairly specific definition (see box 8.1), this is contested, not in terms of what *range* of objects fall within the scope of nanotechnology research (most agree on the size and composition of these, i.e. on the 'nanoscale'), but rather in terms of which *discipline* is best suited to carrying out nanotechnology research. A recent survey by Joachim Schummer of formal science journals which published papers in nanoscale research identified the following principle disciplines publishing 'nano-title papers': physics, chemistry, biomedical sciences (including biomedical engineering, pharmacology, pharmacy), material sciences and engineering (including special materials like ceramics, polymers, etc.), mechanical engineering (including micromanufacturing), electrical engineering (including electronics, microelectronics, microsystems), chemical engineering (including process engineering), information and computer sciences, general technology, and other sciences (mostly earth sciences and environmental science) (Schummer 2004: 12, table 5). This plethora of disciplines and the rapidly expanding number of 'nano-publications' in formal science leads Schummer to speculate that, 'if measured by the number of "nano-title-papers", the current dynamics would, only in a few years, lead to the strange situation that almost the whole of science and engineering might be called nanoscale research' (Schummer 2004: 27). The range of disciplines and arguments over what actually constitutes nanoscale research (let alone nanotechnology) highlights an important issue in social studies of science: where are boundaries drawn, and who draws them?

So what should we consider to be typical examples of formal science nanoscale research? As social researchers, it is unlikely that we will be able to simply select specific journals, read the papers included, and draw conclusions about the status of nanoscale research. However, it is a good idea to look at some examples of this research in its original form, and a quick review of the two major international science journals that publish primary research – *Nature* and *Science* – provide a good range of examples every week (<www.nature.co.uk> and <www.science.com>). More discipline-specific journals, such as *Nanotechnology*, *The Journal of Physical Chemistry*, *The Journal of the American Chemical Society* and *Physics Today* all have a large number of papers oriented towards nanoscale research in every issue. You may experience problems in identifying which papers are actually nanoscale research papers, since titles are often so exact or so esoteric as to be somewhat misleading, and the language used in many papers is difficult to understand. However, it is worth persisting in looking at formal science journals, as this will provide a feel for the range, complexity, specificity and difficulty of this research. Your own survey will also reveal, among other things, just how much research is taking place, and thus how much financial investment is being put into this area of formal science.

Interrogating formal science papers:
Who funded the research?
Why was the research carried out – both the specific aim of a group of experiments and the purposes of the research in general?
Whose names are on the paper, where were they working, and what does this indicate about social organization of the production of this knowledge?
How is the paper written – how will an audience understand this?
What picture of science emerges from formal scientific papers?
Is the paper increasing public expectations of nanotechnology?

There are a number of other sources of formal science nanoscale research, but it is important to note that as we move away from the primary product of the research laboratory (i.e. the formal science paper in a refereed journal), the language of description will change, and it is probable that the representation of the research will alter in a way that begins to hide certain key features of the production of scientific knowledge. For example, university websites often provide accounts of the research taking place in their science laboratories. This can be a very useful resource for social researchers of science, although some caution must be taken as the websites may be providing overviews of ranges of experiments, and amalgamations of total outputs, rather than reflections of individual experiments.

Looking at websites, some questions to ask:
Who does the website address as its readers: prospective students, research funders, business partners, the general public?
What larger narratives are being employed here? For example, is nanoscale research described in terms of nanotechnology, or in more 'traditional' ways such as 'condensed matter physics'?
What visualizations (if any) are offered to explain the research? How are these presented?
Do these websites represent a version of what science and scientific endeavour is?

Similarly, popular science magazines at the 'hard' end of the scale (such as in the UK *New Scientist* (<www.newscientist.com>) and in the USA *Scientific American* (<www.sciam.com>)) provide good general articles about nanoscale research (probably in most current issues), including much material that helps to provide an understanding of the general principles behind this kind of research, but, just by the fact that they are meant to provide general overviews, they obscure details of the complexity, diversity and difficulty of the experiments that have led to the construction of theories of the nanoscale.

Questions to ask of popular science journals:

What wider narratives are being used here? Do stories about nanotechnology make connections to wider social or environmental issues?

Who is the audience? 'Lay people'? Professional scientists? Technology companies? Governments?

Does the text reflect how research is carried out in laboratories? Can you connect this level of description to the primary formal science descriptions of more specialist journals?

Do these journals question the role of scientific research into specific areas?

You will see that there is a continuum of representations of formal scientific knowledge that leads from the esoteric discourses of the community of scientists carrying out specific experiments through the discipline-specific scientific journal to the abstracting scientific journal and to the 'hard' general science magazine. We shouldn't stop here, as there are further connections working in this direction, from esoteric to exoteric. From the popular science journals and textbooks we can see the uptake and representation of nanoscale and nanotechnology ideas in the news media, popular science books, science fiction books; but also in government science policy, environmental pressure groups' activities and publications, and in the general social consciousness of what science is and what it is doing. Diverse esoteric thought communities are constructing discourses involving nanotechnology, just as a diversity of exoteric thought communities in different locations construct discourses of science. This is not a one-way street; the constructions of exoteric thought communities are significant in the formation of ideas in esoteric thought communities – and we'll return to this point soon.

Scientific communities and nanotechnology

Websites, textbooks and popular science articles provide good general information on nanotechnology, abstracting and amalgamating information produced in primary sources such as specialist science journal papers. However, these sources tend systematically to obscure some key features of the production of scientific knowledge, most notably the context within which much of this work is done. The working processes and, particularly, the working conditions of those producing scientific knowledge rarely feature in popular or formal science representations.

It is significant that the vast majority of those working in UK science laboratories are employed on short-term temporary contracts and are offered little or no career progression, and women workers face significant gender discrimination (Erickson 2002). This is despite their being the most highly educated and qualified people in the UK labour force. This situation is replicated in the United States, where women and most minorities, as groups, have lower levels of participation, position and recognition than do white men (Long and Fox 1995).

Understanding of the social aspects of the production of scientific knowledge is best accessed through interaction with scientific workers. It is very useful to visit a number of sites of production of scientific knowledge to get a feel for working conditions, and also to hear first-hand accounts of how scientific knowledge is produced. The conditions of knowledge production vary greatly across scientific institutions, and even between adjoining research teams in the same institution. Getting involved in discussions with scientists about how they do their work is, apart from anything else, a good way of identifying connections between different thought communities. This may not be straightforward as, increasingly, science facilities are much concerned with security, although access is far from impossible. A good starting point is your nearest university: make some contact with those involved in formal science teaching, learning and research, and ask them about their work. From that starting point you may be able to visit laboratories and research facilities, and get opportunities for asking more questions. There are two broad strands of questions to ask scientific workers: about the content of their work as scientists and about their employment.

Questions about employment:
Make sure you include standard interpretive sociology of work questions such as length of service, grade, tasks. Collect demographic data (age, gender, qualifications, etc.)
Are you a member of a trade union? Why / why not?
How much autonomy do you have in terms of everyday work?
How do you get on with your supervisors?
Do you enjoy your work?

Why did you choose this work?
What will you be doing in five years?

Questions about the content of work:
Why is this work being done? Why is it important?
Who funds it?
What will happen to the results of your work?
How do you explain your job to other people, people who don't know
 what you do?
What is nanotechnology, nanoscale research and science? How are these
 things connected?

What you should look for:
Think about how people explain their work to you: What images and
 metaphors do they use to clarify points? Why did they choose these?
 And where did they get them from?
Is there a connection between the discourse of your respondents and
 wider social discourses on science? Do people explain their work
 by reference to a wider social project, e.g. do nanotechnologists
 tell you they are involved in 'the war on hunger', or do they consider
 themselves to be part of the defence industry? Information about
 this allows you to investigate further the structure of science funding,
 or to analyse scientists' motives. It also allows you to make connections to the public representations of nanotechnology and to
 consider whether these are having some impact on an esoteric thought
 community.

Similarly, although questions such as 'What is nanotechnology?'
may look trite, they can be very useful. Asking those directly involved
in the production of knowledge about nanotechnology what they
think may provide you with insight into how people are involved
in science research activities and also involved in promoting those
activities as something else, or as something that holds out promise
for us.

Popular culture and nanotechnology

Science is represented to us in many locations, and through many different media. Formal science represents the products of its endeavours in ways that serve to construct a picture of what the project of
science is. Academic debates and texts (including this one) contribute
to producing a range of images and meanings of what science is.

Popular science texts and TV documentaries represent factual accounts of scientific activity, and science fiction assimilates trends and tendencies in contemporary formal science to promote a picture of science that becomes embedded in our culture, amalgamating with other forms of representation. These are legion, including everyday household technologies, industrial organization strategies such as scientific management, interactions with computers and emerging artificial intelligences, medicines and cosmetic products. All around us are signs, embodiments and representations of science, reminders that we are living in a technoscientific society.

These aspects of science are not just external to us: they are internalized in a number of ways. We internalize science as a concept that has a range of socially constructed meanings. We use the word 'science' to describe the technical and technological aspects of contemporary society, as well as to describe a firmly defined set of people (scientists), practices (doing science) and knowledge (scientific knowledge). This internalized conception represents science to us as an essential object – something with an identifiable core that is separate from us, scientific knowledge as a form of knowledge that is essentially different, bounded and more exact, and scientists as essentially different from non-scientists. This widely shared construction of science has been termed an 'ideology' by many commentators, and this ideology has been named 'scientism'. It infuses our understanding of the world, infuses representations in culture, and infuses the stories we tell ourselves and each other about science. The social construction of science through these processes becomes the critical focus for this form of research.

When we look at nanoscale research and nanotechnology, we find a large range of popular culture representations of the nanoscale, both factual and fictional, and it is also possible to find a well-established public debate concerning nanotechnology and its implications for society. The next sections investigate the connections between formal scientific discourses of nanotechnology and these popular representations.

Science fiction and nanotechnology

Science fiction has had an interest in the very small for a long time. For example, Isaac Asimov's classic novel *Fantastic Voyage* (1966) described how scientists were shrunk to microscopic size and injected into the bloodstream of a human being. Asimov even returned to this theme in 1987 with *The Fantastic Voyage II: Destination Brain*. However, it is in the 1990s, when there was a large amount of popular science reporting of the possibilities of nanotechnology, that we find the emergence of science fiction texts that use nanotechnology as an active component of their narrative.

Science fiction accounts of nanotechnology rarely use that word, preferring to come up with specific terminology such as 'matter compilers', 'neural nanonics' or 'medichines', and it may be that authors want to stress their texts' future orientation by avoiding the obvious term. In all science fiction texts, be they cyberpunk, space opera or hard science fiction, a common attitude towards nanotechnology emerges: that nanotechnology is inevitable, that it will be hugely powerful, and that it will transform our lives. It is worth remembering that science fiction mediates the concerns of the present much more than it predicts the future, and the themes and representations of nanotechnology in contemporary sci-fi are closely related to those appearing in contemporary popular science.

Take, for example, the idea of being able to produce objects using nanoscale manufacturing processes – building up almost any object using basic raw materials. Here is an account of just such a machine – a 'matter compiler' (M.C.) – from Neal Stephenson's *The Diamond Age*: in this example the very young heroine Nell is introduced to the possibilities of nano-manufacturing.

Nell had grown too old for her crib mattress, and so Harv, her big brother, said he would help get a new one. . . . Nell followed him into the kitchen, which housed several important boxy entities with prominent doors. . . .

One of the boxes was called the M.C. It was built into the wall over the counter. Nell dragged a chair and climbed up to watch as Harv worked at it. The front of the M.C. was a mediatron, which meant something that had pictures moving around on it, or sound coming out of it, or both. As Harv poked it with his fingers and spoke to it, little moving pictures danced around. It reminded her of the ractives she played on the big mediatron in the living room, when it wasn't being used by someone bigger. . . .

Harv gave an especially dramatic poke, and then a new mediaglyph came up, a white circle with a narrow green wedge at the top. The wedge got wider and wider. The M.C. played a little tune that meant you were supposed to wait. . . . [Harv] looked at the M.C. disdainfully. 'This one takes so long, it's ridiculous,' he said.

'Why?'

'Cause we got a cheap Feed, just a few grams per second. Pathetic.'

'Why we got a cheap Feed?'

'Because it's a cheap house.' . . .

[F]inally the music came to a bouncy conclusion just as the white wedge vanished.

'It's done!' she said.

Harv paused his ractive, swaggered into the kitchen, and poked a mediaglyph that was an animated picture of a door swinging open. The M.C. took to hissing loudly. Harv watched her scared face and ruffled her hair; she could not fend him off because she had her hands over her ears. 'Got to release the vacuum,' he explained.

The sound ended, and the door popped open. Inside the M.C., folded up neatly, was Nell's new mattress. (Stephenson, Neil, *The Diamond Age*, London, Penguin, 1995: 43–5)

Stephenson's description of the M.C. contains some details, but is vague in places. But it is not unlike the following:

The breadbox assembler is a relatively small (breadbox size) device containing thousands of assemblers, replicators, and nanocomputers. The nanocomputers carry instructions for the manufacture of a host of common household products, such as pots and pans, hairbrushes and mirrors, gloves and underwear, and tennis rackets and baseballs. About the only limitation on the kinds of objects for which the nanocomputer can be programmed is the size of the box in which they are made. To make larger objects, such as a bookcase, one would need to build a larger breadbox assembler. To operate the breadbox assembler, a supply of raw materials is introduced into the box. The raw materials consist of common, readily available, inexpensive substances, such as sand and coal dust. The operator selects the object to be manufactured from a list of those that can be produced. Molecular devices inside the breadbox assembler then begin their work of assembling the desired product by following the instructions stored in the nanocomputer. After some period of time, assembly is complete, and the final product is ejected from the machine.

This list of instructions is not from a science fiction text but from a current popular science book on nanotechnology (Newton 2002: 25–6), i.e. science 'fact'. Although Newton does at times mention (very briefly) that nanotechnological devices of this sort do not exist as yet, he strongly implies that it is only a matter of time before there is one of these on our desktop. And indeed it is the desktop where science fiction writer Peter F. Hamilton places his nanotechnology, in the form of molecular synthesizers that will produce the drug of your choice in a matter of seconds (Hamilton 2002).

Science fiction texts and movies that use nanotechnology as a plot device are commonplace. The science fiction section of a good bookshop will have copies of classic texts such as Michael Crichton's *Prey*

(2002) and Stephenson's *The Diamond Age*. It is worth looking through other contemporary sci-fi novels, particularly British hard sci-fi: many of these are using nanotech and nanoscale themes. In addition, other sci-fi media, such as comic books and TV programmes are also fruitful sources of representations of nanotechnology. A fairly standard cultural studies approach to texts will help reveal key aspects of how texts are involved in constructions of meaning surrounding nanotechnology and science. This involves seeing texts as containing two related instances: the production of meaning by authors and the production of meaning by audiences. Analysis involves making connections between these two instances and placing this in wider context. See chapter 7 of Ann Gray's *Research Practice for Cultural Studies* (2003) for an excellent overview of the use of texts in social research.

Questioning sci-fi:
Production of meaning:
What objects and devices are being predicted?
Do they connect to current research?
What image of science and of technology is emerging?

Audiences' readings:
Who are the imagined audiences for this material, and what knowledge do audiences supply to understand the text?
What picture of science and technology is constructed?

Wider context:
Is sci-fi responding to science fact, or vice versa?
Does sci-fi contribute to the 'promotion' of nanotechnology?
Is the language used to describe nanotechnology similar to or different from that used in other places and genres?

Popular science and nanotechnology

The quotation from Newton above shows that science fiction and popular science narratives can take similar forms, suggesting that connections exist. Newton's book is not an isolated example. The original source-book for many of the current research themes of nanotechnology, Drexler's *Engines of Creation*, is full of such descriptions, and his more recent work has included a number of 'pictures' of the devices he is describing, such as differential gears and nanobots (Drexler's web site, <www.foresight.org>, includes many of these graphical representations). These objects and machines do not exist, and even strong supporters of nanoscale research will point out the 'impossibility' of such objects and devices. Most notable is the dispute between Richard Smalley, the 1996 Nobel laureate, who doubts the possibility of creating nanoscale machines due to the immutable character of the laws of physics, and Eric Drexler, who still maintains that such devices will be produced in the near future (for further details see the debate in the 'nanotechnology' special issue of *Scientific American* (September 2001), the <www.sciam.com> website and Smalley's site at <cnst.rice.edu/reshome.html>). Yet popular science accounts and even undergraduate textbooks persist in producing such representations of future possibilities. In this example, from a current physics textbook, look at the use of present-tense and positive, certain future-tense statements:

> Using nanosystems, better and cheaper products *can be made* than using conventional systems. In the future *we can expect* computer controlled molecular machines much smaller than a speck of dust that have the accuracy and precision of today's target drug molecules. In nanomedicine, *these will* perform controlled surgery at the cellular and molecular level. (Wilson et al. 2002: p. xiv, my emphasis)

Who is the imagined reader of this text? The authors appear to be speaking to undergraduate students, and are making a strong attempt at enthusing young scientists. The future is certain, is bright, and will involve nanotechnology. They take this theme of presenting a strong case for studying nanotechnology much further:

> During revolutions, wealth is made by pioneers. Knowledge of the old science is not important. Think of the sales opportunities for the people who had the first arrowheads, think of horses and carts, candles and electric lights . . . Think of Ford, Gates, Nobel and those two rich cave people Mrs Fire and Mr Wheel. A lot of people are already making plenty of money out of genetic engineering and gene therapy. So what else is coming?
>
> The answer is nanotechnology. What is nanotechnology and why *will it* make a lot of money? Why *is it* more important than all previous scientific advances? Nanotechnology is an anticipated manufacturing technology that allows thorough, inexpensive control of the structure of matter by working with atoms. It *will allow* many things to be manufactured at low cost and with no pollution. It *will lead* to the production of nanomachines, which are sometimes also called nanodevices. *It is* therefore an advance as important as the discovery of the first tool. However, rather than shape what nature offers, we can do it ourselves. Unlike metallurgy, natural substances are not used as the starting materials, but atoms – the ingredients of the universe.

Has this all started? Indeed it has. (Wilson et al. 2002: 3, my emphasis to highlight the use of the positive future tense and present tense)

What will nanotechnology do? The authors identify two things, and make connections to two wider social discourses. The first is money, and readers will identify this reason for being involved in nanotechnology fairly easily. The second is saving the environment, a common theme in public discourse. There are a number of further questions we could ask here. What does science do? Science transforms nature, and nanotechnology goes even further than 'old science' – it can act as nature does. What is science? Science is a set of tools and a project that is external to you, but to which you can get access.

From popular science discourse, science fiction narratives and university level textbooks a common story about nanotechnology emerges. Nanotechnology is coming (or is already here), it will do amazing things and transform our lives and society, and this is inevitable. This narrative is taken up by governments and funding agencies, but also by environmental pressure groups concerned about a new technology.

Questioning popular science texts:
Although the content of popular science texts is different from science fiction, the questions we want to ask are the same: What meanings are constructed by authors? How do audiences read these texts? What are the wider implications of this?

Political discourse and nanotechnology

Given the level of hype surrounding nanotechnology, but also the potential for applications which could be of great strategic and economic importance, it is not surprising that governments around the world are investing very heavily in nanoscale research. In the US alone about $4 billion per annum is spent on nanotechnology research and development, with $849 million being provided by a range of US government agencies (2004 figures). The increase in funding for nanoscale research in recent years has been dramatic: US government nanotechnology funding was 'only' $495 million in 2001 (source: *Aviation Week and Space Technology*, 4 September 2000, p. 89), so has almost doubled in three years.

The rationale behind funding nanotechnology-oriented research is complex, but the prime reason given is that of technology transfer: 'nanotechnology has the potential to profoundly change our economy and to improve our standard of living, in a manner not unlike the impact made by advances over the past two decades by information technology' (US National Nanotechnology Initiative, <www.nano.gov>). We can therefore see the funding decisions as a form of investment, or even as a form of betting. The possibilities for nanotechnology are still very much subject to debate, although there have been a number of technology transfers already (most notably the production of nano-layer insulating films on glass). However, the possibilities that are presented by the scientific community involved in nanoscale research are often highly plausible, possibly achievable, and attractive to a range of investors, not just governments. The facet of science we see here is its economic and strategic role.

Some questions to ask:
What reasons are given for funding nanotechnology?
Which agencies are responsible for funding, and how do they disseminate knowledge?
What nanoscale research is receiving funding?
What connections between commercial and government funding programmes are visible?
What relationships can you identify between the public discourses representing nanotechnology and the funding nanoscale research receives?
Are scientific institutions and scientific research represented as being independent from or connected to government?

Not all public representations of nanotechnology are positive. Classifying public discourses on nanotechnology, Christopher Toumey identifies four main groupings arranged on a continuum from extreme nanophilic hyperbole (exemplified by Drexler's *Engines of Creation*), through childish enthusiasm (Toumey offers the US National Nanotechnology Initiative as an example) to measured scepticism and finally 'extreme nanophobic counter-hyperbole' (Toumey 2005). In the public arena some of the latter voices are represented by organizations such as Greenpeace (<www.greenpeace.org>) and the ETC Group (Action Group on Erosion, Technology and Concentration, <etcgroup.org>) (see illustration 8.1). The UK Green Party MEP, Caroline Lucas, has called for regulation of nanotechnology research, although this kind of meaningless statement may not help her cause: 'The commercial value of nanotech stems from the simple fact that the laws of physics don't apply at the molecular level'

Illustration 8.1.   ETC Group. © Reymond Pagé.

(Caroline Lucas, 'We must not be blinded by science', the *Guardian*, 12 June 2003). Recently, the UK heir to the throne, Prince Charles, presented a speech warning of the dangers of nanotechnology, in particular the danger that self-replicating nano-machines may escape and destroy everything they encounter, the so-called 'grey goo' scenario (Tim Radford, 'Brave new world or menace. Why Prince Charles fears grey goo,' the *Guardian*, 29 April 2003). Ironically, it was Drexler himself, the arch-proponent of nanotechnology, who first predicted the possibilities of 'grey goo':

> Dangerous replicators could easily be too tough, small, and rapidly spreading to stop – at least if we made no preparation. We have trouble enough controlling viruses and fruit flies. Among the cognoscenti of nanotechnology, this threat has become known as the 'gray goo problem'. Though masses of uncontrolled replicators need not be gray or gooey, the term 'gray goo' emphasizes that replicators able to obliterate life might be less inspiring than a single species of crabgrass. They might be 'superior' in an evolutionary sense, but this need not make them valuable. We have evolved to love a world rich in living things,

ideas, and diversity, so there is no reason to value gray goo merely because it could spread. Indeed, if we prevent it we will thereby prove *our* evolutionary superiority. The gray goo threat makes one thing perfectly clear: we cannot afford certain kinds of accidents with replicating assemblers. (Drexler 1990: 172–3)

It is worth pointing out again that there are no such things as self-replicating nano-assemblers, and the possibility that there will ever be such devices is still a matter of conjecture.

Voices critical of nanotechnology provide a useful resource to illuminate aspects of the public understanding of science and, in particular, how contentious science issues are dealt with. Opposition to nanotechnology often takes the form of characterization of scientists as irresponsible and unaccountable; the risks of nanotechnology are portrayed as far outweighing any possible benefits; and the only correct public response to nanotechnology, from this perspective, is seen as being a complete moratorium on research. As Toumey notes, these extreme reactions to nanotechnology are, in form, no different from those offered by similar pressure groups to GM and also to recombinant DNA technology in the 1970s (Toumey 2005).

Questions to ask of environmental campaigns concerned about nanotechnology:

Is the object of concern nanotechnology, the institutions of science, or big business and its use of scientific knowledge?

Which sources of information are used?

How do these sources achieve legitimacy?

What are the aims of the campaign? Are they specific to nanoscale research or wider, asking for changes to science in general?

What picture of science emerges from these resources?

This climate of fear and distrust of nanotechnology and, by extension, science is significant for social investigators of science for at least two reasons. First, it suggests that public understanding of science could be improved, or at the very least that scientists need to improve their communication with the public. This strand of critique is taken by rationalists. Too often the public meet scientists, through the mass media, at times of crisis, when facts are scarce and emotions are running high. Gregory and Miller (1998) suggest that what is needed is more mutual respect, more clarity and a recognition of the need for public participation. They also note that it would be helpful for scientists to begin to recognize the importance of the social in science, and that the questioning of science by outsiders does not equate to being 'anti-science'; indeed, scientists themselves should be part of this process (p. 248).

Secondly, the dominant picture of science that we are presented with confuses and distorts our understanding of science, where it is located and what it does. We need to move to an understanding of science that is more useful, and better represents what science means to us.

The two-way street

The central argument of this book is that the social construction of science is a two-way street. Scientists produce scientific knowledge through a process of social construction, and the rest of society is involved in constructing science. There is not simply a one-way flow of ideas, from formal science to the general public. Not recognizing this is to validate the dominant model of science in society, where 'pure' scientific knowledge that embodies the 'truth' gradually leeches out of the scientific institutions into our society and is watered down as it emerges into the public sphere. This model is inaccurate for a number of reasons, not least of which is the point made by science and technology studies (STS) that scientists are members of communities that set standards for inquiry and evaluate their own knowledge claims. 'Thus ideology and values of many different types are important components of research' (Sismondo 2004: 10). An alternative conception of science starts by recognizing that the social construction of science is a widespread phenomenon. It is not sufficient to note that scientific knowledge is being socially constructed in formal science settings; indeed, if this is all we do, we may reinforce the essentialist idea of science.

We need to start with seeing science as something that is being socially constructed in a great many places by a great many people, not just scientists, and that this phenomenon will have consequences for how formal science is enacted and what formal scientific knowledge is produced. To this starting point we need to add the insights of Ludwik Fleck, particularly his conception of esoteric and exoteric thought communities. We can then begin to see how the public social construction of science that takes place in diverse exoteric thought communities can have effects in esoteric thought communities.

Nanotechnology illustrates this well. At a societal level we hear a number of competing voices that are creating representations of nanotechnology – positive, negative, sceptical, speculative. These emerge from, amongst other things, public discussion of the benefits or otherwise of nanotechnology, science fiction and popular science accounts of the 'inevitability' of the development of nanotechnology, and the generation of technoscientific cultures in which science and technology become fused together. The result is a public culture in which nanotechnology is being placed on the agenda and the public wait with anticipation for products to emerge. If we work backwards from the societal level, we can see a similar process of the dissemination of ideas. We've already noted the construction of an 'inevitability' at a societal level, but this is replicated as we move back from the exoteric towards the esoteric.

From external to internal, exoteric to esoteric

The matter compiler of Stephenson's science fiction may be a flight of fancy, but the idea of the 'breadbox assembler' from Drexler's *Engines of Creation* has taken on a life of its own:

> The availability of a breadbox assembler in every person's home would have profound, perhaps unimaginable, consequences for human civilization. For the cost of the breadbox assembler itself and the raw material needed for its operation, any individual or family could manufacture most of the objects they would need for a safe, healthy, reasonably prosperous life. The most basic human needs – food, for example – could be met by anyone in the world at the minimal cost. Under such circumstances, the state of poverty might disappear or be dramatically altered. (Newton 2002: 25–6)

From a cultural perspective, this use of language to describe an imaginary, but anticipated, technology is of great interest. The object being posited must be around $0.25 \times 0.25 \times 0.5$ metres, neither particularly larger nor particularly small. But why pick 'breadbox' as an analogy? Breadboxes are cheap, universally available (at least in most Western industrial households), and they feed us. They're not luxuries that are just for leisure purposes. They are also generic objects, relatively unsullied by contemporary consumerism and branding. Further, the word 'breadbox' is closely related to 'breadbasket', and we recognize not just the personal importance of bread, baskets and boxes, but also the strategic and geopolitical role of breadbaskets in our history. Popular descriptions of historic or contemporary international conflicts often make reference to the 'breadbasket' region of a state or continent, the place where the food for a large number of people has its origins, and thus an object of immense strategic value. Describing an imaginary object as a breadbox, with the connotations noted, displays connections to concerns much wider than simply the technicalities of how such an object would be produced. At this point we should note that many advocates of nanotechnology, like advocates of GM crops, offer visions of a future where nanotechnology has solved many human social problems, hunger and poverty often being high on the list. To put this in perspective, think what difference it would make if, instead of describing a 'breadbox assembler', we describe an 'Apple assembler' or a 'Sony matter compiler'? Instead of comparing the nanotechnology assembler to a real breadbox, compare it to a computer, TV, DVD player or playstation (which may be a much more likely outcome of their development, assuming it could be made). Attitudes toward the object change according to the description we use.

Nano-assemblers are still just wishful thinking and may never actually exist. However, a culturally oriented analysis of science would argue that the vocabularies of nanotechnology are not innocent, but are part of its social construction and are also part of its contestation. Think back to the idea of 'grey goo': there is no reason why this imagined scenario should be 'grey' or even 'gooey', yet the use of this vocabulary works well in providing a scary image. It reminds us of 'grey matter', a colloquial term for brain cells, and connects to the incipient threat of artificial intelligences replacing human intelligences.

Much of the discourse that is generated inside the esoteric communities involved in nanoscale research is not confined to discussions of formal science; nor should it be. These communities are also involved in bids for further funding and in justifying their current funding. They construct research grant proposals and convince politicians that the continued funding of scientific research is worth undertaking. But the members of these esoteric thought communities are also members of exoteric thought communities: families and households, political groups, local communities, and so on. As well as forming discourses for the continued funding of research, scientists are also involved in expressing strong ethical and moral ideas about what their work involves and what their results should be used for. They are not simply responding to agendas set externally, but are actively negotiating their way through a whole series of considerations that impact on what experiments they do, and how they carry them out. The ideas and attitudes of such exoteric communities are incorporated into the understandings and meanings that scientists attach to their everyday work, in the same way that their work experiences have an impact on their non-work lives. We can thus make a clear line of connection from technoscientific culture to the institutions of formal science.

Making sense of science

This account, the story of science presented in this book, begins to introduce the complexity and extent of science in our technoscientific society. The story suggests that 'science' is a family-resemblance concept that takes on a range of meanings in different locations, but that in general meanings surrounding science coalesce around a collectively held understanding of science that we can call scientism. Different pictures of science emerge in different places, and identifying these pictures and places is an important task for the social understanding of science and its role in contemporary society. As we do this, it becomes clear that the pictures, although different, are all interconnected. It also becomes clear that at the heart of science, at the heart of what we think of as science, there is no essence. Different pictures of science exist interdependently, but this interdependence is contingent rather than absolute.

Locating science in a small number of places – laboratories, popular science, science fiction, social science – is a starting point, but by no means an end-point. Science is increasingly significant in all aspects of our society and culture. It infiltrates our selves and our ways of being. Given the level of institutional investment in science, both financially and ideologically, this state of affairs is very likely to continue and to increase. Similarly, given the level of personal investment that members of society have in science and technology, it is unlikely that science will dissipate and reduce in significance. Science will continue to penetrate further and further into our bodies and our minds, and the scientific will take on greater significance in global competitions for economic and military power. Yet this will not be a simple and straightforward process. Apart from the obvious point that nation-states and multinational corporations will compete against each other and will attempt to control and dominate the production of crucial scientific knowledge, there is the problem of a widespread public ambivalence towards science.

This ambivalence can be identified in almost all public representations of science in contemporary society. For example, the L'Oréal advertisement for shampoo on the part III title-page uses the tag line 'The progress of science shines through your hair'. On the one hand, it could be seen as simply a reinforcement of the dominant 'progressive' image of science, where science delivers greater and greater benefits for us all. On the other hand, the advertisement implies that using science and scientific research to improve shampoos is appropriate, though some would see it as inappropriate, even wasteful. In addition, a number of environmental campaign groups argue that the cosmetics industry in general is a contributor to environmental pollution and degradation, and a range of health problems. Cosmetics companies are increasingly advertising the use of nanotechnology in their products, which has prompted some environmentalists to call for a moratorium until health risks have been fully evaluated. This highlights how science, even in the domestic sphere, becomes significant in everyday life, but is also contested at the level of effect and even definition.

What we can identify here is that individuals may be members of thought communities that have little to do with formal science, but that these thought communities become colonized by a story of science, 'scientized', that promotes an essentialist conception of science, scientific knowledge and scientists. As this happens, the consequences for public understanding of science as a whole are significant. On the one hand, public expectations for science become extended (into new areas) and heightened (promise upon promise on behalf of science is made). On the other hand, members of these exoteric thought communities are presented with an increasing number of scientific 'failures', where the promise of scientific progress is unfulfilled, or, worse still, the deployment of science in places from which science has previously been seen to be excluded results in significant negative consequences for a large number of people. What is occurring is a cycle of public expectation and public disappointment leading to a state of public ambivalence and sometimes outright hostility towards science. There is a continual recirculation of the standard account of science and the entry of science into ever more areas of life. This constructs expectations for the future which are often unrealistic, unachievable, or lead to unintended negative consequences. Ironically, this process reinforces the standard account of science, or at least the aspects of that account that see science as being remote, isolated and impenetrable.

Towards the future

The problem here lies not with the production of formal scientific knowledge, although the often poor levels of public communication that professional scientists allow to emanate from scientific institutions should be noted. The problem lies in the contestable nature of the concept of science, and the denial of this contestability by the dominant culture of scientism. We are presented with a unified and essential understanding of science, yet even a cursory glance inside scientific institutions shows this to be an inaccurate image. We are further presented with a construction of scientists as a unified and separate community, which is, in some way, external to the rest of society, again quite misleading. This picture of science as unified, superior and separate is inappropriate and inaccurate. Public understanding of science rests upon these constructions, but because they constitute an inaccurate picture, the result is a distorted and ambivalent public understanding of science. The essentialist account of science reinforces the esoteric aspects of what science is at the expense of the exoteric. This manifests itself in a number of ways.

At a very general level, this can be seen in the hierarchical model of scientific knowledge, which perceives scientific knowledge and modes of explanation as being superior to other forms. The systematic exclusion of non-scientific methods from formal procedures for making sense of the world can be, and is, challenged. The institutions of formal science can also be challenged and opened up. Centralized funding of science is not necessarily the best way of paying for scientific research: the wider public could have much more input, perhaps even at a local level, into what science is being done, where, for what reason and by whom.

However, still at a general level, the direction and scope of the project of science needs to be challenged. Feminist epistemology and environmental campaigners have begun to do this, although much more action is needed here, since science and the vested interests that surround it are intensely conservative and resistant to change. By adopting an anti-essentialist model, it is possible to see that thought communities external to science have a significant input into what science is done, and why it is done. This recognition provides a starting point for a radical reappraisal of what science is for. It should not be the case that only a small range of thought communities external to science (generally elite groupings) have some input; why not all thought communities that want to?

The debate here is not about the value of science *per se*: few would argue that science is a 'bad thing'. Rather, we need inclusive debates around how science is being applied, who is doing it, in whose interests it is taking place, and what the outcomes of scientific activity are. The current public debates in the UK about GM crops provide a good example of an inappropriate mode of operation for science in contemporary society. Debates about the effectiveness of specific genetic modifications often come to the fore in public discussions of GM – does one modification lead to higher crop yields, and does it have wider environmental effects? But the wider public debate does not focus on such issues: here we see publics scared of what 'science' is doing, sceptical of the claims of science as a whole, and disbelieving that the esoteric science from which they are excluded can have positive impacts on their personal lives. Thought communities collide in such debates: formal science thought communities generate knowledge which is contested and contestable. This knowledge is translated into the understanding of a project of science by a number of competing thought communities – notably those of government and environmental pressure groups – and such understandings translate the knowledge according to their own contexts, interests and knowledge. These thought communities generate understandings of, at one level, GM foods, and subsequently at another, 'science', that are at odds with each other. These descriptions enter other thought communities – the lay public, the farming community, the press, the media, etc. (and these communities of course overlap one another) – and produce more understandings and pictures of GM foods and of science itself. Promoting a dominant picture of science as the province of experts, bounded by institutional barriers that are difficult to cross, leaves the wider public in a situation where knowledge of GM foods is hard to appraise: it is taken out of context by multinational corporations and governments following agendas set by financial imperatives, and, on the other hand, is deployed by campaign groups for specific purposes. Such co-option of knowledge makes public debate difficult. Different starting points provide different imperatives for a community, and provide different understandings of what science is and what it needs to be. Yet the image that receives most validation in public debates is one that excludes these other starting points. As an aside, it will be interesting to watch the development of public debates about nanotechnology to see if they follow a pattern similar to that of the GM debates in the UK.

Public debates that don't start from the position that science is external to us, that scientific knowledge is always superior, and that professional scientists present neutral perspectives, would allow a wider range of voices to be heard, and would also allow all participants to see much more clearly where forces external to science, most notably those of business and the state, are impelling science and scientists towards particular projects and particular outcomes. Such debates might also, one hopes, be more acceptable to the general public, in that people might be able to see that the voices emanating from their communities could be heard and may even make a difference.

The realization that scientific knowledge is produced socially, and that there is a connection between the world external to the science lab and the knowledge that emerges from within it was a huge breakthrough for social science. Sociologists, in particular, saw that to understand science it was necessary to understand society, and the relationship between science and society. However, this is only half of the story. We live with science: science surrounds us, invades our lives, and alters our perspective on the world. We see things from a scientific perspective, in that we use science to help us make sense of the world – regardless of whether or not that is an appropriate thing to do – and to legitimize the picture of the world that results from such investigations. Our lives are dependent on technological devices that have emerged, in part, as a result of scientific endeavour. Every day sees yet more aspects of everyday life being scientized, be it the food we eat, the work regimes that order our labour, or the medicines we take to promote health. While it is important to understand the social aspects of science, the reverse may be even more important: that to understand society and culture, we need to understand science.

Further reading

Scientific American dedicated its September 2001 issue to an examination of emerging trends in nanotechnology, and this provides a good, if detailed, overview of principles and issues. A number of these articles were reprinted in: Editors of Scientific American (eds) 2002: *Understanding Nanotechnology* New York: Warner Books.

References

Agassi, J. 1971: *Faraday as a Natural Philosopher*. Chicago: University of Chicago Press.

Aronowitz, S. and DiFazio, W. 1994: *The Jobless Future: Sci-Tech and the Dogma of Work*. Minneapolis: University of Minnesota Press.

Aronowitz, S., Martinsons, B. and Menser, M. (eds) 1996: *Technoscience and Cyberculture*. London: Routledge.

Asimov, I. 1979a: *Foundation and Empire*. South Yarmouth, Mass.: J. Curley.

Asimov, I. 1979b: *Second Foundation*. South Yarmouth, Mass.: J. Curley.

Asimov, I. 1982: *Foundation's Edge*. Garden City, NY: Doubleday.

Asimov, I. 1983a: *Foundation*. New York: Ballantine Books.

Asimov, I. 1983b: *The Robots of Dawn*. Garden City, NY: Doubleday.

Asimov, I. 1985: *Robots and Empire*. Garden City, NY: Doubleday.

Asimov, I. 1986: *Foundation and Earth*. Garden City, NY: Doubleday.

Asimov, I. 1987: *Fantastic Voyage II: Destination Brain*. New York: Doubleday.

Asimov, I. 1988: *Prelude to Foundation*. London: Grafton Books.

Asimov, I. 1989: *Asimov's Chronology of Science and Discovery*. New York: Harper & Row.

Asimov, I. 1993: *Forward the Foundation*. New York: Doubleday.

Asimov, I., Kleiner, H. and Klement, O. 1966: *Fantastic Voyage*. London: Dobson; Boston: Houghton Mifflin.

Atwood, M. 2003: *Oryx and Crake*. London: Bloomsbury.

Ayer, A. J. 1971: *Language, Truth and Logic*. Harmondsworth: Penguin.

Baldamus, W. 1977: Ludwig Fleck and the development of the sociology of science. In: P. R. Gleichmann, J. Goudsblom and H. Korte (eds), *Human Figurations: Essays for Norbert Elias*, Amsterdam: Stichting Amsterdams Sociologisch Tijdschrift, 135–56.

Banks, I. M. 1987: *Consider Phlebas*. London: Orbit.

Banks, I. M. 1988: *The Player of Games*. London: Orbit.

Banks, I. M. 1990: *Use of Weapons*. London: Orbit.

Banks, I. M. 1991: *The State of the Art*. London: Orbit.

Banks, I. M. 1996: *Excession*. London: Orbit.

Banks, I. M. 1998: *Inversions*. London: Orbit.

Banks, I. M. 2000: *Look to Windward*. London: Orbit.

Barber, B. and Hirsch, W. (eds) 1962: *The Sociology of Science*. New York: The Free Press of Glencoe.

Barker, M. and Brook, K. 1998: *Knowing Audiences: Judge Dredd, its Friends, Fans and Foes*. Luton: University of Luton Press.

Barnes, B. 1982: *T. S. Kuhn and Social Science*. London: Macmillan.

Barnes, B. and Bloor, D. 1982: Relativism, rationalism and the sociology of knowledge. In M. Hollis and S. Lukes (eds), *Rationality and Relativism*, Oxford: Blackwell, 21–47.

Barthes, R. 1993: *Mythologies*. London: Vintage.

Baxter, S. 1998: *Moonseed*. London: Voyager.

Baxter, S. 2000a: *Space*. London: Voyager.

Baxter, S. 2000b: *Time*. London: Voyager.

Baxter, S. 2001: *Origin*. London: Voyager.

Baxter, S. 2002: *Deep Future*. London: Victor Gollancz.

Beck, S. 2002: Natural selection. The *Observer*, Sunday, 2 June 2002.

Bennett, J., Donahue, M., Schneider, N. and Voit, M. 1999: *The Cosmic Perspective*. Menlo Park, Calif.: Addison-Wesley.

Berger, P. and Luckmann, T. 1967: *The Social Construction of Reality: A Treatise in the Sociology of Knowledge*. Harmondsworth: Penguin.

Bradley, H., Erickson, M., Stephenson, C. and Williams, S. 2000: *Myths at Work*. Cambridge: Polity.

Bragg, M. 1998: *On Giants' Shoulders: Great Scientists and their Discoveries from Archimedes to DNA*. London: Hodder & Stoughton.

Brandsen, B. H. and Joachain, C. J. 2000: *Quantum Mechanics*, 2nd edn. London: Prentice-Hall.

Bukatman, S. 1993: *Terminal Identity: The Virtual Subject in Post-modern Science Fiction*. Chapel Hill, NC, and London: Duke University Press.

Callon, M. 1987: Society in the making: the study of technology as a tool for sociological analysis. In W. E. Bijker, T. P. Hughes and T. J. Pinch (eds), *The Social Construction of Technical Systems: New Directions in the Sociology and History of Technology*. Cambridge, Mass.: MIT Press, 83–103.

Cartmell, D., Hunter, I. Q., Kaye, H. and Whelehan, I. (eds) 1999: *Alien Identities: Exploring Difference in Film and Fiction*. London: Pluto Press.

Case, E. and McDonald, M. 2003: Life after man: an interview with Margaret Atwood. *New Scientist*, 178 (2393), 40–3.

Cavallaro, D. 2000: *Cyberpunk and Cyberculture: Science Fiction and the Work of William Gibson*. London: Athlone Press.

Chalmers, A. F. 1999: *What is this Thing called Science?* Buckingham: Open University Press.

Cho, A. 2001: Lost and found: the Sun's missing neutrinos were there all the time. *New Scientist,* 170 (2296), 7.

Clark, A. 2003: *Natural-born Cyborgs: Minds, Technologies, and the Future of Human Intelligence.* Oxford: Oxford University Press.

Clarke, A. C. 1973: *Profiles of the Future: An Inquiry into the Limits of the Possible.* New York: Harper & Row.

Clarke, A. C. 1977: *Prelude to Space.* London: Sidgwick & Jackson.

Clarke, A. C. 1984: *1984, Spring: A Choice of Futures.* London: Granada.

Clarke, A. C. and Baxter, S. 2000: *The Light of Other Days.* London: Voyager.

Clarke, A. C. and Lee, G. 1991: *Rama II.* London: Orbit.

Clarke, A. C. and Lee, G. 1992: *Garden of Rama.* London: Orbit.

Clarke, A. C. and Lee, G. 1994: *Rama Revealed.* London: Orbit.

Cohen, R. S. and Schnelle, T. (eds) 1986: *Cognition and Fact: Materials on Ludwik Fleck.* Dordrecht: D. Reidel.

Cole, J. R. 1979: *Fair Science: Women in the Scientific Community.* New York: The Free Press.

Collins, H. 1981: Stages in the empirical programme of relativism. *Social Studies of Science,* 11, 3–10.

Collins, H. and Pinch, T. 1993: *The Golem: What Everyone Should Know about Science.* Cambridge: Cambridge University Press.

Collins, H. and Pinch, T. 1998: *The Golem at Large: What You Should Know about Technology.* Cambridge: Cambridge University Press.

Collins, H. M. and Yearley, S. 1992: Epistemological chicken. In A. Pickering (ed.), *Science as Practice and Culture,* Chicago: University of Chicago Press, 301–26.

Cotgrove, S. and Box, S. 1970: *Science, Industry and Society: Studies in the Sociology of Science.* London: George Allen & Unwin Ltd.

Couvalis, G. 1997: *The Philosophy of Science: Science and Objectivity.* London: Sage.

Crane, D. 1972: *Invisible Colleges.* Chicago: University of Chicago Press.

Crichton, M. 2002: *Prey.* New York: Harper Collins.

Curtis, P. 2002: UK 'left behind' in GMdebato. *Guardian Unlimited.* 10 June 2002.

Curtis, P. 2002: Call to explode 'mythical academic duide'. *Guardian Unlimited,* 5 July 2002.

Davies, P. 2001: *How to Build a Time Machine.* London: Allen Lane.

Drexler, K. E. 1990: *Engines of Creation.* London: Fourth Estate.

Drexler, K. E. 1992: *Nanosystems: Molecular Machinery, Manufacturing, and Computation.* New York: Wiley-Interscience.

Drexler, K. E. 2001: Machine-phase nanotechnology. *Scientific American,* 285 (3), 66–7.

Ebright, R. H. 2000: RNA polymerase: structural similarities between bacterial RNA polymerase and eucaryotic RNA polymerase II. *Journal of Molecular Biology*, 304, 687–98.

Einstein, A. 2001: *Relativity*. London: Routledge.

Erickson, M. 2002: Science as a vocation in the 21st century: an empirical study of science researchers. *Max Weber Studies*, 3 (1), 29–52.

Erickson, M. 2004: Jean-François Lyotard: Narrating Postmodernity. In D. Robbins (ed.), *Jean-François Lyotard*, Vol. 3. London: Sage Publications, 293–315.

Feyerabend, P. 1978a: *Against Method*. London: Verso.

Feyerabend, P. 1978b: *Science in a Free Society*. London: New Left Books.

Feyerabend, P. 1988: Knowledge and the role of theories. *Philosophy of the Social Sciences*, 18, 157–78.

Feynman, R. P. 1999: *The Meaning of it All*. London: Penguin.

Feynman, R. P. 2000: There's plenty of room at the bottom. In J. Robbins (ed.), *The Pleasure of Finding Things Out: The Best Short Works of Richard P. Feynman*, London: Penguin, 117–39.

Fieser, L. F. 1964: *The Scientific Method: A Personal Account of Unusual Projects in War and Peace*. New York: Reinhold Publishing Corporation.

Fisher, L. 2002: *How to Dunk a Doughnut: The Science of Everyday Life*. London: Weidenfeld & Nicolson.

Fleck, L. 1979: *Genesis and Development of a Scientific Fact*. Chicago: University of Chicago Press.

Foucault, M. 1967: *Madness and Civilization: A History of Insanity in the Age of Reason*. London: Tavistock.

Foucault, M. 1970: *The Order of Things: An Archaeology of the Human Sciences*. London: Tavistock.

Foucault, M. 1973: *The Birth of the Clinic: An Archaeology of Medical Perception*. London: Tavistock.

Frakes, R. and Wisher, B. 1991: *The Terminator*. London: Sphere.

Franklin, A. 2001: *Are There Really Neutrinos? An Evidential History*. Cambridge, Mass.: Perseus Books.

Friedlander, M. W. 1998: *At the Fringes of Science*. Boulder, Colo.: Westview Press.

Fuller, S. 1997: *Science*. Buckingham: Open University Press.

Fuller, S. 2000a: *The Governance of Science: Ideology and the Future of the Open Society*. Buckingham: Open University Press.

Fuller, S. 2000b: *Thomas Kuhn: A Philosophical History for our Times*. Chicago: University of Chicago Press.

Fuller, S. 2003: *Kuhn vs Popper: The Struggle for the Soul of Science*. Cambridge: Ikon Books.

Galison, P. 1997: *Image and Logic: A Material Culture of Microphysics*. Chicago: University of Chicago Press.

Gardner, M. 1957: *Fads and Fallacies in the Name of Science*. New York: Dover Publications, Inc.

Gibson, W. 1984: *Neuromancer*. New York: Ace Books.

Gibson, W. and Sterling, B. 1991: *The Difference Engine*. New York: Bantam Books.

Gould, S. J. 1997: Ladders and cones: constraining evolution by canonical icons. In R. B. Silvers (ed.), *Hidden Histories of Science*, London: Granta, 37–67.

Gould, S. J. 2000: *Wonderful Life: the Burgess Shale and the Nature of History*. London: Vintage.

Gray, A. 2003: *Research Practice for Cultural Studies: Ethnographic Methods and Lived Cultures*. London: Sage.

Gregory, J. and Miller, S. 1998: *Science in Public: Communication, Culture, and Credibility*. New York: Plenum Trade.

Gribbin, J. 1998: *Q is for Quantum: Particle Physics from A–Z*. London: Weidenfeld & Nicolson.

Gribbin, J. 1999: *Get a Grip on the New Physics*. London: Weidenfeld & Nicolson.

Hacker, P. M. S. 1986: *Insight and Illusion: Themes in the Philosophy of Wittgenstein*. Oxford: Oxford University Press.

Hacker, P. M. S. 1997: *Wittgenstein*. London: Phoenix.

Hacking, I. (ed.) 1981: *Scientific Revolutions*. Oxford: Oxford University Press.

Hacking, I. 1983: *Representing and Intervening: Introductory Topics in the Philosophy of Natural Science*. Cambridge: Cambridge University Press.

Hacking, I. 1988: The participant irrealist at large in the laboratory. *British Journal for the Philosophy of Science*, 39, 277–94.

Hacking, I. 1999: *The Social Construction of What?* Cambridge, Mass.: Harvard University Press.

Hagstrom, W. O. 1965: *The Scientific Community*. New York: Basic Books.

Hamilton, P. F. 1993: *Mindstar Rising*. London: Pan.

Hamilton, P. F. 1996: *The Reality Dysfunction: Book One of the Night's Dawn Trilogy*. London: Pan.

Hamilton, P. F. 1997a: *A Quantum Murder*. New York: Tor.

Hamilton, P. F. 1997b: *The Neutronium Alchemist: Book Two of the Night's Dawn Trilogy*. London: Pan.

Hamilton, P. F. 1998: *The Nano Flower*. London: Pan.

Hamilton, P. F. 1999a: *A Second Chance at Eden*. New York: Warner Books, Inc.

Hamilton, P. F. 1999b: *The Naked God: Book Three of the Night's Dawn Trilogy*. London: Macmillan.

Hamilton, P. F. 2002: *Misspent Youth*. London: Macmillan.

Haraway, D. J. 1991: *Simians, Cyborgs and Women: The Reinvention of Nature*. London: Free Association Books.

Haraway, D. J. 1992: *Primate Visions: Gender, Race and Nature in the World of Modern Science*. London: Verso.

Haraway, D. J. 1997: *Modest_Witness@Second_Millennium: FemaleMan©_ Meets_OncoMouse™: Feminism and Technoscience*. New York and London: Routledge.

Harré, R. 1981: *Great Scientific Experiments: Twenty Experiments that Changed our View of the World*. Oxford: Oxford University Press.

Hawking, S. W. 1988: *A Brief History of Time: From the Big Bang to Black Holes*. New York: Bantam Books.

Hawking, S. W. 2003: *On the Shoulders of Giants*. London: Penguin.

Heisenberg, W. 1958: *The Physicist's Conception of Nature*. London: Hutchinson & Co.

Heisenberg, W. 1959: *Physics and Philosophy: The Revolution in Modern Science*. London: George Allen & Unwin, Ltd.

Henry, J. 1997: *The Scientific Revolution and the Origins of Modern Science*. London: Macmillan.

Hess, D. J. 1995: *Science and Technology in a Multicultural World: The Cultural Politics of Facts and Artifacts*. New York: Columbia University Press.

Hoch, P. 1992: The development of the band theory of solids. In L. Hoddenson, E. Braun, J. Teichmann and S. Weart (eds), *Out of the Crystal Maze: Chapters from the History of Solid-state Physics*, Oxford: Oxford University Press, 182–235.

Hoddenson, L., Schubert, H., Heims, S. J. and Baym, G. 1992a: Collective phenomena. In L. Hoddenson, E. Braun, J. Teichmann and S. Weart (eds), *Out of the Crystal Maze: Chapters from the History of Solid-state Physics*, Oxford: Oxford University Press, 489–616.

Hoddenson, L., Braun, E., Teichmann, J. and Weart, S. (eds) 1992b: *Out of the Crystal Maze: Chapters from the History of Solid-state Physics*. Oxford: Oxford University Press.

Horgan, J. 1996: *The End of Science: Facing the Limits of Knowledge in the Twilight of the Scientific Age*. London: Abacus.

Hunter, I. Q. (ed.) 1999: *British Science Fiction Cinema*. London: Routledge.

Hutchings, P. 1999: Satan Bugs in the Hot Zone: exploring microbial pathogens as alien invaders. In D. Cartmell, I. Q. Hunter, H. Kaye and I. Whelehan (eds), *Alien Identities: Exploring Difference in Film and Fiction*, London: Pluto Press, 11–30.

Jacobs, S. 1987: Scientific community – formulations and critique of a sociological motif. *British Journal of Sociology*, 38 (2), 266–76.

Jacobs, S. and Mooney, B. 1997: Sociology as a source of anomaly in Thomas Kuhn's system of science. *Philosophy of the Social Sciences*, 27 (4), 466–85.

Jancovich, M. 1996: *Rational Fears: American Horror in the 1950s*. Manchester: Manchester University Press.

Jastrow, J. (ed.) 1967: *The Story of Human Error*. New York: Books for Libraries Press, Inc.

Jones, S. 2000: *Almost Like a Whale: The Origin of Species Updated*. London: Anchor.

Kember, S. 2003: *Cyberfeminism and Artificial Life*. London: Routledge.

Kirkpatrick, D. 1970: *Eduardo Paolozzi*. London: Studio Vista.

Kuhn, A. (ed.) 1990: *Alien Zone: Cultural Theory and Contemporary Science Fiction Cinema*. London: Verso.

Kuhn, T. S. 1970: *The Structure of Scientific Revolutions*. Chicago: University of Chicago Press.

Kuhn, T. S. 1977: *The Essential Tension: Selected Studies in Scientific Tradition and Change*. Chicago and London: University of Chicago Press.

Larrain, J. 2000: *Identity and Modernity in Latin America*. Cambridge: Polity.

Latour, B. 1987: *Science in Action*. Cambridge, Mass.: Harvard University Press.

Latour, B. 1996: *Aramis or the Love of Technology*. Cambridge, Mass.: Harvard University Press.

Latour, B. 1999: *Pandora's Hope: Essays on the Reality of Science Studies*. Cambridge, Mass.: Harvard University Press.

Latour, B. and Woolgar, S. 1979: *Laboratory Life: The Social Construction of Scientific Facts*. London: Sage.

Law, J. (ed.) 1986: *Power, Action and Belief: A New Sociology of Knowledge?* London: Routledge & Kegan Paul.

Law, J. (ed.) 1991: *A Sociology of Monsters: Essays on Power, Technology and Domination*. London: Routledge.

Law, J. 1994: *Organizing Modernity*. Oxford: Blackwell.

Law, J. and Hassard, J. (eds) 1999: *Actor Network Theory and After*. Oxford: Blackwell.

Lewontin, R. C. 1993: *Biology as Ideology: The Doctrine of DNA*. New York: HarperPerennial.

Lindqvist, S. 2001: *A History of Bombing*. London: Granta.

Lloyd, G. S., Niu, W., Tebbutt, J., Ebright, R. H. and Busby, S. J. W. 2002: Requirement for two copies of RNA polymerase alpha subunit C-terminal domain for synergistic transcription activation at complex bacterial promoters. *Genes & Development*, 16 (19), 2557–65.

Long, J. S. and Fox, M. F. 1995: Scientific careers – universalism and particularism. *Annual Review of Sociology*, 21, 45–71.

Lucas, C. 2003: We must not be blinded by science. The *Guardian*, 12 June 2003.

Lykke, N. and Braidotti, R. (eds) 1996: *Between Monsters, Goddesses and Cyborgs: Feminist Confrontations with Science, Medicine and Cyberspace*. New York: Zed Books.

MacIntyre, A. 1977: Epistemological crises, dramatic narrative and the philosophy of science. *The Monist*, 60 (4), 453–72.

MacKenzie, D. 1998: *Knowing Machines: Essays on Technical Change*. Cambridge, Mass.: MIT Press.

MacLeod, K. 2000: *Engines of Light, Book 1: Cosmonaut Keep*. London: Orbit.

MacLeod, K. 2002: *Engines of Light, Book 2: Dark Light*. London: Orbit.

MacLeod, K. 2003: *Engines of Light, Book 3: Engine City*. London: Orbit.

Martin, J. 1996: On Healing Self / Nature. In N. Lykke and R. Braidotti (eds) 1996: *Between Monsters, Goddesses and Cyborgs: Feminist Confrontations with Science, Medicine and Cyberspace*. New York: Zed Books, 103–19.

Matthews, R. 2003: Researchers' links with biomed industry lead to bias in clinical trials. *New Scientist*, 177 (2380), 8.

Mayberry, M., Subramaniam, B. and Weasel, L. H. (eds) 2001: *Feminist Science Studies: A New Generation*. London: Routledge.

McCaffery, L. (ed.) 1991: *Storming the Reality Studio: A Casebook of Cyberpunk and Postmodern Science Fiction*. Durham, NC: Duke University Press.

Merton, R. K. 1967: *Social Theory and Social Structure*. New York: Free Press.

Midgley, M. 2001: *Science and Poetry*. London: Routledge.

Monk, R. 1991: *Ludwig Wittgenstein: The Duty of Genius*. London: Vintage.

Mort, M. 2002: *Building the Trident Network: A Study of the Enrolment of People, Knowledge, and Machines*. Cambridge, Mass., and London: MIT Press.

Moss, N. 1987: *Klaus Fuchs: The Man who Stole the Atom Bomb*. London: Grafton.

Muir, H. 2003: Underground lab fills with water. *New Scientist*, 178 (2400), 6.

Nelkin, D. 1987: *Selling Science: How the Press Covers Science and Technology*. New York: W. H. Freeman & Co.

Nelkin, D. and Lindee, M. S. 1995: *The DNA Mystique: The Gene as Cultural Icon*. New York: W. H. Freeman and Co.

New Scientist 2002: Conduct unbecoming (editorial). *New Scientist*, 5 October 2002, p. 3.

Newton, D. E. 2002: *Recent Advances and Issues in Molecular Nanotechnology*. Westport, Conn.: Greenwood Press.

Nowotny, H., Scott, P. and Gibbons, M. 2001: *Re-thinking Science: Knowledge and the Public in an Age of Uncertainty*. Cambridge: Polity.

Olby, R. C., Cantor, G. N., Christie, J. R. R. and Hodge, M. J. S. (eds) 1990: *Companion to the History of Modern Science*. London: Routledge.

Orwell, G. 1954: *1984*. Harmondsworth: Penguin.

Oster, M. (ed.) 2002: *Science in Europe 1500–1800: A Primary Sources Reader*. London: Palgrave/Open University.

Park, R. 2000: *Voodoo Science: The Road from Foolishness to Fraud*. Oxford: Oxford University Press.

Pearson, F. 1999: *Eduardo Paolozzi*. Edinburgh: National Galleries of Scotland.

Penley, C. 1989: *The Future of an Illusion: Film, Feminism and Psychoanalysis*. Minneapolis: University of Minnesota Press.

Penley, C. 1997: *NASA/Trek*. London: Verso.

Peters, J., Lane, N., Rees, T. and Samuels, G. 2002: *Set Fair: A Report on Women in Science, Technology and Engineering from the Baroness Greenfield to the Secretary of State for Trade and Industry*. London: DTI.

Phillips, D. L. 1977: *Wittgenstein and Scientific Knowledge: A Sociological Perspective*. London: Macmillan.

Pickering, A. 1984: *Constructing Quarks: A Sociological History of Particle Physics*. Edinburgh: Edinburgh University Press.

Pinch, T. J. 1986: *Confronting Nature: The Sociology of Solar-Neutrino Detection*. Dordrecht: D. Reidel Pub. Co.

Plait, P. 2002: *Bad Astronomy: Misconceptions and Misuses Revealed, from Astrology to the Moon Landing 'Hoax'*. New York: John Wiley & Sons, Inc.

Polanyi, M. 1958: *Personal Knowledge: Towards a Post-critical Philosophy*. London: Routledge & Kegan Paul.

Popper, K. 1945: *The Open Society and its Enemies*. London: Routledge & Kegan Paul.

Popper, K. 1981: The rationality of scientific revolutions. In I. Hacking (ed.), *Scientific Revolutions*. Oxford: Oxford University Press, 80–106.

Popper, K. 2002: *The Logic of Scientific Discovery*. London: Routledge Classics.

Rabinow, P. 1996: *Making PCR: A Story of Biotechnology*. Chicago: University of Chicago Press.

Radford, T. 2003: Brave new world or menace. Why Prince Charles Fears grey goo. The *Guardian*, 29 April 2003.

Radnitzky, G. 1973: *Contemporary Schools of Metascience*. Chicago: Henry Regnery Company.

Rae, A. I. M. 1981: *Quantum Mechanics*. Maidenhead: McGraw-Hill Book Co. (UK) Ltd.

Rae, A. I. M. 1986: *Quantum Physics: Illusion or Reality?* Cambridge: Cambridge University Press.

Ridley, B. K. 2001: *On Science*. London: Routledge.

Rose, H. 1994: *Love, Power and Knowledge: Towards a Feminist Transformation of the Sciences*. Cambridge: Polity.

Rose, H. and Rose, S. (eds) 2001: *Alas, Poor Darwin: Arguments against Evolutionary Psychology*. London: Vintage.

The Royal Society and The Royal Academy of Engineering 2004: *Nanoscience and Nanotechnologies: Opportunities and Uncertainties*. London: The Royal Society.

Russell, B. 1923: *The ABC of Atoms*. London: Kegan Paul, Trench, Trubner & Co. Ltd.

Russell, B. 1985: *ABC of Relativity*. London: Unwin Paperbacks.

Sagan, C. 1996: *The Demon-Haunted World: Science as a Candle in the Dark*. New York: Ballantine Books.

Samuel, E. 2002: Rising star of electronics found to have fabricated his ground-breaking results. *New Scientist*, 5 October 2002, pp. 4–5.

Samuel, E. 2003: How nuclear power plants in Japan helped uncover the Sun's secrets. *New Scientist*, 177 (2376), 13.

Sardar, Z. 2000: *Thomas Kuhn and the Science Wars*. Cambridge: Icon Books.

Schummer, J. 2004: Multidisciplinarity, interdisciplinarity, and research collaboration in nanoscience and nanotechnology. *Scientometrics*, 59 (3), 425–65.

Scientific American 2002: Editorial. *Scientific American*, 287 (6), 8.

Scientific American (eds) 2002: *Understanding Nanotechnology*. New York: Warner Books.

Shermer, M. 2001: *The Borderlands of Science: Where Sense Meets Nonsense*. Oxford: Oxford University Press.

Shermer, M. 2002: The shamans of scientism. *Scientific American*, 286 (6), 25.

Seed, D. 1999: *American Science Fiction and the Cold War: Literature and Film*. Edinburgh: Edinburgh University Press.

Silver, B. L. 1998: *The Ascent of Science*. New York: Oxford University Press.

Sismondo, S. 2004: *An Introduction to Science and Technology Studies*. Malden, Mass.: Blackwell Publishers.

Stephenson, N. 1995: *The Diamond Age*. New York: Bantam Books.

Toumey, C. 2005: Historical comparison for anticipated public reactions to nanotechnology. In M. C. Roco and W. S. Bainbridge (eds), *Societal Implications of Nanoscience and Nanotechnology*, Springer Science, forthcoming.

Trenn, T. J. and Merton, R. K. 1979: Descriptive analysis. In T. J. Trenn and R. K. Merton (eds), *Genesis and Development of a Scientific Fact*. Chicago: University of Chicago Press, 154–65.

Trigg, G. L. 1975: *Landmark Experiments in Twentieth-Century Physics*. London: Edward Arnold Ltd.

Trigg, R. 1993: *Rationality and Science*. Oxford: Blackwell.

Tudor, A. 1989: *Monsters and Mad Scientists: A Cultural History of the Horror Movie*. Oxford: Blackwell.

Tulloch, J. and Jenkins, H. 1995: *Science Fiction Audiences: Doctor Who, Star Trek, and their Fans*. London: Routledge.

Turner, B. S. 1992: *Max Weber: From History to Modernity*. London: Routledge.

van Frassen, B. 1980: *The Scientific Image*. Oxford: Clarendon Press.

Velody, I. 1989: Socialism as a sociological problem. P. Lassman (ed.), *Politics and Social Theory*. London: Routledge, 123–37.

Vonnegut, K. 1976: *Wampeters, Foma and Granfalloons*. Frogmore: Granada.

Watson, J. D. 1968: *The Double Helix: A Personal Account of the Discovery of the Structure of DNA*. London: Weidenfeld & Nicolson.

Weber, M. 1989: Science as a vocation. In P. Lassman and I. Velody (eds), *Max Weber's 'Science as a Vocation'*. London: Unwin Hyman, 3–31.

Wilson, M., Kannangara, K., Smith, G., Simmons, M. and Raguse, B. 2002: *Nanotechnology: Basic Science and Emerging Technologies*. London: Chapman & Hall.

Wittgenstein, L. 1958: *Philosophical Investigations*. Oxford: Blackwell.

Wittgenstein, L. 1993: Lectures on freedom of the will: notes by Yorick Smythies (1939). In J. Klagge and A. Nordmann (eds), *Ludwig Wittgenstein: Philosophical Occasions 1912–1951*, Indianapolis: Hackett Publishing Company, 429–44.

Youngson, R. M. 1998: *Scientific Blunders: A Brief History of How Wrong Scientists can Sometimes Be*. London: Robinson.

Ziman, J. 2000: *Real Science: What it Is, and What it Means*. Cambridge: Cambridge University Press.

Zuckerman, N. and Cole, J. R. 1975: Women in American science. *Minerva*, 13 (1), 82–102.

Index